IF IT WASN'T FOR
GOLF . . . !

By the same author

Start-Off-Smashed!
In Search of Eastern Promise
Victory In 'Site'!

IF IT WASN'T FOR
GOLF . . . !

People, Places, Parties, Pictures,
joined by a common link

Sam Morley

Aedificamus Press

First published 1988 by
Aedificamus Press Ltd., The Ridgeway,
Northaw, Herts EN6 4BG

© 1988 Sam Morley

ISBN 0 9511701 2 0

Production in association with
Book Production Consultants, Cambridge.

Typeset by Omnia Ltd, Cambridge.

Printed in Great Britain by
Billings, Worcester.

Contents

Chapter	Title	Page
Foreword	The Author – by Alex Hay	ix
PART ONE	**The British Collection**	**1**
One	For Whom the Bell Tolls	3
Two	Ted Ray	7
Three	In the Beginning	18
Four	The Night I Played in the Esso Open!	32
Five	The BBUGS	38
Six	Of Mice and Men	51
Seven	Totteridge Village Barber-Shop Quartet	61
Eight	The Cavendish Open	68
PART TWO	**The Springbok Connection**	**77**
Nine	The Scenic Route to Simonstown	78
Ten	Eccentric Brits in the Transvaal	92
Eleven	Eccentric Lawmen at Tolworth!	113
Twelve	Stanley Baker and the Zulus	122
Thirteen	Sun City Serenade	131
PART THREE	**The Nashville Confection**	**153**
Fourteen	Enter Skinny Huggins	154
Fifteen	How Not to Plan a Banquet	169
Sixteen	Over-the-Sticks in S. Carolina	188
Seventeen	New York, Washington and the Vanderbilt Gridiron	197
Eighteen	Way Down Yonder in New Orleans	213
Nineteen	The High – and Dry – Road to Chattanooga	226
Twenty	Postscript	240
	Epilogue	247
	The Artist	249
	Index	251

To Sarah-Jane Morley (7½) and Lauren Morley (6), my two South African grand-nieces.
I first met them eight weeks ago, since when Sarah-Jane has written to tell me we both have the same initials, that she can swim a mile, and would I write her a book. Not being into children's literature, I'm afraid she'll have to settle for a Dedication – plus a brief walk-on part in Chapter 13.

Samuel John Morley
Cuffley, Herts
30 March 1988

List of Illustrations

2 'Let me guess – Sam Snead – Turnberry, 1952?'

6 'God loveth a cheerful giver . . . Corinthians 9:7'

17 'You want it in writing?'

31 'Congratulations – it's been interesting watching a business associate who chooses a quick profit rather than long-term steady growth.'

37 'What d'you chap'sh think . . . couple of shix irons enough?'

50 'Fire!'

60 'Remember old Arthur – same putt – same competition – same hole – suddenly clutched his heart and fell stone dead.'

67 'I remember that one last year – he sharpened my woods!'

76 'Dunlop "65", Penfold, Warwick, Slazengaire . . . ze re-paints?'

91 'If we hurry we could just about finish.'

112 'Throw him your own ball – mine's 2 feet from the pin!'

121 'Mind you, it's some time since I last played.'

130 'What's the name of the doddery old feller sitting between young Thingammy and old Whatsisname?'

152 'For your information, Madam Captain, the place for Fairy Liquid is the bloody kitchen not the ball cleaner.'

168 Casual Water

187 'At this hole it's customary to tee up on a pinch of Past Captains.'

196 'By the way, if you hear a loud klaxon blast at any time, it'll be my anti-rape device!'

212 'For the rich you SING!'

225 'Well, we've talked enough about my prostate – how about your prostate?'

239 'I propose that 5-Day membership for ladies should be restricted to Christmas Day, Boxing Day, Pancake Day, Mother's Day and Guy Fawkes Day!'

The Author
by Alex Hay

In the early seventies I was taken to the Eccentric Club of St James's, in London's Ryder Street, by Leslie Noble – a very dear friend who was also my accountant.

To me, as a young golf professional, the membership appeared styled on living life to the full and enjoying all the pleasures that the mixture of sport and pleasure could muster. It was made up of a complete cross-section of the community – barristers, actors, high-ranking police officers, bookmakers, prizefighters, bankers, industrialists, property developers, barrow-boys, and a multitude of likeable rogues.

In such an atmosphere it would seem certain that villains would abound; so when I met Sam Morley for the first time and he was introduced as a man who 'was away a lot' I assumed, bearing in mind the look of him, that he made a habit of doing 'time'. What was meant, of course, was that he was a man who spent as much time as possible combining business and golfing abroad. He was in fact one of the group of nine Eccentrics who opened up reciprocity with South Africa in 1965, the story of which he presents so colourfully in Part Two of the book. The second such trip was made in 1973 and I was privileged to be in that party, travelling as the Honorary Professional to the Club – a position I held until the Club closed in 1985.

Sam Morley is a man whose company I have enjoyed many times over the years, yet I am still confused by him. From his often fierce countenance one can hardly believe he has the ability to pick the fun from life's experiences and put it on paper in his inimitable style – so often highlighting that fun at his own expense.

Our meetings are now unfortunately less frequent, but when our paths do cross there is alway laughter – the ingredient all too often missing from sport today.

Alex Hay. Woburn 1988

ix

PART ONE

THE
BRITISH
COLLECTION

" Let me guess - Sam Snead -Turnberry 1952?"

——— 1 ———

For Whom the Bell Tolls!

'Bertie Troubridge' was once a 'high-rolling' wheeler-dealer in the City of London. Word has it that not only was he a 'Mr Big' in the machinations of reinsurance, but also a much-vaunted figurehead in the industrial corridors of power. His entrepreneurial flairs brought him chairmanship of a score or more businesses scattered around the country. But 'was' is the operative word in these opening sentences.

Things did not go too well for Bertie when the management of certain Lloyd's syndicates came under scrutiny a year or two ago. So much so, he was obliged to depart from these shores in somewhat of a hurry, abandoning many of the 'goodies' acquired during the fat years. Like the chauffeur-driven Silver Cloud Rolls Royce; luxury penthouse apartments in Knightsbridge; spacious home with swimming pool complex abutting Sunningdale Golf Course; to name but a few of the more pleasurable things in life that only a money mountain will buy. But his friends are confident he will rise again from the ashes of former glories to achieve even bigger and better things. But the same friends have their doubts whether he'll ever want to come back to this country to achieve them – there are too many awkward questions on file waiting for him to answer.

'Bertie Troubridge' is, therefore, a fictitious name I've chosen to mask the identity of a very real person. But only the name is an invention; the ensuing story – give or take a word – is vouched for as authentic by a mutual friend. A friend to whom Bertie recounted the detail on the golf course shortly after the event and during the period when Bertie's star still shone brilliantly from its zenith.

3

We go back to a day early in 1979. The day that Bertie's dear old grandad breathed his last in the remote Hampshire village where he had lived out his declining years. Bertie's father having been killed in World War Two, it was left to Bertie to take care of the formalities. Except that, being a very busy man, he found it difficult to finalise a time and date for the cremation. His diary was full of business and social commitments for many weeks ahead. After rescheduling a number of his appointments, and discussions with undertakers and crematorium authorities, Bertie was able to advise all concerned that the ceremony would take place in Hampshire at 9.00 on a Saturday morning. This would allow Bertie just enough time to travel down from Berkshire, go through the ceremony, mix a little with family and friends at the scene, and get back to Sunningdale in time for his usual Saturday afternoon four-ball.

Word went out. Although many were a little bewildered by the unusual hour and day that had been chosen, a goodly number attended the appointed place to pay their last respects to the old gentleman. Bertie swept his Rolls into the crematorium car park and hastened, being a few minutes late, towards the buildings.

It was rather a bleak morning and most of the mourners were seated patiently in the pews. The pall-bearers, too, had brought the coffin in out of the cold and placed it in readiness on the platform to the side of the altar. All waited in comparative gloom as none of the chapel staff had yet arrived to put any lights on.

Bertie entered hurriedly, peering around to take in the scene and try to identify some of those present. 'Why's everybody sitting around in the dark?', he demanded peevishly. He was told that nobody had yet shown up to take care of that sort of thing. 'Well, we can soon take care of that for ourselves, can't we?', was his immediate reaction. He looked around and, noticing a bank of a dozen switches or so by the door, put them all on with one impatient sweep of the hand. To say the effect was dramatic would be the understatement of the year.

The overhead chandeliers sprang to life and bathed the congregation in suffused light. The vestry was illuminated. The porch lights at the front, side, and rear entrances lit up, as did the long line of post-top lanterns illuminating the drive from the main road to the chapel. The chapel exterior walls, roof, tower and clock were attractively floodlit.

From a concealed tape-recorder started the solemn resonant chords of a Bach fugue played on a mighty church organ. Full-length heavy velvet drapes glided noiselessly across the chapel from wall to wall, discreetly screening off its business end from the sorrowing congregaton. The platform on which the coffin sat started to glide from view – slowly but inexorably conveying the earthly remains of Bertie's grandfather to their final destination.

Everybody watched, spellbound in shocked and silent disbelief. A spell broken only by the arrival of the duty chaplain, with apologies for tardiness dying, stillborn, on his lips. Without even removing his bicycle clips, he asked, 'What in Heaven's name is going on here?' or words to that effect. 'Well, everyone was sitting here in darkness when I arrived', pleaded the crestfallen Bertie, 'so I thought I'd put some lights on!' 'Well, you've certainly done that', said the chaplain. 'But how am I now going to conduct the burial service I had mind for your grandfather, without having him here among us, so to speak?'

They talked it over until the chaplain came up with a bright idea. He had another cremation due at 10.00 a.m. when the last rites were to be administered to an old lady who had died recently in a local old people's home. No mourners were anticipated. If those currently assembled didn't mind waiting another half-hour he would conduct the service intended for Bertie's grandfather over the old lady's coffin. Not only would it be giving her a far more impressive farewell than she could ever have hoped for, but it would help resolve a situation that must be bordering on unique in the annals of cremations and crematoria. And so it was done. I believe it made Bertie a little late for his four-ball at Sunningdale – but then you can't win 'em all!

5

"God loveth a cheerful giver ... Corinthians 9:7"

—— 2 ——

Ted Ray

If it wasn't for GOLF . . . Nedlo, Hugh Neek, or even Charlie Olden, might well have been as much a household name as is the title of this chapter.

It was August 1958, at the ripe old age of 41, that I first set foot on an 18-hole golf course, as described in a later chapter of this book; but not until a fine Saturday morning in August 1960, did I make my maiden appearance as a full member at Crews Hill Golf Club, Enfield. With a handicap of 17, earned over the previous 12 months at Whitewebbs, the local public course, I hoped to find one or two people prepared to play a round with the new boy.

I knew nobody. The highly respected member and business neighbour who proposed me into Crews Hill, together with his friend – a past-Captain – who seconded the proposal, both played their golf on Sunday afternoons, whereby they could follow it up with a pot of tea and a rubber of bridge in the lounge.

Standing by the bar that Saturday morning I asked the steward how a newcomer went about getting a game amidst strangers. 'Oh', he said, 'somebody will soon sing out to ask if anyone wants to make up a four.' Over the next three-quarters of an hour sixty or seventy members arrived in twos and threes, greeted friends, got changed, and went out to play. But singing-out was marked by its absence. True, one or two did wander around a little to ask another if he was fixed, but nobody took a lot of notice of the hopeful but shy stranger propping up the corner of the bar.

When the steward said there was not much chance now of any more arrivals, I dejectedly went and changed in readiness for a little solo practice. On leaving the locker room,

I popped back in the bar and told the steward that I'd be round the corner on the putting green for the next fifteen minutes or so just in case a belated arrival needed me. With that came footsteps down the corridor and in hurried the flushed and unmistakably familiar face of Charlie Olden. Not just the face, but the rest of him too, making up a total height of about 64 inches. What he lacked in height was certainly compensated for by ambience. One of Britain's greatest stand-up comics, Charlie Olden had been packing 'em into the nation's music halls for as long as I could remember. (In the mid-1930s two or three of us would traipse across London each week after work, just to catch his act. Before TV it was usually a word-for-word repeat of what he had done the previous week! But who cared? If Max Miller was on the same bill it was a double-bonus.) And now, twenty-five years later, he turns out to be not only a member of my new golf club but, as I was soon to learn, one whose membership went back to the early 1930s.

The steward looked at him in surprise. 'Your regular crowd were under the impression you were in a provincial show and had opted out of coming back for today's game. So they invited Mr. So-and-so to make up their four.'

Now for those who find it difficult to get all starry-eyed at the mention of Charlie Olden, there might be comfort in knowing that he didn't go a lot on his name either. So much so, that soon after breaking into show business he considered it was that poor in charisma as to justify changing. This he did by reversing the spelling and having himself billed as Nedlo. Amazingly, that didn't prove much of a show-stopper either. Then, with his characteristic corn-laden wit – and considering his stage performance to be something of a speciality – he changed from Nedlo to Hugh Neek! You must admit he had guts!

By this time he'd put a good act together and was in regular demand – despite his appalling choice in naming it. His London agents told him for the love of God to go out and find himself a distinctive 'handle' – something to match the quality of bookings they could get if only he'd offer them a name that would look good on the contract documents. Charlie knew they were right and cast around for ideas.

He was already a confirmed golf addict and, as his work took him all over the country, he would spend as much time as possible each week on whichever course happened to be nearest the town he played. He read up everything on the history of the game and idolised the great players of bygone days. A Channel Islander, Harry Vardon, was the greatest and reigned during the early part of this century. He needs little introduction from me. Then along came another Channel Islander who won the British Open in 1912 and the U.S. Open in 1920. He was a taciturn giant of a man with an unkempt walrus moustache and huge hands in which the club he held looked like a toothpick. The very antithesis of dapper little Charlie Olden, who was never known to stop talking, and so often complained that he was unfairly handicapped with hands he could just about wrap around a standard toothpick.

Charlie never did meet his hero, but chose to give the latter's name a second lease of immortality by discarding Charlie Olden for ever, in favour of calling himself 'Ted Ray' for the rest of his colourful and highly successful life as one of England's greatest entertainers.

In his book *My Slice of Life* (published in 1972 at about the same time as my *Start-Off-Smashed!* and for which we did a straight swop of personalised copies), Ted – the comic now, not the golfer – describes how a listener to his radio series of the 1960s, *Ray's a Laugh*, wrote him a touching letter. She owned a souvenir of Ted Ray the golfer. Her late husband had worked for the great man as assistant, and been given it as a gift on retirement. About to leave England and live out her days in the South of France, she wanted to pass the said precious souvenir to somebody who would appreciate it. 'Who better than you?', she wrote.

It was a handsome ornamental French clock, with a gold plate bearing the inscripton: 'Presented to Ted Ray by the Oxhey Golf Club, to commemorate his winning the American Open Golf Championship, 1920'.

Ted wrote how highly honoured he felt by the kind lady's gesture and proudly kept the clock on the mantelpiece in his North London home. Visitors would look at the clock, read the inscription, look at their host, and marvel how well he looked for his age. When playing golf with him, however, he said they'd also marvel over how much his game had deteriorated.

Before we get back to Ted's arrival at Crews Hill on that sunny Saturday morning in 1960, I must explain that introducing him as Charlie Olden was just a bit of dramatic licence, whereby the ensuing potted biography could be told. Nobody had known him as anything other than Ted Ray for at least twenty-five years prior to the steward telling him that his mates had gone without him that morning. We take up the story again from that point.

Ted looked around him with unseeing eyes. He was completely bewildered at being 'dropped'. It was only through knowing him and his regular playing pattern so well over my next twenty years at the Club, that I still wonder at the unique (Hugh Neek?) and memorable start to my golfing career that day. I don't believe he was ever alone and without a game before or since. He always played with the same three fellows every Saturday morning, and a different three on Sundays. Only when one of them fell ill, went on holiday, or passed away, did the remaining three ever seek a replacement to make a fourth. But for the reason given, his friends were now out playing without him and he stood at the end of the bar wondering what to do next.

The steward then told him that I was a brand new member and had come up for the first time that day hoping, but failing, to find somebody to play with. We exchanged polite nods and 'how d'you do's' from opposite ends of the bar, but he said he thought he'd better get changed and practice a few chip shots around the ninth green until his friends came by, in case there was some mistake and there were still only three of them. I told him I understood perfectly, and carried on out to the putting green where I started trundling a couple of balls around.

Pretty soon, Ted came out to practice little chip shots in the long grass near the ninth green. He then walked across to tell me he felt I must have thought him rather rude back there in the clubhouse, but he had no intention of being so – just momentarily put out due to chasing like mad to meet his friends. He'd phoned one of them the previous evening from where he was appearing, to say he planned to motor down in the morning for their game but might be a little late. 'But they didn't wait', he said, 'so sod 'em. Now how about you and me playing a few holes, and as you don't seem to know anybody yet I'll introduce you to as many as possible on the way round.'

We played an unforgettable 18, and stopped Lord knows how many times, as my partner took me over to shake hands with members on adjacent fairways; many of whom are now long-standing friends but, at that time, no doubt speculated on the unknown left-hander playing a two-ball with their Ted.

A wonderful introduction to a great golf club and a truly great man, with whom I remained good friends until his death some twenty years later. Incidentally, the clubhouse was the lovely old single-storey building with its bow-fronted lounge overlooking the eighth and ninth holes. Not the two-storey planning 'disaster' that went up to take its place in the early 1970s.

Ted was a true professional and never stopped working. Walk into a restaurant, clubhouse or pub bar with him and, no matter how serious or banal the conversation, directly he noticed that the waiter, barman or folks at the next table had recognised him, his voice would rise by half an octave and a handful of decibels; he would switch the subject to whatever suited his patter; and he was 'on stage' – pretending to be unaware of the rising interest all around, but noting every titter and guffaw out of the corner of his crinkled blue eyes.

And just as Royalty travels with courtiers in attendance – as does the Pope, or Billy Graham, with their faithful acolytes – so Ted Ray would go on planned visits to golf clubs in this country and abroad with a band of loyal followers, founded in 1964 and called the One-Over-The-Eight Golfing Society. Ted, of course, was the One – to whom homage was usually paid at their festive dinners by the eight 'homagers' drawn from the ranks of Crews Hill and elsewhere.

Having always preferred to plan and do my own thing, I never did go much on organised 'homaging' – so have had to rely on what's been told to me by others about the fun and games Ted's party enjoyed on their various junketing jaunts. Two of them dwelt, perhaps, a little closer to Ted's shadow than the other six, and were sometimes involved with him in hedonistic jaunts outside of their Society activities. They were Jack Stone, a transport contractor, who first got to know him well when a vacancy occurred in Ted's Sunday morning four-ball in the mid-1960s; and Albert Stevenson, a BBC producer who played his golf near his home in Blackheath. And all that has gone before in this chapter is by way of being a lead-in to a tale concerning the three, and as told to me by one of them. Here it is.

Esso, the international oil conglomerate, had planned a sales conference lasting a week at Gleneagles, Perthshire, during the late 1960s, and engaged Ted Ray to entertain the assembly after dinner each evening. For a healthy fee, no doubt, and all expenses paid.

Ted, anticipating the need for familiar company while 'locked in' for a week with all those 'oil-burners' and 'haggis-addicts', asked Jack Stone if he felt like spending the week, or part of it, up there with him. Jack, being a bachelor and almost his own boss, didn't need his hero to ask twice. But Albert Stevenson, who was not asked even once, wished he had been.

Ted and Jack travelled up by car on the Sunday, checked into the hotel, had their dinner, and went to bed ready for whatever the morrow had to offer. This consisted of a good old Scottish breakfast, an introductory meeting with the Golf Manager, an allocation of starting times for the King's Course in the morning and the Queen's in the afternoon, followed by 36 glorious holes played in a truly magnificent setting.

Once back in the Gleneagles Hotel, cleaning up and preparing for dinner that evening, Ted had a phone call from London. It was Albert Stevenson. The conversation went something like this:

'What's it like up there, Ted?', asked Albert.

'Smashing!', answered Ted, describing highlights of the day's play, events, and the place in general.

'Well, I was thinking of coming up to join you for a day', said Albert.

'That's a long way to come for a day's outing, surely?', replied Ted with surprise.

'No, I don't mind, really', answered Albert. 'I've looked up the trains and I can get the sleeper from Euston on Tuesday night; Jack can pick me up from Auchterarder station on Wednesday morning and take me back to the hotel where we can all have breakfast together; we can get two rounds of golf in like you did today; have dinner together; and then you can drop me back to the station in time for the sleeper home. I'd like that.'

And that's just what happened, enhanced by Albert – a high handicap player whose addiction to the game was as steadfast as his difficulty in putting two good shots together – achieving a near miracle during the afternoon round on the King's Course.

There are no less than four full-size golf courses at Gleneagles, and each of the 72 holes is individually named in picturesque 'Rabbie' Burns style. There's a 'Muckle Bookit', a 'Dun Whinny', a 'Pass o' Pinkie', and so on. The 13th on the King's Course, the longest and most formidable of the four, is 446 yards long and named 'Braid's Brawest', after the legendary James Braid, who designed the course.

And on that Wednesday afternoon, Albert Stevenson strung together the two greatest shots of his life. Following a magnificent drive of some 230 yards, his second shot – with a fairway wood – travelled the remaining 216 yards straight to the heart of the green, bounced a bit, rolled a bit, and finally fell into the hole itself for an eagle two!

It's hardly necessary to describe the congratulations and celebrations in the crowded bar once the round was over, with vocal replays *ad nauseum* of how he did it. The party went on right through dinner until the time came to drive the hero of the day to the station, tip him out the car, and carry him into the train. No doubt the sleeping-car attendant had to listen to a detailed, but by now, incoherent, retelling of the afternoon's play, before Albert fell into the bunk and knew no more until he woke up in a siding at Euston the next morning.

Back at Gleneagles, Ted and Jack went on to complete their week, and on Friday were seated in the Secretary's office paying bills and chatting about the fine time had by all. During the temporary absence of that gentleman when called away for some reason or the other, Ted helped himself to a few sheets of Gleneagles printed stationery and envelopes. Whether he arranged for the Secretary to be called away so that he could snaffle them for what's to follow, or whether it was on impulse, is anybody's guess; but knowing the man as I did I'd settle for the former.

While Jack drove back to London they discussed and composed a letter to Albert Stevenson. It went something like this:

Dear Mr. Stevenson,

It has come to the attention of my Committee that while playing on the King's Course in the company of Mr. Ted Ray and Mr. Jack Stone on 13th June, 1968, you holed out with your second shot on the 446-yard 13th hole.

Having examined our records we can find no trace of this ever being achieved since the course was laid out.

The Committee have given consideration to the best means whereby your feat could be commemorated in some tangible fashion, and have asked me to seek your approval on their decision.

The individual holes on Gleneagles Courses have traditional names, and these are featured on the score cards, the name boards at each tee, and on all Gleneagles marketing literature. The 13th on the King's, our Championship course, is 'Braid's Brawest'.

The Committee now seeks your permission to place your achievement on permanent record by re-naming this hole, 'Stevenson's Rocket'.

It is hoped you will have no objection and I look forward to hearing from you at your early convenience.

Yours sincerely,

A draft was typed when Jack got back to his office and, once they were both satisfied with the wording, it was set out on a sheet of the Gleneagles stationery. As Jack had trucks hauling goods all over the country, he gave the letter to one of his drivers doing a Scottish run with instructions to post it when in the Perthshire area.

Then came excited phone calls from Albert Stevenson who insisted on reading the letter to him, having already done so to Ted, and no doubt to anybody else prepared to hear him out at his home, club, pub or place of work. 'What do you think I ought to do?' was his theme. 'Why, write a nice letter accepting the honour' was the general advice.

This he did. But before sending it, there were meetings with both Ted Ray and Jack Stone to assist in couching the reply in terms suitable to such a gracious offer. Worded to the satisfaction of all concerned it was finally posted to the Golf Secretary at Gleneagles.

Weeks passed into months and our friend was bewildered by the lack of reaction from Gleaneagles. Ted explained there was no reason for him to expect any. Gleneagles had sought his approval in writing to change the name of a hole to commemorate his feat and he had given the approval in writing. End of story.

'But I thought they might have written or sent a photograph when they made the change', complained Albert. 'Not at all', was Ted's reasoning, 'with all their international activities your little bit of glory has long since been forgotten. They've no doubt made the change and it must now wait until you next visit Gleneagles to take your own pictures and read about it on the score card or handbook.' Or words to that affect.

And there the matter rested.

Or should I say did rest, until Albert and Jack were at a golfing function in 1983, when Jack decided to relate the story – more or less as set out here – while making an after-dinner speech.

Jack was no great friend of Albert's for quite some time after that dinner; and as Ted Ray departed this earth in 1981, I expect Albert'll have a few words to say when he joins him on the first tee up there. But as there's no hurry, let's hope that won't be for quite a while yet – especially as being the good sport he is, Albert took my write-up in good part when I sent him a draft; just correcting a few dates and the like where necessary. 'It means', he said, 'that having waited a further twenty years, the world at last is going to learn through your book, Sam, what a great golfer I turned out to be twenty years after my four-year stint in a Japanese prisoner-of-war camp!'

In the Beginning

According to family history, there was hardly a childhood disease or ailment that passed me by. Whooping cough, scarlet fever, mumps, measles, chicken pox, convulsions – to name but a few – each gave me a whirl before making way for the next one in line. But once having hosted a particular virus and hit the road to recovery, that was it. For, in accordance with popular belief, they never came back.

With appendicitis licked at 11, staying free of contagion for the next 37 years must have made me over-confident; for I then fell victim to one of the most virulent bugs known to mankind. A physical and mental disease from which, once contracted, few people are expected to recover. Learned students of the subject may have coined a Latin name for it, but its four-lettered Anglo-Saxon title is recognised instantly and universally. Treatment and isolation centres spring up in increasing numbers as the epidemic spreads worldwide, but amputation of both upper limbs is the only known escape from its dreaded clutches. Its name? – Golf!

Until the age of 39, my only knowledge of golf, and the background against which it was played, was from word-pictures created by some of the greatest books on the subject. Not boring old tomes on wrist-pronation, hip-rotation, or clubhead speed – written by cunning professionals to destroy what tiny skills may have developed before deciding to study the subject. Studies that created a need for another half-dozen expensive lessons to help rebuild a shattered golf-swing (caused by trying to follow complicated texts and line drawings of deformed or double-jointed people in vain attempts to improve one's game). But wholesome fun-laden stories by P. G. Wodehouse – like 'The Clicking of Cuthbert' or 'The Heart of a Goof' – whose countless hilarious plots unfolded around the Royal and Ancient game. Or the smooth-flowing anecdotes of Henry Longhurst, with a lifetime of writing on the golfing scene in *The Sunday Times, Golf Illustrated* and other magazines, besides at least a dozen hard-back books to his credit. In all of which he wrote elegantly of the pleasures associated with the game, rather than of the game itself.

Back in 1972, when trying to write my first book, I was introduced to Henry at a Club lunch, where I told him what a struggle it was to get lumpiness out of sentences when trying to construct them, and how I envied his oh-so-easy-to-read writing style.

'Thank you, dear boy,' he replied with a deprecating smile, 'but you must just persevere. If you're aware of lumpiness then you're aware of the one problem that besets every writer worthy of the name.' He went on to quote Richard Sheridan, a great English writer of Napoleonic times.

One writes with ease to show one's breeding
But easy writing's demned vile reading!

'And by the same token', said Henry, 'easy reading is demned hard writing.' (Not half! I will have rewritten or retyped much of this chapter myself once or twice, for instance; before sending it to be retyped professionally by the fair Helen in readiness for the printer – only to disfigure her well-presented final copy yet again with a further spate of Tippex erasures and ball-pen afterthoughts before letting it go.)

He told me about his home in the shadow of two old windmills, Jack and Jill, on the Sussex Downs near Brighton. The cap of Jack had been lined with pine boards and converted into a cosy study, where he did most of his writing. He said he knew from memory every knot-hole in the ceiling – having spent hundreds of hours tilted back in his chair gazing at them, while trying to smooth 'lumpiness'

– as I chose to call it – from whatever he happened to be writing at the time. It was nothing, he reckoned, to spend an hour or more mentally fumbling with 19 ways of constructing one sentence before deciding on the twentieth, in which the syntax met with his approval.

Being told this first-hand by one I considered to be master of the written word – and the spoken one, too, as any fortunate enough to have heard him responding to an after-dinner toast will confirm – was great encouragement to persevere with descriptive writing. The pendulum swung full distance when I read a flattering 750-word review of *Victory in 'Site'!* in a March 1987 trade magazine. It began with, 'Sam Morley has produced a very easy-to-read book'.

Thank you, Henry Longhurst.

It was my fascination with the writings of both Wodehouse and Longhurst, each as good at the game as they were with the pen – they were both scratch golfers in their time – that took me up through 'O-levels' on the complexities of birdies, mashies, stymies, etiquette, and clubhouse life, without my every placing a foot into a spiked shoe or a sand-filled bunker. Together, over the years, they had built for me a haunting mental picture of good fellowship and broad, smiling fairways.

Came one day in 1957 when, returning to my Holloway office after a business meeting, I drove through Regent's Park and saw a sign near the entrance to London Zoo. It read 'Holdright's Indoor Golf School', and the establishment consisted of a number of single-storey wooden huts at the end of a short walk from the road. On impulse I stopped the car, walked up the path, and entered the door marked 'Enquiries'.

'Do you take left-handed idiots and beginners?', I asked in ringing tones of a benign and elderly gentleman, having noticed a flex dangling from a hearing-aid to the battery in his jacket pocket. 'Why, of course we do', said Mr. Holdright courteously, hastily turning down the volume, 'come right in.' He explained that he'd lost count of the number of idiots and beginners who had come through his door over the years, only to finish up as world-beaters once he'd finished with them. 'But the first thing we're going to do is turn you into the makings of a top right-handed golfer'.

'But I don't want to be a right-handed golfer', I protested, 'I'm naturally left-handed, -shouldered or -footed in all sports and games, with guns or bows-and-arrows, and with screwdrivers, hammers or pens.' He explained that the right-hand golf swing was really the equivalent to a good leftie backhand-shot in tennis, with the left arm fully extended and hitting against a braced left side. The right hand was a steadying influence that just went along for the ride while sitting on the left. With a naturally strong left side, he explained carefully, once a left-hander had overcome the unfamiliarity of playing the wrong way round, it shouldn't take him very long to win his club scratch competition. There ended the first lesson!

'Then why don't you teach all right-handed people to use left-handed clubs and learn to hit against their strong right side?', I asked. 'Ah', he sighed, 'there are far too many of them and too many manufacturers producing conventional clubs to suit the conventional 95 per cent in the land. Look at Ben Hogan', he went on, 'a natural left-handed golfer like you until he realised he'd never get to the very top trying to beg, borrow or buy the limited choice of left-handed clubs there were around in those days. So he went out of circulation for a couple of years while teaching himself to play the other way round, and just look what he achieved once he overcame those early difficulties.'

Mr. Holdright then turned me over to one of his assistants who, as we walked toward one of the practice huts, went through the Ben Hogan routine again and said he'd have me hitting the ball a country mile once he'd got me through the teething stage of playing right-handed.

(But he made no mention at the time that, early in the course, the School usually managed to sell a nice new matched set of golf clubs to a beginner after the first series of lessons. The ploy being, the sooner you start taking your lessons with your own clubs, which they will help you choose to suit your build and swing, the sooner you will reach a higher standard of consistency than you would wielding that miscellaneous collection of old tools standing in the corner of the practice shed. A very good selection of brand-new matched sets were always on show for that purpose in Mr. Holdright's front shop. All of them right-handed, and for each set sold the assistant would, no doubt, receive a reasonable reward for his sales 'pitch'.)

Be that as it may, there seemed no point at the time in opposing the expert advice of those to whom I'd agreed to pay good folding money to teach me how to do it right.

So, with jacket and tie on a hook, and looking into full length mirrors in front, behind, and to my right, I stood on a large coconut mat, trying to wrap unwilling fingers – in what I was told was the Vardon grip – around the shaft of an old right-handed 5-iron. Before me was a series of overlapping nets protecting three sides and the ceiling of the shed, with a sheet of canvas behind the back net, into which the ball would rocket with a resounding thwack! if hit correctly.

With a succession of thwacks! the young man demonstrated effortlessly what was expected of me, and at the end of an hour I was awash with perspiration – having swung at something like 250 balls and hit 33 of them! All the time to encouraging compliments that I was showing great promise.

After another six lessons over the ensuing month or so, I was swinging easier and making reasonable contact with the ball more often than not. So much so that the young man called in Mr. Holdright to show what a star pupil he had made me and didn't he think it was time I got measured up for a nice new set of clubs of my own. The boss was suitably impressed when I proceeded to hit one air-shot and two thwacks!

But sloshing a right-handed 'screamer' never did compare with the sweet smell of success a good leftie shot in football, tennis or cricket once provided. It just didn't seem to be me swinging at and thwacking that ball with a right-handed 5-iron or 2-wood. (Yes – I'd graduated into the two-or-three-club league by this time.) Each time I complained that I felt like a disembodied machine, my mentor would resurrect Ben Hogan as a shining example of a dedicated man who saw the light and found 'right' was might!

But I thought about Ben's lovely big green book called *Golf*, with its wonderful anatomical drawings explaining the golf swing. (The work of a perfectionist and the finest instructional book on the subject I've ever seen. I bought it in Holdright's shop after that first lesson, and would still have it today if, like a fool, I hadn't lent it to somebody or other who never returned it.) Being a determined perfectionist, Ben's photographs in both his book and the golfing magazines usually showed grim, unsmiling features dedicated to the perfection he pursued. And from what I remember, the fun-filled spin-offs of the game – as described by Wodehouse and Longhurst – played about as much a part in his off-course life-style as they would in that of a Trappist monk!

By changing from the way Nature ordained that I play my games was I risking a possible change of personality? Some will say I should have persevered, because any change in what I turned out to be could only have been an improvement. But then how many all-time 'greats' were able to please all the people all the time? Proceeding with the soliloquy, I decided that even if I stayed with the right-handed approach to the game, I was now too long in the tooth to believe the American Open could ever be mine – and even the British equivalent wasn't going to be that easy. Came the decision that right-handed golf and Sam Morley weren't cut out for each other, the whole thing lost its first exciting momentum. As a result and without ever yet knowing the thrill of striking a ball into the wide blue yonder, I shook the dust of Holdright's off my feet and returned to pursuing the path of a mini-tycoon.

Two years went by, and came one hot summer morning in

1959. A midweek morning with more than the customary frustration and irritation in the post, on the phone, and from those with whom I shared the daily round. Feeling an urgent need to vent some spleen, I didn't know how to start. I had no idea of (a) where to look for a spleen, and (b) just how to vent it once located. But instinct said it was something best done in natural surroundings – such as are found on a rural golf course. Brookmans Park, thirty minutes from the office and four minutes from my home, came immediately to mind. With the help of the telephone directory I got through to their professional, a Mr. Ron King.

'I want to start playing golf immediately', I said, 'but have never before ever set foot on a golf course. Yours happens to be nearest my home in Cuffley. I am a natural left-hander and will need to buy the necessary equipment to suit one so afflicted. Can you fix me up if I came straight over? And having once bought what was needed can I go straight out into the good clean fresh air and get down to some private spleen-venting?' 'Of course', said the genial Mr. King, 'this is great spleen-venting country. Just hang on a minute while I check our left-handed stocks.'

He took the best part of three to come back and tell me that all he could find was a 4-wood and a 3-iron. He suggested that I ring the Professional Golfers Co-operative, then in Baker Street, W.1, but now defunct, for a left-handed half-set to be booked against his name.

'All you need', he said, 'is a 3-, 5- and 7-iron, a 3-wood and a putter. Once you've learned to use them properly you will play down to 12-handicap without any need to add to them.'

But the Pro's Co-Op, as it turned out, carried about as much left-handed stock as Ron King, and promised that if I cared to wait a week or two they'd get some in for me. When told it was an emergency, the man suggested I ring Lilleywhite's, Piccadilly. Lilleywhite's said that sets or half sets of left-handed clubs were only bought in to order, although they might manage to find one or two odd ones. Simpsons, also in Piccadilly, could only promise that they'd get something in for me within three or four days if it was that important. It was, and also beginning to become abundantly clear why Ben Hogan chose to do it the hard way.

Remember this was 1959. The stores mentioned are no doubt bristling with left-handed clubs today, but thirty years ago it was a different story.

My secretary then suggested I try Gamages, where she'd seen a very well-stocked golfing department when out shopping recently. Before it was pulled down for yet another office block, Gamages was in Holborn opposite Fetter Lane, and somewhat similar to what Selfridges is today. The store was especially popular with City folk and shoppers coming in from North and East London.

'Come along and take your pick', said the man, when asked my stock question over the telephone, 'we've dozens of sets for you to choose from.' And so they had.

Equipped with my five shiny new golf clubs, a shoulder bag, and a book on how to use them – including a chapter on course etiquette – I drove as fast as possible to Brookmans Park. When Ron King learned of the hurdles that had to be overcome since speaking to him on the telephone, he commiserated and planned to have a few things to say about the failings of the Pro's Co-Op at the next meeting of the P.G.A. But in the meantime and in answer to my question, he was fully booked for lessons that afternoon. In any case, he didn't think I was ready for any yet.

'You know the rudiments of the swing', he said, when told of the right-handed lessons two years back, 'so all you've got to do is reverse the procedure and start getting the feel of your nice new clubs. Why don't you just pay a five shillings' green fee' (that's 25p, for the sake of future generations that might come across this book) 'and go and enjoy yourself? There's nobody out there and if you say you've never walked a golf course before I couldn't think of a prettier one on which to start. You'll find your way around quite easily, as the direction to each tee is clearly marked from the preceding green.'

So, having bought myself a pair of spiked shoes, a dozen GBD golf balls, and some wooden pegs, I hung my jacket and tie on a hook in the locker room and stepped out to the first tee. It was just after 1.00 p.m. and there wasn't a soul about. Everything looked and smelt beautiful, with a tractor-driven gang-mower plodding slowly away in the distance. Lovingly I removed the crinkly paper from the first of my twelve new balls and placed it carefully on one of my new wooden pegs. Just as lovingly I drew my new 3-wood from my new shoulder bag, and took up the stance as taught at Holdright's and in Ben Hogan's book – but of course in reverse. After a couple of practice swings just to get the feel of it, I took up position, swung slowly back, and launched myself into a brand new world.

It would be useless to pretend I know where that ball went, or the next one come to that; all I knew was that all that delightful greenery was at my disposal, and it didn't matter what happened to the odd ball that went to ground. After all I had 12 of them, and whatever it was that niggled me back there in the office was now a million miles away. Nothing now remained but to suck this beautiful afternoon dry, peel the skin off another GBD when necessary, and walk in the footsteps of the great men I'd read about.

But the euphoria had to end. Half way down the third, my twelfth and last GBD flew into a thick and inpenetrable hedge, never again – like its predecessors – to be seen. Not by me, at least. The hot sun belted down, a skylark twittered up aloft, and the freshly-cut grass never smelt sweeter as I began the long trudge back to the clubhouse.

To my delight the bar was still open. Samuel Whitbread started his brewing business in the middle of the 18th century, since when his firm must have produced goodness knows how many hundred million gallons of their celebrated bitter. But never could they have improved on that perfect pint pulled for me by the Brookmans Park steward that afternoon. It slid down my parched throat in one long refreshing draught without once touching the sides.

Then back to the pro's shop, where I bought another dozen GBDs; and was told by the kindly Mr. King that they'd last me a lot longer this time if I remembered not to take my eye off the ball – even after I managed to hit it. He apologised for not being able to provide me with old balls to learn with, but didn't have many and needed them all for his lessons.

Not only was his advice sound, but my game must certainly have improved because, starting again from the first, I got as far as the eleventh hole this time before the twenty-fourth ball I'd unwrapped that afternoon disappeared with a musical 'plop' into a broad and tranquil lake. (That's another thing the unfortunate golfer entering the game for the first time during recent years will never know – the thrill of taking the crinkly paper off a lovely new ball before trying to knock the stuffing out of it. Although now six or seven times dearer than what they were 27 years ago, and with ten times as many people buying golf balls, they now come naked in cartons of three; for some unbelievably obscure reason, the makers do not seem able to afford clothing their £1.50 product in a piece of decorative wrapping paper, similar to that still found around a tuppenny toffee! (Or around the other traditional 'packet-of-three' enjoying a new lease of popularity with the promiscuous!)

Anyway, although through with unwrapping balls for that particular day, I was now irrevocably hooked. The following day I went back to Holdright's place in Regent's Park and, with a new assistant, booked in a for a dozen lessons – my way! Indoor tuition is something I'd recommend to any beginner or 'rabbit' at the game. Grooving a swing is far better achieved by hitting three times the amount of balls into a net than would be hit on a practice fairway in the same amount of time. Remember how much of that time in the latter instance is spent in watching wayward ones; and then walking around collecting between bouts of actual sloshing at them.

When an old business pal, Ron Garner, learned I'd taken an interest in the game, he was delighted, and suggested I join him, his partner Bert Meddings, and their pal Charlie Marshall, at the local public course, Whitewebbs. They had played there together almost every Saturday and Sunday for ten years or more, I was told when I first joined up with them somewhere around November 1959.

It was a cruel winter in which to start playing regularly each weekend – but I learned a lot. Like how to paint those old Spitfires and Lobbies bright red so they showed up better on frosted ground; how to carry a bag of clubs so that both hands could be thrust deep in trouser-pockets between shots, round a couple of hand-warmers; how to stop at Charlie Marshall's favourite 'watering place' – a thicket by the side of the sixth tee and screened from those coming behind – where he'd complain of his most difficult task of the morning – how to get three-eighth-of-an-inch of frigid 'willie' through five-eighth-of-an-inch of knitted woollie! (Just wouldn't sound the same in millimetres today, would it?)

The Eccentric Club of St. James's, of which I'd been a member since 1955, had an established golfing section. I joined it early in 1960, having achieved a 21-handicap at Whitewebbs; and went on to experience playing illustrious courses like Sunningdale, Wentworth, St. George's Hill and Moor Park. I just couldn't believe there was so much pleasure to be had, around bunker or bar, at 43 years of age.

Wanting more out of golf – in keeping with the stories I'd read and those related by my Eccentric friends – than Whitewebbs had to offer, I applied to join Crews Hill Golf Club in June 1960. Chapter Two tells the eventful story of my first day there.

A year after leaving Whitewebbs, I invited Ron Garner and his wife to join me for an Eccentric weekend at Le Touquet. On his return he learned his partner and life-long friend, Bert Meddings, had died suddenly. Without his old pal, golf lost its appeal to him until he joined me at Crews Hill, where he was to become Captain 14 years later.

Going back to 1960, when I was still playing at Whitewebbs, I supplemented those five Gamages clubs with a 2-wood, a 9-iron and a sand wedge from the same store. By dint of spending about as much time on a golf course as I did in the office, my handicap came down to nine (as did, almost, the staff in my electrical engineering business) over the ensuing three years.

But I learned so much more than how to hit a ball reasonably well and less inconsistently. I learned how many of the friends I made in golf had started at it much earlier in life, but never read the kind of books referred to at the beginning of this chapter. Playing the game with an urgent need to make every shot a telling one, so many had never 'stopped to smell the flowers', as Walter Hogan once put it.

There's so much more to golf than just the game we see serious-minded young men – and some old enough to know better – posturing over and pacing out on greens and fairways up and down the country. (With the result that a round that once took three hours often takes nearer five today.) Ask many of them the name of a particularly magnificent old tree en route to wherever their ball happens to be lying, and they'd ask 'What tree?' Or else complain that it should have been cut down 'yonks' ago because it fouled up a well-drawn shot designed to beat the dog-leg approach to the green.

The true meaning of golf is far too complex and profound for young people to take seriously before reaching their mid-thirties – at the earliest. Oh, by all means let a youngster go and bash an old ball at his dad's club, but it's got to be treated like a ride on the cross-bar of his big brother's bike. He's far too small to reach the pedals or be trusted out on his own in traffic. There are so many pleasures better suited for those in their teens, twenties and early thirties before they try to enter the hallowed portals of Golf.

I say 'portals' because, to fully appreciate the point, think of it as a means of entry into a new way of life. A way of life that should not be savoured until a man has resigned himself to the depressing thought that middle age approacheth, and that opportunities for active hedonism are becoming noticeably fewer.

Then, with one pull of the curtain, the self-pitying wretch will behold, for the first time, a magnificent array of stimulating people, places, parties, pranks and prattle; something the Kingdom of Golf will continue to provide for him, in infinite variety and abundance, for the ensuing fifty years. Or even sixty, if he paces himself!

Now try to reconcile that picture with the grim-faced youths of our time, hitting five thousand golf balls a day on practice fairways, in pursuit of some transient honour like next Saturday's monthly medal!

Alas, the true multi-coloured Kingdom of Golf can never be theirs!

" Congratulations —
It's been interesting watching a business associate
who chooses a quick profit rather than long-term
steady growth "

—— 4 ——

The Night I Played in the Esso Open!

If it wasn't for GOLF . . . many high-spirited people, having become even higher and a little more spirited after a session on high and spirited stimulants, could turn troublesome and do things they'd forget, or would like to forget, come next morning. But not golfers. Certainly not the kind of golfers featured in this story.

Reg Davies, Fred Tebbs and Hugh Donald are still three great friends with whom, together and separately over the past thirty years, I've had enough four-star outings to fill half-a-dozen of these books – and there'd be at least as many again best left unchronicled.

This one concerns the four of us returning in my car from a day with the Eccentric Club Golfing Society at Addington, near Croydon, Surrey. It was sometime in the early 1960s, when all four were fairly new into golf, but heavily addicted to the magic of it all.

Pre-breathalysers, if a gregarious man found himself with a thirst, he'd work untiringly at quenching it in the best company he could find. And flogging round 36 holes of Addington on a hot sunny day with three fellow-floggers raised one hell of a thirst that took a lot of quenching. But with prize-giving over, all bets paid, ball-sweep completed, and the drinks-pot – into which winners were religiously expected to transfer their hard-won sweepstake-money for the benefit of all – emptied, the bar-staff pulled the shutters down with professional indifference to fingers still pleading for that last and truly final one for the road.

Living as we did within a few miles of each other, it was normal practice after full days such as this to get about two-thirds of the journey done back to our part of the world, before stopping for some solid back-up to the evening's liquidity. A further couple of hours would then be spent over steaks and a flagon or two while dissecting the highlights of the day.

On this occasion the decision on where to stop was made when Fred spoke highly of The Dorice, Swiss Cottage, in the open Finchley Road. The place is still there, as is the filling station opposite, but readers familiar with the area should remember that at the time in question, there were neither pedestrian barriers lining the pavements nor a central island making a dual carriageway of the busy road between them.

It was about 10.30 p.m. as we parked about ten yards past the place and trooped inside. Once decisions were made on how steaks, chops or Wiener schnitzels were to be cooked and how many bottles of what were to be opened without delay, we got back to our favourite topic of conversation.

Immaturity at golf was matched only by our wild enthusiasm for the game, as seated round that table, each in turn – and quite often out of turn – pontificated with pet theories on how some of the shots that we'd made such a hash of on the course should really be played. Opinions varied and, as the wine flowed, so did each of the four insist that his was the only correct way.

Emerging into the night air a little after midnight, the principal bone of contention was how to play a delicate 30-yard chip with a 9-iron. We stood outside the Dorice, hotly debating the subject. Feeling the time had come to press my point with deeds, not words, I broke away, went to the boot of the car, drew out my 9-iron and a ball, went back to the others, and put the ball down on a crack between paving stones. I suggested we each play the shot in question at the second petrol pump from the left in the brilliantly lit all-night garage across the road, and the one to finish closest to the target would receive half-a-quid from each of the others.

Then, taking my stance in the classic style of all great left-handers, I waited for a break in the traffic before playing, to my astonishment, a perfectly shaped chip shot. It cleared the low parapet wall in front of the garage, bounced off the hard tarmac forecourt and hit the pump in question with a resounding metallic crack. The attendant came charging out of his kiosk, peering around bewildered at his empty filling station. In the meantime Fred had selected his club from the car, placed a ball on the pavement and with a shower of sparks as the sole of the club struck the unyielding stone, hit what he always maintains to be the darlingest little chip shot of his life. It sent the ball into an invisible high lob across the murky highway to land with a resounding wallop against the target pump.

The poor old attendant jumped and cried out in alarm as he peered into the night and tried to fathom out why his pumps were clanging. Still grasping his club, Fred nipped sharply across the road, thrust half-a-quid into the astonished bloke's hand, and quickly explained that, of some thirty thousand filling stations in Greater London, his had been chosen by four exponents of the game to help resolve a golfing problem. As an independent witness, would he assist by deciding which of the four shots now being played finished up nearest to the second pump on the left?

In the meantime Reg had his club at the ready and a ball in position on the pavement. By this time a small knot of interested spectators had halted in a half circle at a reasonably safe distance behind the point of play. At a bus-stop immediately to the right, there were now two late-night buses parked, while their crews and some of the passengers stood on the pavement spellbound at what was taking place. But their stationary vehicles now made it difficult for the player to see traffic approaching from the right. On realising this, the driver of the leading bus kindly stood by its offside front wing and stopped all vehicles heading north, whilst Reg coolly played his shot through the intermittent flow in the southbound direction. Once again the blow was a true one, landing in the target area and bouncing merrily around the forecourt. Fred and his now-enthusiastic 'referee' watched and waited for it to stop careering around in order to pace out its distance from the pump in comparison with the other two, now-stationary balls.

Finally, Hugh Donald, who was by far the most experienced and proficient golfer of the four, carefully adjusted his stance, surveyed the hazards, checked the wind direction, firmed up his grip and swung effortlessly through the ball.

Whether a little restlessness on the part of the crowd disturbed his concentration, or a reflex action on sensing a southbound cyclist pedalling like mad into the line of fire as his wrists pronated through the hitting area, we never really found out. But instead of the ball soaring in a triumphant parabola across the midnight sky and landing even more accurately than its three predecessors, it rocketed viciously across the road at a little below knee-height, smashed against the low parapet wall of the garage and, in rebounding into the front wheel of the offending bicycle, unseated the rider.

He was a big burly chap who, glowering at the laughing Fred as he approached from the filling-station end, castigated him as a dangerous and stupid idiot, old enough to know better than chucking stones at cyclists in the middle of the night. 'Not at all,' replied our man, 'you had no right taking your bike across our fairway while a game was in progress!' Before he could take that in, the cyclist got another wigging. This time from the approaching white-coated petrol attendant, who accused him of riding in a reckless manner into an area where any fool could tell from surrounding stationary vehicles and crowds that it was necessary to proceed with caution. Glancing nervously from one to the other the poor chap jumped on his bike and, with one final glance over his shoulder, pedalled off madly into the night.

The traffic moved on and the crowds dispersed as the clubs were put back into the car. The petrol attendant came over to bid us goodnight and, as a little more largesse found its way into his willing hand, thanked us warmly for choosing his garage to hold our competition. He went on to tell us he was on nights for the rest of the month – during which time we were welcome to come along and play there again whenever we fancied!

Thinking back, I don't believe we ever did.

"What d'you chap'sh think?.... couple of shix irons enough?"

5

The BBUGS

A Golfing Society is a 'closed shop' of dedicated golf addicts. It usually begins when people sharing a common interest – be it to work, play, teach, learn, cure, protect or amuse – form an inner circle among those of its number familiar with the game.

So just as the House of Commons and the House of Lords have their own Golfing Society among those who make our laws, so does each of the Police Divisions that enforce them, and the Barristers and Judges who interpret them. Not to mention the Prison Officers guarding those who break 'em.

They can be found as frequently among Freemasons, Rotarians, Buffaloes, Trade Associations, Chambers of Commerce, Airlines, Town Halls, H.M. Forces, Hospitals, Colleges, Polytechnics and Old Boys Associations, as among British Airways, Gas, Oil, Telecom, Electricity, Water, Rail. And while some of the foregoing don't yet carry the national tag at the time of writing this book, it's odds on they will before it goes out of print.

Devotees of the game among Writers, Publishers and Journalists generally form themselves into Societies, as do Jockeys, Stage Performers and Income Tax Inspectors. Most of the Gentleman's Clubs around Pall Mall boast one among their members, as do similar establishments around the provinces. Bunny Langford, daughter of the late Larry Webb, Chairman of the Eccentric Club and responsible for Chapter II, formed the Lady Eccentric Golfing Society in the 1970s. A choice of name abbreviated nicely to those shapely feminine appendages that cause grown golfers to gaze and drool – LEGS!

Doctors, Dentists, Architects, Lawyers, Engineers,

Publicans, Broadcasters, Surveyors, and Lord-knows how many more brainy and brawny groups, have their local and national Golfing Societies. There's a left-handed golfing society in most civilised countries, as there is among one-armed, one-legged, and no doubt one-eyed enthusiasts for the game. Most golf clubs have their own inner 'closed shops' – made up from those of its members who choose to form a society because they share a common experience, activity or peculiarity. Hence the Over-forties; Over-sixties; Past-Captains; Hole-in-one; ex-Army, -Navy or -R.A.F. Golfing Societies. Back in 1963, a few of us at Crews Hill formed 'The CHEDDARS'. Or to give it its full title, The Crews Hill Eating Drinking Debauching And Rug-making Society. I must admit that 'Rug-making' was a bit of an afterthought. 'Raping' was the original word when dreaming up the title, but some of the boys didn't think they were up to it any more!

Whether they meet weekly, monthly, quarterly or annually, all Golfing Societies have one thing in common. A pre-arranged plan to take time off from the daily round and get together at a chosen golf course other than the one they normally play at weekends. It could be in the next parish, village, town, county, country or continent.

The day, or days, away with a good society is usually made up of competitive golf, prize-giving, sweepstakes for golf balls, possibly too much food, certainly too much drink, and nowhere near enough sleep. At least, with most of the folks I've been away with.

Golf clubs usually welcome societies, as much revenue is derived from green fees, catering and general extravagance in both the bar and professional's shop. Some of the more prestigious clubs are selective over which societies they will accept and the maximum number of players they may bring. Despite charges being sometimes double those of the more parochial clubs, the prestigious ones are so much in demand that bookings need to be made two, or even three, years ahead.

To ensure the good times will roll as planned, each society

needs a tireless enthusiast as its Honorary Organiser or Secretary. It is he who makes bookings, collects dues, pays bills, circularises members, chooses menus, buys prizes, decides competitions, scrutinises scorecards, plans ball-sweeps, and deals with all the problems that arise before, during and after the day. Like the bloke who rings the night before to say he's just lost his licence to drive and is there somebody who can give him a lift; or the one who's not going to play with slow-old-cheating Percy Preethfingle again, and wants a different partner to the P.P. he's paired with on the starting sheet; or he who left his 7-iron somewhere out there on the course – or can of Brut-spray in the shower room – and wants the honorary 'minder' now to ask around if anybody's handed it in and arrange for it to be sent on.

Where societies have a number of meetings in a year, one or more can be declared a guest day; whereby each member brings along a pal. Often the same pal each time. I suppose Reg Davies was my guest at Eccentric meetings about as often as I was his at those of the British Dental Association Golfing Society. It has been said we each knew more among the other's society than did many of its own less gregarious followers. As a result, his 'trophy-room' shelves are stacked with about as many Eccentric cut-glass drinking goblets as mine are with silver tankards engraved BDAGS.

It was as his guest at Thorndon Park Golf Club one year that I learned of the history of an exclusive little society that's worth retelling. It happened like this.

After golf, prize-giving, ball-sweep and speeches we went down to a hot meal in the Thorndon Park dining room. I sat across from Millice Freeman – a dental officer with the Ministry of Health. His plain blue silk tie with a single large golfing motif had me asking what the letters HCCG woven into it stood for. 'Horrible Company of Cambridgeshire Golfers', he replied, and with little further prompting told the story behind it.

When he was a young man at Cambridge, and a member of its famous Gog and Magog Golf Club, he decided –

together with three equally-addicted, low-handicap pals –
on a golfing holiday in Scotland, playing some of its great
courses. The oldest and one of the most hallowed clubs is at
Muirfield, on the south coast of the Firth of Forth, and bears
the splendid title of 'The Honourable Company of
Edinburgh Golfers'. It is still recorded in Donald Steel's *Golf
Course Guide to the British Isles* as providing 'No facilities for
lady golfers'!

But, despite his unusual Christian name, there was
nothing lady-like about Millice Freeman, or his three
companions, when they presented themselves at the
Secretary's office at Muirfield and asked permission to pay a
green fee and play a round of golf. Especially as a fellow-
member at Gog and Magog was also a member at Muirfield,
and had assured them that if they just mentioned his name
to the Secretary the doors would be flung open wide by way
of a welcome. Well, they mentioned the name good and loud,
but the doors remained bolted and barred. In vain they told
of their prowess at the game and awareness of the behaviour
and etiquette expected of them, but the man in charge was
adamant. Without a letter of introduction from their own
club secretary, or from the friend and member to whom they
referred, they remained *personae non grata* at the illustrious
home of the Honourable Company of Edinburgh Golfers,
and were barred from placing mortal feet on its sacred
fairways.

They pleaded how far they'd travelled just to walk on the
hallowed turf, and took an oath that should any of it be
disturbed by their efforts it would be carefully reinstated,
right way up, before attempting another shot. For all the
effect it had, they might just as well have pleaded with the
granite blocks of which the clubhouse was built. The door
remained firmly closed.

Turning away in despair, one of the four said bitterly, 'It's
not fair, when you think of the number of Scots who come
sightseeing around historic old Cambridge, and are allowed
to play golf on our historic old "Gogs" without ever being
asked to produce credentials. We wouldn't dream of being

discourteous to folks who'd come all that way to enjoy our treasured heritage'. Or words to that effect.

This must have found a chink in the old curmudgeon's armour because he relented sufficiently to growl, still with some reluctance, 'Ah weel, ye can play a roon o' gowf the noo, but ye canna use the clubhooose'. To which the boys replied with genuine delight, 'That's very kind, Sir, and thank you very much. But surely you'll let us use the locker rooms to change our clothes?' 'Nay', was the firm response. 'The clubhoose and locker rooms are for members and their guests only. Ye'll have to make do as best ye can in the trolley-shed or in yer ain motor-car'. And that was final.

Well, they made do as best they could in the trolley-shed and motor-car. Once having played, they went in search of a pub or hotel to rinse the dust from parched East Anglian throats. While doing so they mulled over the day's events and discussed their traumatic brush with The Honourable Company of Edinburgh Golfers. To commemorate the day they formed the 'Horrible Company of Cambridgeshire Golfers'!

They would meet each year at the scene and on the anniversary of their experience, and play a Stableford competition at the Honourable Company of Edinburgh Golfers – having, of course, first ensured that they'd brought the vital written credentials with them. They would book into and stay at one of the best hotels in Gullane, a few miles along the coast from Muirfield, where the quality of food, wine and service would serve to remind them of the Muirfield catering standards denied them on the day. After dinner there would be prize-giving, toasts and speeches, followed by the Annual General Meeting of the HCCG. A Captain, Treasurer, Secretary and Vice-Captain would be elected for the ensuing year. Well, not exactly elected because with but four positions to fill from a full membership of four, the honours would be passed around in rotation each year. The new Captain would call for a magnum of champagne to celebrate his appointment and to launch the society on yet another successful year.

A special tie was designed, to be worn at all official meetings of the society, and as frequently as possible when in the company of other golfers, so that its origin could be explained to those curious enough to ask about it.

And this ritual they continued to follow for the next thirty years or more, with the exception of time spent while otherwise engaged in playing their part in World War Two.

Finally, Millice Freeman, like so many of those responsible for these ramblings, has now gone to join his illustrious ancestors. But having made reference to war service, it should also be known that he was awarded the Military Cross in 1944 for carrying a succession of wounded men to safety on his back in the jungles of Burma, while his stricken ambulance was under fire from Japanese guns – something I learned for the first time when checking my facts with a surviving member of the Horrible Company of Cambridgeshire Golfers in June 1987. Yes, he was a great man in many ways, was George Millice Freeman.

Then there's the Stuart Raybold Golfing Society – founded about ten years ago and still going strong. It also meets once a year – to mark Stuart Raybold's failure to win the monthly medal, on a technicality, at his golf club. This is how it was told by the founder of the society.

The Secretary in question, now long replaced, was a rather ludicrous character with Walter-Mitty-like tendencies. My memories of him comprise fruity banalaties about the thoroughbred horses he claimed to own; a flying-officer-Kyte-type moustache; a pepper-and-salt hacking jacket; cream-coloured cavalry-twill jodhpurs – against which he'd slap a riding crop as he strode around the course near the clubhouse; and a tendency never to refuse a pink gin.

He was a constant source of amusement and wonder to the rank-and-file membership, by whom he was generally referred to as Biggles, or Peter Prawn – neither of which happened to be his real name.

The event that earned the immortality of these pages was the August Monthly Medal. A competition played each month at most clubs whereby a fun round that should take three hours becomes a masochistic one of four-and-a-half. Players record the shots taken to complete each of the 18 holes – whether three shots or 13 – deduct their official handicap from the total, and are judged by the lowest nett score handed in. Usually something around the seventy mark wins the day.

I am told that on the day in question, and with most of the completed score-cards deposited in the box as players came off the course, my friend and the rest of his four-ball stood at the bar discussing the highlights of the morning over a glass or two. Watching the officious Biggles leave his favourite corner from time to time in order to collect the latest returns and take them back among his array of pink gins for scrutiny and stacking in order of merit, they decided to enliven his day.

On a blank score-card they entered the name of a fictitious competitor, Stuart Raybold, and gave him a handicap of 15. They put a score down for each hole whereby, when his handicap was deducted from the total, he finished up with a nett score of 70. From the general chat around the crowded bar and with not many returns still to come, that might very well finish up as the best score. To make it authentic a couple of indecipherable squiggles were pencilled in where the signatures of player and marker were called for and, while Biggles was busy acknowledging the latest drink offered him, one of their number slipped the card into the box without being noticed.

Came the moment when, after another couple of four-balls had entered from the course, Biggles decided to gather in the latest batch of returns. Back on his bar stool he went through them, and stopped to concentrate on one. Our quartet watched with sidelong glances, while pretending to be deep in their own conversation.

Biggles looked puzzled and was heard to ask if somebody would point out Stuart Raybold, as he couldn't put a face to the name himself. He drew three blanks before one member, allegedly a bit of a 'know-it-all', replied, 'Stuart Raybold? Of course I know him. He was playing behind us this morning, and he and his partner were standing just here a few minutes ago having a drink!' He turned to his companion and asked if 'he'd noticed where Stuart Raybold had disappeared to. 'He's gone. I heard him say he didn't want to be late home for lunch today', glibly replied the other.

Biggles went to study the Handicap Board, on which every member's name and his handicap changes are entered. He came back to buttonhole a committee member standing at the bar with his pals. Being not too far away from the 'conspirators', they overheard the conversation. 'I've got a problem', he complained. 'It seems that someone named Stuart Raybold has won the Monthly Medal. I don't know him, can't find him because hardly anybody knows him, and his name is not on the Handicap Board. What do you think I ought to do?'

But his committee man was too deeply engrossed in discussing affairs of state – or swapping dirty stories – with his cronies to bother his head with the problems of Biggles – or the elusive Stuart Raybold. 'You're the Secretary – sort it out yourself', was the abrupt answer.

The unhappy Biggles went to study the Board again – long and hard – and then disappeared into his office. Only to emerge shortly afterwards, his face set in triumphant indignation. Walking straight to the aforesaid committee man he announced in a firm voice that would brook no denial, 'That Stuart Raybold won't be getting any prizes from me. He hasn't paid his subs this year!'

Choking with suppressed laughter, the culprits were eventually obliged to admit their responsibility for Stuart's existence, and duly reprimanded by the hierarchy for being so irresponsible and heretical about something as hallowed as the Club's Monthly Medal.

Once they'd finished digesting the humble pie forced upon them, in the form of an apology to Biggles, they formed the Stuart Raybold Golfing Society. It meets once a year on the anniversary of Stuart's great achievement, in order to eat, drink, play golf and indulge in the usual pattern of merriment practised by hedonistic devotees of this great game!

The BBUGS is a final example of how small societies are formed and function. It is best introduced in the form of my letter to the Honorary Secretary of the Eccentric Club Golfing Society; another of the many old pals written about in these pages who now play down to scratch in that 'Great Golf Course in the Sky!'

Leslie Newman, Esq.,
Eccentric Club Golfing Society,
Ryder Street,
LONDON. W.1.   24th May 1966.

Dear Leslie,

On Wednesday 18th May I invited my friend, Reg Davies, to be my guest at a meeting of the ECGS at Burhill Golf Club.

We left his home in Totteridge at about 7.30 and arrived in glorious sunshine at Burhill a little after 9.00 a.m. It was to be the first time either of us had played there and, driving along the road that crossed the course, we wished we'd brought a larger car. There was just not going to be enough room in my Healey for all the prizes we felt bound to win on such a beautiful course on such a beautiful day.

On entering the car park we commented on the dearth of Bentleys, 'Rollers', Jaguars, and Aston Martins – vehicles usually well in evidence when Eccentrics are around in force – but soon learned the reason on checking with the Club Secretary. According to his diary we were twenty-four hours too early for the ECGS fixture.

That being too long to wait, we decided to pay a green fee and form a new society – consisting of one member and one guest. We had morning and afternoon competitions, with sweepstakes and prizes, and held a ball-sweep in the evening after prize-giving. All in the best tradition of the ECGS. And as the BBUGS is a spin-off from that noble fraternity, I feel you should be kept informed on its activities.

A report on the day is attached.

Yours sincerely,

And here's a copy of that report:

THE BURHILL BALLS-UP GOLFING SOCIETY

(THE BBUGS)

Members Present	*Guests Present*
Sam Morley	Reg Davies
(Captain)	(Captain's Guest)

The first meeting was held at Burhill Golf Club on Wednesday 18th May 1966, with a record 100 per cent turnout. The weather was perfect and the course in excellent condition.

Concern that we may have clashed with another and larger Society, belonging to the Eccentric Club of St. James's, proved to be groundless, and the BBUGS had the course almost to itself.

The Members' prize for the morning round was won by the Captain, Sam Morley, with the useful score of 25 points. The Guest prize went to Reg Davies, who amassed a total of no less than 31 points. It might well have been a mere 29, there being some doubt whether his ball had moved while addressing it for his second shot on the 11th. The BBUGS Rules Committee met immediately in situ and, after deliberation, it was decreed that the ball had not moved, but only rocked.

Thirty-one points were therefore recorded, as was the fact that this was the highest guest score ever at an official BBUGS meeting.

The BBUGS have an interesting rule going back to its early days, whereby the winner of the morning Guest prize is invited to become a full member of the Society. With the result that, before they all sat down to lunch, Reg Davies completed the formalities for membership, was co-opted on to the Committee, and elected vice-Captain of the BBUGS. Another interesting tradition is that, following his appointment, the vice-Captain buys all the liquid refreshment during lunch. A lunch that consisted of devilled whitebait, steak and kidney pudding and two ample wedges of Burhill's celebrated treacle tart. As all the foregoing was liberally laced with the vice-Captain's contribution, the members retired from the table to bask by the lake at the rear of the clubhouse, and did not wake for their afternoon round until 4.00 p.m.

This was a match-play competition for the BBUGS BBOWL, won by Reg Davies (11) who met and beat Sam Morley (11) in the final by the narrow margin of 2 and 1.

The Scratch Championship of the BBUGS was also won by Reg Davies, with a score of 178 over 36 holes. It was indeed a great day for Reg – incidentally, his first outing with the BBUGS – especially as he had some difficulty in walking. Partly due, I understand, to a touch of gout in the morning and DT's in the afternoon. When presenting the prizes in the bar (hastily-made but tasteful purchases from the pro's shop at lunch-time) the Captain of the BBUGS asked for the Club Secretary to join them from his office. Once the vice-Captain had called for silence, the Burhill Secretary, Head Steward and Head Greenkeeper were thanked in the Captain's speech for the excellent attention and catering received and the condition of their course.

The prizewinners generously put all their sweepstake

winnings over the bar, and a syndicate, consisting of Sam Morley and Reg Davies, was lucky enough to hold all winning tickets in the ball sweep. The bar closed at 8.30 p.m. with all BBUGS members staying through to the end. On their drive back to Hertfordshire they stopped for an informal steak and chips in a little bistro off the King's Road, Chelsea.

The meal was enlivened by a spirited debate on a wide variety of topics including: the Rise and Fall of the Roman Empire, Harold Wilson, Apartheid, Homosexuality, and whether Reg's ball had really moved and not just rocked back there on the 11th that morning.

At an extraordinary General Meeting, held in the car on the journey home, it was agreed that further golf meetings would be arranged for the BBUGS, but only on courses whose names began with a B and incorporated a 'hill' in their title. Only one guest would be invited each time and rewarded with membership of the BBUGS on winning the Guests' prize.

I look forward to a good turn-out at our next meeting.

Captain of the
Burhill Balls-Up Golfing Society.

There never was another meeting of the BBUGS, and this must be the longest report on the smallest and shortest-lived Golfing Society on record!

6

Of Mice and Men

If it wasn't for GOLF . . . *Victory In 'Site!'* might never have been written. In which case it is quite probable that Aedificamus Press would not have been founded, nor the title of this chapter credited to other than John Steinbeck or Robert Burns.

Admittedly, none of the foregoing would rank as a national disaster in itself, but the combined outcome would have left me an aimless wanderer in my declining years. Instead of which, here I am madly scribbling away on yet another contribution to modern English literature. Or so I like to believe. It happened like this . . .

In 1967, Colin Troup founded a trade magazine called *Lighting Equipment News*. Besotted with golf rather late in life, he circulated his readers with the suggestion that a Golfing Society be formed – inviting those interested to be his guests at the R.A.C. Golf Club, Woodcote Park, Surrey, in May 1977. There were 12 of us present to play a round that morning, and the name, Lighting Industry Golfing Society, was decided upon at the lunch table after golf.

Colin sold out his publishing interests but continues to run the LIGS from his home. It now has a membership of about seventy. There are four or five meetings a year, where the editor and advertising manager of *LEN* – although both non-golfers – attend to help in the day's admin, and mingle in an atmosphere of festive goodwill with the paper's readers and advertisers.

For the past eight years, Colin has also organised an annual dinner for LIGS members at the R.A.F. Club, Piccadilly – during January or February – where previous and forthcoming activities are mulled over by the twenty to thirty stalwarts who attend. It's always pleasant recalling soft summery days on lush green swards when wintry conditions prevail outside.

In October 1984, *In Search of Eastern Promise* was published. Travelling to and from the Far East in pursuit of orders for my business was the light-hearted theme of the book, and review copies were sent to a number of trade magazines. Rodney Abbott, editor of *Lighting Equipment News* at the time, phoned during late November to tell me he'd read the book but would not be publishing a review. Instead could I join him for lunch the following week and discuss writing an article for his paper.

We lunched at Shekey's, an old-established fish restaurant off Charing Cross Road, where the hot stewed eels have long been a speciality of the house and a particular favourite of mine. Rodney explained that having enjoyed my style of writing, he would like about 1500 words on any subject I thought would appeal to his readers, and that I'd get an editorial plug for my book plus the going journalistic fee for the article.

When we parted I thanked him for an excellent lunch and descended to the northbound platform of nearby Leicester Square station, en route to the car I'd left parked at British Rail's Cuffley depot. While waiting for a train I pondered on what to write about. Idly watching a couple of mice scampering over a pile of rubbish under the rails at the entrance to the tunnel, the thought occurred that London Transport could do with some good mousetraps. This spun off to what I remembered of Emerson's immortal lines, linking mousetraps with marketing. By the time the train roared in above the mice, I had the opening theme and a title. The journey from Finsbury Park to Cuffley passed all too quickly, being spent in scribbling away and scratching out at the bones of the article, while searching for rational continuity.

For the next three or four evenings I'd work on it at my desk, go to bed about midnight, wake one and a half hours later bursting with inspiration, turn up the heating control on the boiler, and go back to scribbling at the desk. Until – hearing the morning papers being popped through the letter box – a strange weariness would descend and I'd sneak back to bed for an hour. After mucking about and re-hashing it a few times my story seemed to fit the bill and Rodney Abbott published it in the January 1985 issue of his magazine.

As I think the theme is still relevant today here's the first half of that article.

OF MICE AND MEN
by Sam Morley

'*HAVING built his house in the wood,*' once observed Ralph Waldo Emerson, '*if a man were to make a better mousetrap than his neighbour, the world would beat a path to his door*'.

That's how it used to be with mousetraps. Though nobody's yet discovered why there had to be two of them down there in the woods competing for the mousetrap trade.

Emerson was born in Boston, Massachusetts, in 1803, and died 79 years later at Concord, 17 miles away from his birthplace. At that time Britain led the world as an industrial nation. We didn't just make mousetraps, either. Requiring anything from an Aardvark-snare to a Zymosis-pipette the world would look to Britain to produce it, and the country waxed fat.

Men of ideas, skills and courage boldly struck out at the head of thousands of little enterprises – making both mousetraps and history. Usually each employed a humble clerk, seated on a high stool in a dingy counting house, to write up that history in fat dusty ledgers.

Business was simple: 'How much do you want for your better mousetrap and how soon can you deliver 5000 if the price is right?'

The master would have the chap on the stool do a few quick sums on his abacus while 'Himself' popped his head into the 'Dark Satanic Mill' to check stocks of parts and progress on current orders – and the deal was done.

At the end of the year they had made enough profit to put in another 3M's (Mousetrap Making Machine); thereby his suppliers and sub-contractors prospered with him.

Cancer

Income Tax was first introduced by William Pitt to help pay for Napoleon's war; but repealed in 1816 once the shooting stopped. It was resuscitated by Robert Peel in 1842 to pay for his free trade policy, and has been with us ever since. Although only 2d in the £ in the early 1870s, like malignant cancer its insistent demands have grown stronger; something one or two reading this may already have noticed.

As its hold on the body (corporate) increased and the patient weakened, secondary and tertiary cells were introduced – Profits Tax; Corporation Tax; Capital Gains Tax; Capital Transfer Tax; Land Development Tax . . . the outcome being that money manipulation became the prime concern of big business, instead of old-fashioned buying, making and selling. With the result that sound businesses of yesteryear are no longer led by starry-eyed and highly-skilled adventurers, each preoccupied with the basic principles of industry . . . Design, Production, Sales, Profits.

Instead too many hard-eyed, figure-orientated moguls are at the head of affairs, each obsessed with their own brand-version of 'Monopoly' . . . Finance, Acquisition, Taxation and Property.

Pestriddance

'Fred Bloggs – Better Mousetrap Maker – established 1864', is now 'Pestriddance 20th Century Products plc'.

The Chairman is a direct descendant of the old abacus-manipulator on the high stool in old Fred's counting-house. Fred's great, great grandson heads a project design team in the Pestriddance drawing office. But he will never get to boardroom level. Its members enjoy their Monopoly too much to allow their game to be interrupted by practical-minded enthusiasts.

Ah! – but supposing they decide there's a need for somebody with more than a passing knowledge of the product to sit in with them. Does Fred's great great grandson get the promotion he so richly deserves? Not on your Nellie! He's far too valuable on the drawing board.

Instead, astronomical fees are devoted to staffing consultants who then spend vast sums on display advertisements in the top dailies. Curricula vitae are passed around, applicants are interviewed, assessed and short-listed.

Finally, some glib nomadic type, whose last job was marketing, say, pencil sharpeners or boiled sweets, is appointed Executive Technical Director – Mousetrap Division. He knows he's going to be safe for years.

Nobody in the boardroom knows enough to challenge him – and Fred Bloggs g.g.g. will go on doing the real work. Once they've taught the newcomer their methods of playing the game, the enlarged board will continue convening regularly for a 'rubber of Monopoly'.

Periodically they will take over a latter-day entrepreneur in order to impress the shareholders. And then quietly knock the stuffing out of whatever enterprising spirit there was in the new acquisition by sending in a middle-management team with a new set of rules. Rigid rules to suit the spacing of the squares on their Monopoly board!

Exports

Competing for trade against the type of organisation described above is like taking candy from a child. That's why today Britain has less than 4 per cent of total world trade, compared with about 90 per cent a hundred years ago. We used to sneer at the pathetic attempts by foreigners to emulate the peerless masterpieces of Fred Bloggs and his ilk.

Now every 'half-hard' emergent nation has factories making the 'currency' we once used as exchange for the native goodies – glass beads, tin trays, coloured cloth and, of course, mousetraps – not to mention motor cars, electronic gadgetry, bombers, battleships and spacecraft.

And making them cheaper, faster – and often better – than so many of our muscle-bound giant corporations like 'Pestriddance 20th Century Products plc' and its contemporaries.

As long as big business boardrooms continue to enlarge their 'Monopoly' sets with mergers and takeovers, captive home-market prices will continue to rise to pay for their vanishing exports.

What can be done about it? Very little with the likes of 'Pestriddance'. One day it will have to grind to a halt as a trading force. Asset-strippers will then step in and dispose of its property and plant. With regard to its personnel, many would be suffering from chronic Pestriddancitis and be of little use to the new get-up-and-go enterprises.

Yet there's still a lot of 'poke' left in the old country and – like an a.c. sine-wave – weather, tides, seasons and business trends move in cycles. The Fred Bloggs era is returning, and the woods once again echo with the cries of eager customers searching for firm delivery dates of Mark 2 mousetraps.

Let's explore the Fred Bloggs syndrome and see what guidelines we can introduce to stave off the 'Monopoly' boys.

Small is beautiful but – like Topsy – healthy small things, or people, have a habit of growing bigger naturally. An enterprising chap starting his own small venture must prepare for its development into not-so-small a venture.

Cone-shaped

To keep it beautiful during development, a business – like a healthy spruce tree – should retain its effective cone-shape throughout its growth, with the top man dictating from the all-seeing position at the apex. Financial and administrative staff, when needed, should be advisers, not employers.

A business without a customer is not a business. That's why **selling** should take precedence over everything. To pave the way for **selling** there must be **marketing**. Fred Bloggs only got the big crowd-scenes in the woods thanks to good **marketing**. Emerson should have made that point clear.

In the beginning Fred Bloggs did his own selling and marketing. After all nobody could match the enthusiasm and technical knowledge that went into his brain-child. This meant nobody could describe or demonstrate it better. He knew to a penny what the materials cost and to a second or two how long it took to put together.

He knew how and where to make savings when the situation demanded it. His ready wit, born of confidence in his product, was infectious and customers enjoyed his presence. They were pleased to do business with him. They liked him. He sometimes picked up orders when he wasn't the cheapest or fastest.

So, the first maxim is – **'sell yourself'**.

Prepare for the day when you're going to need help with the selling. Fred Bloggs would never squander his hard-earned cash with staffing consultancies. He'd get youngsters fresh out of school each year and vet them carefully himself. He wouldn't care too much about their school reports or academic achievements. He'd use his own judgement. Providing they looked alert and could read, write and do a few sums, he'd remember how gormless he must have seemed at that age and put them to work. He'd watch their progress and weed out the weak and lazy ones. He'd pick the bright-eyed and saucy lads and see they were given experience in every department of the business.

After a few years he'd take the best one out to sit in on meetings with customers and explain on the way back the reasoning behind such decisions or comments he might have made.

Eventually he'd be sending that young man out alone to call on those customers. They'd feel proud that Fred was entrusting his protégé to their good graces and try to help him. In fact, he might well pick up business where Fred might not have done so.

So, the second maxim is – **'build from within.'**

(As this is meant to be a fun book and not a business advisory service, I'll skip the rest and move on to the closing words on marketing and selling.)

Remember what Geoffrey Chaucer said in 1374:

He who whispers down a well
About the goods he has to sell;
Can never hope to make the dollars,
Like the man who stands on a tree and hollers!

Well, if it wasn't Chaucer I bet he wished he'd thought of it!

At the annual dinner of the Lighting Industry Golfing Society some two weeks after publication, Rodney Abbott suggested another article. This time on how a supplier or contractor in the Lighting Industry – which is part of Construction – might curry favour with consultants, whereby his firm was chosen – or specified – for a project in preference to its competitors.

'But no more than a thousand words this time', he warned, 'otherwise I'll have to do some chopping'. He said the last was really too long for the space he had planned for it, but being loth to whittle it down he finished up giving it a full centre spread; complete with a photograph of myself and Lord Matthews – who wrote a highly complimentary foreword to the book – at the launch of *In Search of Eastern Promise*.

It was quite an evening, with lots of congratulatory comments from those fellow-members who'd read the article and/or the book. The one sour note was being seated at dinner alongside one who would insist on asking – and repeating the question two years later when my next book was published – 'Who wrote it for you?' My only regret was not asking who read it to him. Obviously the poor chap couldn't grasp that writing wasn't the exclusive perks of academics with 'Oxbridge' vowel sounds. So if lucky enough to have this one read to him, too, he can feel free to visit me at Cuffley any night and, with glass in hand, browse round the book-lined shelves in between watching a creative author at work. He shouldn't be too bored as some of the books have pictures in them!

Be that as it may, let's get back to the fresh challenge of writing that second article and the spin-off therefrom. When given the brief, I had mentally linked the key word, 'specify', with my insider knowledge of a steeplechaser of that name that won the Grand National for Sir Fred Pontin in 1971. But sad to relate, Rodney Abbott never did get that thousand-word story. To coin a phrase from 'Of Mice and Men' – Morley's version, not Burn's or Steinbeck's – 'like Topsy, it just grew', and finished up as my third full-length book, *Victory In 'Site'!*

It just could never have happened – if it wasn't for GOLF . . . !

" Remember old Arthur?— same putt — same competition—
—same **hole** — suddenly clutched his heart and fell
stone dead "

7

The Totteridge Village Barber-Shop Quartet

If it wasn't for Golf – a now well-established Barber-Shop Quartet might never have found its way into the village life of Totteridge. Some will dispute the title and claim it to be misleading, conjuring up as it does an image of mustachioed songsters in a mid-twenties gents hairdressing saloon. Especially as little singing, if any, is known to take place. But the title is a factual one. As will be seen.

It all started when the Germans invaded Poland in 1939. Steve Przyblski lived in a small town called Naklo, about 80 kilometres north of Poznan, and was 21 at the time. Being just a little over five feet, he was overlooked when so many of his family and friends were marched off for slaughter, or conscripted into forced-labour battalions. It also helped being a barber, as several of the occupying troops needed his services to maintain the image of a well-groomed master-race.

But the continuing German demand for manpower, after the mauling they received from the Russians, had Steve sent off for forced military training in 1941. Once they found him a mini-uniform that didn't envelop him completely, he was given a gun and shipped out in the general direction of the French Channel coast. His instructions were to stop Allied Forces at all costs until such time as they chose to start the Second Front. Being only a little chap, he wasn't expected to do it on his own. He was to be one of tens of thousands of reluctant cannon-fodder from the occupied countries, intended to blunt the initial onslaught of the Allies as they tried to advance from the beach-heads. It was supposed to give them some zest for fighting, knowing that crack SS regiments were in reserve close at hand and ready to avenge the destruction of Steve and his mates should they fail to halt the invaders in their tracks.

Came D-Day, Steve, together with his fellow reluctant heroes – Poles, French, Belgians, Hungarians, Czechs, etc. – were spread across the plains of Normandy. Eagle-eyed battalions of German sharpshooters were ranged not far behind, ready to open up on any of the 'buffer-brigade' that tried to surrender, failed to shoot fast and straight ahead, or were seen to point guns over the heads of their would-be liberators. Nevertheless he still succeeded in getting taken prisoner by the British.

After interrogation by free-Polish Intelligence behind our lines, he was sent with many of his fellow conscripts to be measured for a new suit, albeit a khaki one, and shipped up to Scotland for retraining as one of ours. In as short a time as possible they were due to be sent back across the Channel to advance across Europe with the rest of the boys. But not Steve. He was part of a defence force stationed in Scotland, protecting the country from a possible German counter-invasion, and its womenfolk from the blandishments of nylons-gum-and-candy-toting GIs held in reserve up there while awaiting marching orders.

When there was no longer the possibility of an enemy landing in Scotland, and with most able-bodied US Forces engaged elsewhere, Steve was put on stand-by to go help liberate his country via a massive Allied push on Berlin. But as Hitler chose to shoot himself before Steve could embark, he never did get on that boat to France.

Unfortunately he couldn't return to his native soil either. Joe Stalin was now in charge of poor old Poland and behaving even more nastily towards its citizens than the Germans. Expatriate Polish soldiers returning home with enlightened tales of life in the 'decadent' West were not welcomed, and were made to disappear before they could talk. With the shooting over, Steve stayed in Britain as a Polish political refugee. And, 42 years later, is still classified as such.

He married the British-born granddaughter of a fellow

countryman, and after a couple of years working in an East Barnet factory, went back into his old game at a hairdressing saloon in Totteridge Lane, London N20. Due to its adjacence it numbered many members of South Herts Golf Club among its customers.

He had been put on the waiting list for a US visa, having decided to try his luck, once demobbed, with an uncle in Minnesota; but there were too many displaced persons in Europe with priority over Steve. As a result it was 11 years before they told him his number had come up, by which time he was too well-rooted in N. London. And there he stayed for the next thirty years.

The owner of the shop in which he worked decided to sell it to an investment company in 1981, first giving Steve the option of a lease on the premises. Not being too taken with the asking rent, Steve reckoned the time had come to hang up his scissors.

But his old-established customers were loth to look around for another barber shop with a tonsorial operator of Steve's calibre, and suggested he consider bringing his skills to their homes.

Reg Davies was one of his regulars and believed it would be in Steve's interests if there were more than one head to be shorn at each port of call. To prove the point he went on to organise for the Davies ménage to be the venue for a party of four, and invited me to join it. 'Party' was the operative word and as far as I was concerned it couldn't have come at a better time.

My regular barber at the Eccentric Club of St. James's, one Alfred Freeman, had retired about six months earlier, having completed 25 years of coping with my ever-spreading wide-open spaces. The new incumbent was not cast in anything like Alfred's Jeeves-like mould, and those four-weekly visits for haircut and lunch were no longer the hedonistic trips they used to be. The invitation was a welcome one.

Another of Steve's regulars in the Whetstone shop was Laurie Wootton, past Captain of South Herts and also a

Totteridge dweller. The fourth member was Dai Rees, CBE, professional golfer at South Herts from 1945 to 1983 and another of Steve's old customers. Which means we were really a quintet for the first three years. But having now introduced Dai, who died in 1983 at the age of 70, I'll just tell the story as it is today.

Each fifth or sixth Saturday morning, well before the session is due to start, Reg trundles his heavy old oak carver chair into the kitchen from its regular place at his desk in the study. Joan props a mirror from her dressing table on the working surface in front of it. Bowls of potato crisps and salted nuts are set on the 'waiting-room' table; plates of open smoked salmon sandwiches, prepared earlier that morning and decoratively garnished, have been stashed inside the hostess trolley; and a goodly stock of wine and lager placed to cool its heels in the fridge.

At the appointed hour, usually 11.00 a.m., Steve arrives, opens up a little attaché case, and sets out his tools of the trade on the kitchen table, together with a freshly-laundered navy-blue nylon sheet for tucking around the neck of each 'victim' in turn.

More often than not our host 'opens the batting'. Such time as Laurie or I arrive – usually bearing some contribution toward the day's 'goodies' – his lady bustles round bringing a fresh glass into play; she would already have laid out a mini-party for Steve on his work table.

Each in turn, while under treatment in the chair, is regaled with Steve's latest newsflash on the health of his friends and family, holiday experiences or plans, memories from the old days, and latest 'funny thing happened to me on my way from –', or 'Did you hear the one about the –?' But, to coin a phrase, 'It's the way he tells 'em', and the less said about that the better! Barbers the world over being noted for incessant patter, our man can hold his own with the best – for both craft performance and running commentary on the passing show.

The last of the three being shorn, the waiting room reverts to a dining one where, munching, tippling and chattering away, we are joined by Steve once all the bits and pieces are stowed back in his case.

Over a final glass and nibble before departing to the next appointment, he'll produce his pen and diary for future plans.

When these meetings started back in 1980, it was decided that for each to go fumbling through pockets in order to pay our individual dues to Steve was a bit plebeian. Instead we'd take turns for one to pay for all three, in the sequence laid down by the Reg Davies' desk diary. This would now be produced and a convenient date agreed for the next sheering session. From it we would be told who paid for all three last time, whose turn it was this time and who'd better bring plenty next time. I remember one Saturday, amid difficulties over finding change for a little sweepstake on the races that day, a confused Steve – somewhat befuddled with vino – fishing currency out of his own wallet to pay Laurie for the haircuts!

Steve's departure signifies the closure of the barber shop for the day; but by no means is it the end. Having exchanged views on Steve's chosen topic for that morning, the 'crack' continues until Laurie decides it's time to go and show off his new haircut at South Herts, where he'll regale his friends with highlights of the morning before going out to play a few holes.

If I haven't plans to do something similar at my club, Reg will open the morning papers at the racing page. Taking it in turn to use his reading glasses, we'll check out the form and where the action is to be televised from that day. Once decided on our individual fancies, Joan's included, comes the need to agree where to watch it from. The big colour set in the lounge is the obvious choice, but the 'waiting-room' table spread with what's left of the 'goodies' is always too comfortable to leave. That's why a veteran little black-and-white portable from the bedroom is usually brought down and plugged up in readiness on haircut days. There also happens to be a more modern coloured portable up there somewhere, but we found it hard to back a winner when watching racing on it. It took quite a few sessions to discover that our selections liked the going better on the black-and-white set than they did on the coloured one!

Bets are then phoned away, glasses topped up, and in a euphoria of thundering hooves and whoops of joy or chagrin, another glorious episode in the annals of the Totteridge Village Barber Shop Quartet draws to a memorable close.

They could never have started – if it wasn't for GOLF . . . !

" I remember that one last year – he sharpened my woods!"

—— 8 ——

The Cavendish Open

In October 1945, the Royal Navy decided that, after Hiroshima and Nagasaki, they could manage fine without me. So I planted my own acorn of a one-man electrical engineering business, and sold it 37 years later as a sturdy young oak tree. By so doing I was able to turn my back on industry and venture further into writing.

During those 37 years the same firm of accountants kept me clear of major financial disasters. I was first introduced to its senior partner – an old school friend of my elder brother – when the first over-trading disaster threatened four years after starting up. Since then that partner – and my brother – departed for their Old Boys reunion in Elysian Fields, but the current incumbent learned his skills at the old maestro's knee and is just as good a personal friend as was his predecessor.

But not until he had hauled himself past the age of forty did he get his leisure priorities right, by supplementing his squash racket with a nice new set of golf clubs. He honestly believed that his good eye for a fast-moving ball would stand him in good stead when it came to mastering the stationary one. In no time he was overwhelmed with rage, frustration and intense hatred for the little white, pimple-faced pill, and obsessed with pounding it into submission.

In other words, folks, just like you and me – he was hooked!

Two of his partners being similarly affected, they seldom needed something to talk about under 'Any other business' when grouped round their boardroom table. Came the day they discovered that, between them, they knew of many a client on the firm's books who might well have had a more thriving business had he just spent a little more time at a desk and not quite so much on the green, green grass of his local golf club. Believing that anybody putting golf before work couldn't be all bad, the partners decided to hold a 'convention' at Walton Heath Golf Club, Surrey, where they could research the subject and meet customers who never seemed to be in their office when the sun shone.

Personal invitations were sent to selected clients, requesting their company at a golf-fest to be held on 8 July 1986. It was to be a full and hedonistic day. Golf competition in the morning; golf competition in the afternoon; gourmet lunch at the Club; and prize-giving to take place after a *cordon bleu* dinner at the Gatwick Moat House Hotel, some fifteen miles from Walton Heath. Each invited guest was welcome to indulge in all or any part of the festivities. All that was asked of him was that he return the accompanying form, on which he was asked to state his handicap, preferred starting time for the morning round or whether only coming for lunch and afternoon golf, and if he would be staying to dinner. He was also asked to provide his chest measurement.

No reason for the last unusual request was given, but none was needed when I arrived for lunch on that hot summer's afternoon and checked in with their reception committee. Once my name was ticked off, I was presented with two new balls, tee-pegs, ball-marker, pencil, pitchmark-repair fork, miniature bottle of J & B whisky and – in addition to all these 'freebies' – a handsome pearl-grey V-necked slipover, to the chest size I'd given on the form and emblazoned with a distinctive crest bearing the words 'Cavendish Open'. The title, of course, being taken from the prestigious West End square in which the practice had its offices.

During lunch came introductions to golfing partners and opponents, plus instructions on what kind of competition had been planned for that afternoon. To be more correct I should say competitions, for each member of each four-ball was to play his part in no less than three. First, there was the straightforward Stableford score achieved over 18 holes with his own ball. Next, came the better-ball Stableford score achieved by the pair playing together as partners, where only the better score of their two attempts went down aginst each of the 18 holes. And then there was the Pink-ball score, of which an explanation will follow.

Everybody played off his full handicap, which meant that those with the maximum permitted handicap of 28 – of whom there was no shortage that day – received two free shots on no less than 10 of the 18 holes, and 1 on each of the remaining 8. And as the scoring in Stableford is 2 points for par and 1 for one-over-par, a 28-handicap man playing a par-5 hole would be entitled to 8 goes at his ball before he could consider himself to be out of that particular hole. Sorry about all the technicalities but as the story unfolds they become relevant.

Now for the sake of the uninitiated – and before the 1986 'Cavendish Open' I was one of them – the Pink-ball Competition went something like this.

Each four-ball was issued with one brand-new, fluorescent-pink golf ball when they checked in at the first tee. Not a ball that can be bought in the nearby pro shop – but a special one, numbered and stamped 'Cavendish Open', and its number recorded against the four-ball to which it was issued. Each player had his personal score-card clearly marked with a pink pencil at every fourth hole. Player A at 1, 5, 9, 13 and 17; player B at 2, 6, 10, 14 and 18; player C at 3, 7, 11 and 15; and player D at 4, 8, 12 and 16. And each was obliged to use that official pink ball for playing the allocated holes. At the end of the round the pink ball would need to be returned to the scrutineers when handing in the score-cards; the four-ball returning the best pink-ball score over the 18 holes, irrespective of how badly they each might have done in the single and better-ball competitions, were to be rewarded with elegant prizes. (I think we were still out there on the course somewhere when those were given out, so never did learn just how elegant they really were!)

Even a non-golfer should now appreciate that, no matter

how abysmally an individual player performed with 'pinkie', the other three – like hungry falcons – would anxiously follow its every movement through the air to ensure they stayed in the 'hunt'.

Now that sort of thing would be a real fun game played on a nice flat par-three course, with each team consisting of four well-seasoned golfers. But on Walton Heath! – with a carry of something like a hundred and fifty yards from tee to fairway on so many of the holes, and most of it over a tangled mass of heather up to four feet high; and a goodly proportion of those present in the first flush of Golf, with a nominal and highly flattering 28-handicap?

(Golfers everywhere reading this will have now become increasingly aware of a dry mouth, trembling hands and speeding pulse, as the full impact of these words begin to sink in.)

So, without further ado, and avoiding possible embarrassment with names, let's say I was player C in the team that went in to bat at 2.15 p.m. in the 'Cavendish Open', on that sunny Tuesday afternoon in July 1986. It was hot, and both A and I had hired caddies. B pulled a trolley with a very large expensive-looking bag on it, and my partner, D, being a fit young man, carried his clubs. At that time we were each strangers to the remaining three, although I believe A and D my have played together during the morning round. While waiting for the starter to send us on our way, the usual polite pre-play chat about our handicaps and home clubs broke any ice there may have been between three of us – but B stood aside and was strangely uncommunicative.

To murmurs of appreciation, A then struck a fine shot down the middle with the pink ball. Then came a pause while everybody waited for B; including B, who just stood empty-handed on the edge of the tee, looking around for all the world like a landscape designer. After a few moments somebody politely hinted it was his turn to play. Once that had registered he walked to take a club from his bag, and then went back for a ball, and then back for a tee-peg.

Somebody pointed him in the right direction and, after an air shot or two, his ball was in play. The rest of the expedition then struck off and moved down the fairway.

Once guided to where his ball lay cowering close to the ground, player B had a number of further attempts at getting a bit nearer to the target area – during which time there was a quiet council of war between his three companions. His partner A was delegated to explain, as inoffensively as possible, that there was now no chance of him scoring on that particular hole; and that etiquette of the game demanded he pick his ball up, put it in his pocket, and save his energy for what was to come.

As we milled around the second tee – those ahead seemed to be finding trouble, too – player A confided that his partner had told him he was once 12-handicap, but had not played for quite a long time. By his apparent bewilderment and performance to date, a kindly observer would say 300 years!

Be that as it may, it was now that gentleman's turn to play with our precious pink ball. Player A had started us off in grand style with a par on the first. With his shot, that gave us three points for openers.

Although nobody by now expected the score to have changed much once B had finished with the second hole, the important thing was not to lose that ball. So, with the exception of B and after we'd each struck off, the remaining three rushed to the clump of bonny blooming heather into which he'd trundled it. I say with the exception of B, because he didn't seem to be with it at all. Just stood on the path with one hand on his trolley, staring about him at the picturesque scenery surrounding us on all sides, but not terribly interested in what was next expected of him; until somebody called to show him where the ball lay trembling with its hands over its eyes, so to speak, midst a tangle of roots. Taking a club from his bag he struck it into another clump a few yards away, and then into another – while all the time we watched its harrowing progress with gimlet eyes.

Before he was able to reach the fairway his quota of shots for that hole was used up, and old 'pinkie' – still miraculously intact and playable – then came into my possession for tackling the third.

Now this is not going to be a boring hole-by-hole account of one of the most traumatic – but memorable – rounds of golf I've ever know. Sufficient to say that, whatever was taking place among our four-ball, seemed to be repeating itself in one way or another all round the course that afternoon. Despite the time taken in searching for balls – and let's be fair, by no means was B's the only ball in the 'Cavendish Open' that went to ground in deep heather that afternoon (in fact, it got so that as we wended our way round Walton Heath, he even managed to score on one or two holes) – arrival on the next hole to be played would find a knot of players on the tee in front, waiting or just about to strike off.

Somewhere round the fifth hole we caught up with what was obviously about to be another long hold-up. We'd now been out a good hour and a half or more. Picture the scene: A, C and D stand chatting in the shade of a nearby tree, while taking a swig from their 'freebie' J & B minatures, when B is noticed in a squatting position some twenty feet away, facing his golf bag and with his back to us. Thinking he was a secret 'lush', A walked over to tell him there was no need for secrecy because we were all on the bottle. But it wasn't that at all. In fact, it turned out he was so indifferent to whisky, that he later passed his unopened 'freebie' to partner A, who kindly shared it with C and D.

No, it was a large Radiophone handset that B had taken from the pocket of his golf bag, and with which he was now busily occupied in dialling his office. Earlier he had said that he ran some form of wholesale business in which he had two sons playing executive roles. Apparently it was crucial that he be kept fully informed on what earth-shattering events were taking place 'back at the mill' during his half-day away from all the action. Or so it seemed. On the other hand, he might just have wanted to tell his boys not to worry as he was having a great time playing great golf with some really great guys!

Now we all know those midweek days when, out with friends or golfing societies and on finishing the morning round, there's no shortage of hookey-playing tycoons searching for a phone in the clubhouse – whereby they can contact their H.Q. and learn what orders, cheques and writs have come in with the post that day. Lord knows, I've done my share of ringing in, and from some of the finest locker rooms in the country. But never before have I witnessed or heard of anybody doing it with his own portable telephone from somewhere out on the course itself. Especially one already well on the way to being unforgettable as a player anyway.

At least three more times before we got to the 17th did that phone come out for another quiet chat with base when the hold-up looked to be longer than normal. Anxious to avoid any show of curiosity, we kept well out of earshot, considering it infra dig to overhear – even accidentally – any decisions he might make on whether to buy, sell, sack or sue!

By this time all felt we'd known each other for life. It was 7.35 p.m. before that round of golf ended with a sub-aqua trudge back into the clubhouse. Yes, the little expedition that set out in glorious sunshine at 2.15 that afternoon, took 5 hours and 20 minutes to complete; and it was as we approached the 16th green that the sky was seen to darken from a beautiful blue to the colour of old lead. Rain suddenly lashed down like diagonal stair-rods and with such windswept fury that, in less time that it takes to tell, waterproofs and umbrellas were completely useless. Everybody was soon three times wetter than if they'd fallen fully clothed in the river.

But it was on that par-three 17th tee that this story reached its climax. We had to wait to play it of course, while those in front splashed their way on to the green and in accordance with the rules of golf related to waterlogged greens, sought the least-waterlogged path for putting up to the hole. It gives some idea of the general high standard of play when I recall the official adjudicator complete with note book, ball pen and tape measure, stationed to the rear of the 17th green. It was his duty to record which of the 54 tee-shots struck at the pin that afternoon finished nearest to the hole, whereby the winner would receive some accolade at the dinner to mark his achievement. When we, the last four-ball but two, reached the half-drowned, non-playing member of the accountancy firm delegated to that task, he said he'd only had to measure two shots so far – and the best of those was over fifty feet away!

Before the 17th could be played, however, we must have spent ten minutes sheltering as best we could in the lee of a rhododendron bush, while waiting for the green to clear. The bags of clubs huddled together unattended on the path some thirty feet in front of the tee. Suddenly, above the lashing rain and wailing wind, came the faint unbelievable but unmistakable sound of a telephone ringing. Looking round nonplussed, it took a few moments to realise it had to be from B's golf bag. But he was standing a little further away and hadn't heard until D called and offered to answer it. He'd have loved to tell the caller that B was on the other line and would they mind waiting! But our friend rushed down the slope, unzipped the pocket, pulled the phone out, and was soon 'back at the office' again.

The memory of that 17th tee on the Old Course at Walton Heath, with its camouflaged 'telephone-box-on-wheels' in a hazy Arcadian setting, and torrents of rain bouncing off a central and somewhat bulky figure squatting in front of his golf bag – talking earnestly to whoever decided to ring and catch him still at 'work' at that late hour – hangs like a picture, forever fresh – and still slightly damp – in the space between my ears. It could never have been 'painted' . . . if it wasn't for GOLF . . . !

"Dunlop '65', Penfold, Warwick, Slazengaire...ze re-paints?"

PART TWO

THE
SPRINGBOK
CONNECTION

9

The Scenic Route to Simonstown

Southern Africa was mainly an uninhabited land mass until 1652, when the Dutch first used the Cape as a staging post for their shipping to and from the Far East. It took 291 years, and the ensuing sequence of naval hits and misses, before I discovered why Jan van Riebeck was so enamoured with the place.

In October 1942, as leading seaman Sam Morley, I joined HMS *Redoubt*, a brand new 'R'-class destroyer, nearing completion in John Brown's yard, Glasgow. My job was to look after the ship's electrics. Prior to that I'd done about twenty months' Atlantic and North Sea convoys aboard the *Verdun*, a World War One destroyer taken out of mothballs for the current emergency, and about half the size of *Redoubt*.

Compared to No. 1 mess up in the starboard bow of *Verdun*, No. 14 mess on the port-side aft of *Redoubt* was like a VIP suite at the Savoy. True, the 17 ratings to whom that 16-foot by 9-foot space was home, were without room-service, en-suite loos, or complimentary shower caps, but with a war on everybody made sacrifices.

With a heavy beam sea running, slinging a hammock in the only crack of a gap left between 17 others and then trying to swing into it, needed a lot more agility than just sliding between silken Savoy sheets. Many would come off watch and just crash down on lockers or mess table, rather than sling up among the swaying sacks of those who had collared the best positions first. One hazard of lying on lockers or table was being pitched to the deck by an extra steep roll, sudden change of course, or a sharp jolt such as might occur when bouncing off a submerged rock, friendly ship or unfriendly torpedo. There were other reasons for not sleeping under occupied hammocks, about which more later.

The ship's company mustered about 230, and together we wandered around five or six of the seven seas – like a latter-day *Flying Dutchman* – over the ensuing two and a half years. But as this is to be a golf-orientated book – not a personal history of Sam's war at sea – I'll just touch on the relevant bits of wandering that lead into the title of this chapter.

In mid-November 1942, our flotilla of brand new 'R'-boats – destined to reinforce HM's Far-Eastern Fleet – steamed out of the Clyde estuary on its first job; part of a large force escorting a convoy of troopships and supply vessels bound for Egypt and India via the Cape. Two days later an enemy blockade-runner was reported by a reconnaissance plane as heading for the French Atlantic coast. *Redoubt* and *Racehorse* – our sister ship – were ordered to leave the convoy and intercept her. That one unexpected chore was the forerunner of a chain of events, some of the ripples of which are still quietly bubbling today. As will be seen.

Searching for that doomed blockade-runner involved high-speed steaming for half a day or more. When sighted she quickly hove-to after getting a couple of traditional warning shots across her bows from our 4.7s. (Incidentally, 1917 nameplates on the breech mechanism of these guns showed how shipyards must have scoured scrapyards for vital parts, when building like mad to replace ships lost between 1939 and 1942.) Her crew were ordered to take to their boats and pull across to us within two minutes unless preferring posthumous gallantry awards for going down with their ship. None did, and before the ultimatum ran out they were treading into each other's faces in their efforts to be first up the scrambling nets lowered over *Redoubt*'s side.

They were mostly Italian. As was their beautiful white ship; now, alas, to be used for target practice at point-blank range. It was like throwing bricks through the windows of an empty – but stately – house; and just as effective if the object was to demolish the target. Despite firing two or three dozen rounds into her she showed no sign of sinking, and it took a couple of torpedoes to put her out of the way. Otherwise she'd have been a floating hazard to our shipping – especially at night – and the East Atlantic Ocean was quite hazardous enough in those days. Once she'd gone to the bottom we belted back to Gibraltar to drop off her crew – destined for internment camps – and then prepared to steam off south again to catch up with our convoy, now a good 24 hours ahead.

While filling up with oil and water at Gib. came a fresh Admiralty order. *Redoubt* and *Racehorse* were to return to the Clyde immediately. We just couldn't believe our luck in completing what was probably the shortest foreign service commission on record. Speculation was rife on that mad dash back. Maybe the two crews were to be decorated and would march down Whitehall between cheering crowds because of the intrepid way they'd knocked off that blockade-runner? But not until sailing off again, sad and disillusioned, into the wide blue yonder – just 24 hours after our arrival in Scottish waters – did we learn what it was all about.

Our shipyards being over-crowded, or over-vulnerable to enemy air attack, it had been arranged that one of Britain's newest and most powerful aircraft-carriers, HMS *Victorious*, would receive a much-needed refit in the US navy yards at Norfolk, Virginia. Needing an anti-submarine destroyer escort, and we being the two nearest and newest at a current loose end, so to speak, the Admiralty had called us back for the task. All three ships sailed out of the Clyde estuary on Christmas Eve 1942.

That transatlantic voyage was eventful enough to fill a couple of chapters, if not a book, on its own; but because of their 'knock-on' effect, I'll stick to describing one or two of those still-vivid memories – like trying to refuel from *Victorious* in mid-ocean, having run our tanks nearly dry through steaming a high-speed zig-zag Asdic watch over the previous five days.

It involved both ships – 'mini David' and 'maxi Goliath' –

steering a dead parallel course, about ten yards apart, and maintaining an identical speed of about three knots. A difficult thing to do on a flat inland lake, never mind in a heavy Atlantic swell. And the slower the speed, the more both ships rolled at the mercy of wind and sea, and the more apprehensive everybody became.

Once the two ships were in position, a gun-line operator from *Victorious* fired a cord across to us. On to this was tied a thicker line, and then a rope with which the vital 'umbilical' oil-hose was pulled across.

Getting that 6-inch diameter armoured hose linked up between the two ships was quite a feat as – for all the world like a skyscraper and a bungalow – they tried to avoid over-straining or over-slackening it during the evolution. Our Chief Stoker, with a large axe, stood by the hose where it was coupled up to *Redoubt*'s deck valve, just in case we got wind of a lurking U-boat and had to galvanise into action.

But danger came from a far friendlier source than an enemy submarine. Hardly had *Victorious* begun pumping the precious stuff through that 'umbilical' link than the huge aircraft carrier started to lean toward us in a playful wallowing roll. Her massive grey wall heeled over and seemed never to stop descending, as she blotted out the sky and crunched her AA gundecks into both our bridge and after-superstructures. Stricken with awe we waited to be flipped on our side like an old sardine can, but just when that looked almost inevitable she stopped shoving, paused, and started to rise, before going into her reverse roll. A string of orders from *Redoubt*'s bridge had the engines scream into full-speed-ahead, the deck take a 30-degree list as the wheel went hard-a-starboard, and horrible black sludge gush everywhere when the Chief Stoker sliced right through that hose in one crashing swing of his axe! As a result we were well out of the way by the time *Victorious* decided to roll back for another playful nuzzle up against her little friend!

It's an ill wind, etc. Seeing that both destroyers were now too low on fuel to risk continuing to Chesapeake Bay without a 'top-up', it was decided that *Victorious* would go it alone through the comparatively safe waters of the western Atlantic until she could rendezvous with a couple of US escort ships – now on their way out of Norfolk in answer to her signal. Meanwhile *Redoubt* and *Racehorse* headed for the nearest 'filling station' – Bermuda.

It was 9.00 a.m., New Year's Day 1943, when they moored-up in the harbour at Ireland Island, the Allied naval base in the most westerly of the chain of islands that make up that idyllic archipelago. The sun shone, we swam and fished from the ship's side and from the pink sandy beaches ashore for the next three days, during which time the ship underwent first-aid repairs from the dockyard staff.

After the war, I would often tell my wife that of all the exotic places visited during my seafaring years, it was Bermuda I most wanted to show her. It took another 23 years before that could come about – and then only by tacking it on to a business trip to Canada and having her fly out to meet me in New York. Four years after selling that business and taking up writing for pleasure, we returned to Bermuda for a week at Christmas 1986 – and found those subtropical islands every bit as picturesque and evocative as they had first looked to me 44 years earlier.

It was seven hundred miles from Bermuda to the Chesapeake, where the two 'R'-boats made a spectacular high-speed 'Admiralty sweep' into its sheltered waters at 7.00 a.m. on the morning of 5 January 1943. Harbour ferries plying between Norfolk and Newport News were crowded with early-morning travellers on their way to work. They were seen to heel over dangerously – the ferries, that is – as the said E-MTs threw down newspapers and rushed to the sides, cheering and waving, at the unexpected spectacle of two British warships racing through the 'dawn's early light' – each with a huge white 'bone-in-its-teeth' and a brand new white ensign streaming aft above its boiling wake. A most impressive piece of 'showing-the-flag', that.

The general belief over there at the time was that Britain was clapped out and almost on the point of defeat – which didn't quite fit in with our swashbuckling, grandstand entry into their 'holy' waters. As was said more than once during the ensuing five days that *Redoubt* spent in dock at Newport News, where technicians, shipwrights and mechanics made good the damage caused by both the Atlantic and HMS *Victorious*. Those of us who went ashore wallowed in good old Southern hospitality, while gawping in disbelief at the displays of food and confectionery in the first brilliantly-lit shopping streets seen for almost three-and-a-half years.

Then down to Curaçao in the Dutch West Indies, escorting a convoy of tankers carrying US crude oil to the refining plants that dominated the island – so much so, the whole island smelt permanently like the sump of an old banger! Five days later we left Curaçao with a convoy of petroleum tankers bound for the North African war zone.

Half-a-day out from Gibraltar came a panic call to 'Action-stations', when our Asdics picked up the echo of a lurking submarine. After tossing about half its ready-use stock of depth charges at it, *Redoubt* tore in at something like 30 knots to ram the enemy as it neared the surface. Came a heavy thud and everybody cheered as two halves of an ominous black shape drifted one either side of our bow wave. But the cheering slowly subsided when they were recognised as the two halves of a rather large and much-bloodied whale!

(Unfortunately the skipper wouldn't allow our artistic chief ERA – who usually painted Dorniers, Heinkels and Messerschmidts on the side of gunshields credited with hitting an enemy plane – to go over the fo'c'sle rails in a bosun's chair and paint a sperm whale above the buckled bows!)

In the ramming quite a lot of no good had been done to the ship below the waterline. It meant that we had to limp at half speed into the nearest Allied-occupied harbour. Capital and principal naval base in French Morocco, Casablanca had been bombarded from the sea and taken from the Vichy

French by US forces a couple of months earlier, thereby giving me the chance to take wine in its Casbah while our hull was inspected and patched. Three days later we steamed off and into dry dock at Gibraltar.

It took about a week for the dockyard boys at Gib. to make *Redoubt* into a decent warship again, after which we did some work in the Med. for a couple of months, in the wake of the First Army's invasion of North Africa. I've vague memories of a few hours spent ashore in newly-won places like Algiers and Oran – local vino one-and-a-half francs a glass and 300 Allied francs to the pound probably account for the vagueness.

Then came a recall to Gibraltar to join up with the escort force of a large convoy of reinforcements and stores on its way round the Cape, like the one with which we left Scottish waters when the commission started. This time there were no grounds to leave the convoy except to escort one or two ships joining or leaving it at places like Gambia, Freetown, Lagos, Leopoldville or Point Noir. But as the convoy approached the Cape of Good Hope, *Redoubt* and *Racehorse* received instructions to stay with it round to Durban and Mombasa, but then to return to Cape Town's naval base, Simonstown – from which we were destined to operate over the ensuing nine months as part of a newly formed arm of the Far Eastern Fleet, engaged in escort and patrol duties from Freetown on the west coast of Africa, round to Mombasa, Aden, Bombay and Ceylon.

Lord knows how many impressions of Table Mountain have been written by those approaching Cape Town from the sea for the first time. None can do the scene justice. When it was my turn I just couldn't believe how tidily the 'white cloth' was laid on the 'table' – as though to welcome us to high tea. (The 'white cloth' is a dense white cloud often to be seen sitting on the plateau-top of the mountain.) 'The Table' would normally come into view several hours before we'd reach Cape Town harbour and the approaches to Simonstown in False Bay. As the end of a three or four week spell at sea drew nigh – during the tens of thousands of miles steamed by *Redoubt* while based there – those on deck would anxiously scan the horizon for the first glimpse of the 'Table', symbol of South Africa's warmth and hospitality toward the wandering 'Brit'. I loved the country and its people. Still do, and said as much in a letter to our Prime Minister in August 1986, asking her to resist pressure by the US and Commonwealth to interfere in its internal racial problems by imposing ill-advised sanctions. Got a very understanding reply too.

Traditionally, naval ships were due for a refit, or major overhaul, after 100,000 miles. This usually took four to six weeks, during which time fifty per cent of the crew were sent on leave for half the period she was to be in the dockyard, and the other fifty per cent when the first lot returned. Those on board would again be split into two, each half taking 24 hours local leave in turn. That way there weren't too many needing the ship's limited facilities while dockyard workers swarmed around.

When the time came for *Redoubt*'s refit in Simonstown, those due to go on leave were given three options: (a) billeted in the Union Jack Club, Cape Town, from which volunteer groups of civilians would organise sightseeing tours, dances, dinners etc; (b) invited guests of a South African farming family somewhere within a hundred and fifty miles of Cape Town; or (c) invited guests of a civilian family in an inland town. Wanting to get as far from the Navy as possible for a while I chose (c), and with three messmates was made welcome at Kimberley, about six hundred miles up-country from Cape Town at the home of Jim Palmer – the town's Postmaster General (at least, I think it was Jim). The South African Women Auxiliary Services – of which Mrs. Palmer was a member – organised everything, including the 18-hour journey on what is now the super luxury Blue Train, and the reception committee that met us at Kimberley Station.

Hospitality knew no bounds and every day was a gala event – from the time we finished breakfast and took a mile-long stroll to a friendly pub for our first Castle beer of the day, to the time we fell into our welcome beds from wherever the action happened to be that evening. Which brings me to the one anxious moment with which each day started during that fortnight in Kimberley.

At the beginning of this 'sea-saga', there's mention of the risks accompanying the urge to 'crash down' on lockers or mess table rather than go through the hassle of slinging one's hammock. Well, one or two of those risks might be fairly obvious – like when the one above gets a bit careless and drops his book, fags, or a grotty seaboot on your unsuspecting head; or sinks his large and smelly foot in your face when anxious to scramble out for some urgent reason or the other. Urgent calls of 'Action Stations!', 'Abandon Ship!', or just one of nature, come immediately to mind. But the most hazardous – in our mess anyway – was caused by one of its most inoffensive and longest-serving members, who also happened to be somewhat incontinent. And nothing can be more disconcerting when crashed-out on the lockers shortly after completing a four-hour middle-watch, than awakening to a steady drip-drip-drip on one's weary 'crust' through the fabric of the hammock above!

The poor devil couldn't help it, and tried all sorts of ways to overcome his problem; but he'd be a good boy for weeks and then, usually after a run ashore, there'd be a relapse. And now here he was with us in Kimberley, drinking solidly throughout the day and sleeping each night on snowy-white linen in the home of generous and kindly people.

They'd given us three rooms – two of them each had a single bed, and one had a king-size double. It was decided unanimously that Robbo, to give him a fictitious name somewhere near his real one, qualified for one of the singles. (Nobody in his right mind was going to share a double bed with Robbo!) My old Cockney mate, Alfie Gould, whose home was not too far from my own, shared the big one with me; thereby leaving 'Doc', the ship's SBA (Sick Berth Attendant), with the sole occupancy of the other single, as befitted an ex-St. John's Ambulance man and current 'first mate' to the ship's doctor.

Those 14 days in Kimberley were absolute heaven. All we had to do was go to bed at night, get up in the morning, get dressed, eat the breakfast served us in the dining room below, and let the good time roll. There were a number of servants around to prepare and serve food, clear tables, clean rooms, make beds, tend gardens, and generally see to the household needs of both the family and its guests.

Every night, however late it happened to be, we'd check on Robbo to ensure he'd done his bathroom drill before turning in. And anybody feeling the call of nature through the night would give Robbo a friendly shake on the way back from the bathroom; on the basis that if a disciplined cistern needed emptying, an undisciplined one might well be near leaking point. It meant his sleep was broken more often than ours – something he didn't enjoy judging by the harsh and unfriendly things said when so awakened – but if it got him through the night without mishap all was forgiven. Each morning we'd each show an anxious face at his door, to be greeted by a cheery smile and a thumbs-up sign. At least for the first seven days or so.

Then came one big party night, when everybody got back well loaded and just fell into bed. The next morning, one look at Robbo's face was enough to know the worst!

As it was no use crying over spilt . . . well, anything, we went into a council of war to spare old Robbo further embarrassment when the girl came up later to do the rooms. It was decided to breakfast quickly, get back to his room before she got there, lock the door, make up his bed, tucking the dry bedspread tightly all round over the damp sheets, whereby she'd see there was no need for her to tackle it. Then, once back at the house after the morning session at the pub, the bed could be stripped and sheets hung around the room to dry during the hot afternoon. Later, and before getting ready to sally forth on the evening's festivities, it could all be put together again before she came up to draw the curtains and turn back the beds – as was her wont. That way, nobody would ever know of our mate's little accident.

So, all lighthearted and carefree, we strolled through the quiet lanes back to base for lunch and turned the final corner with what we thought was a situation well under control. Only to be greeted with – like a string of bunting fluttering from a flagship's signal deck – the sight of all Robbo's bed-linen, freshly laundered, blowing gaily on the line at the back of the Palmer house! But never a word was said or implied. Nor would the laughing girl responsible accept the bit of cash Robbo tried to give her in appreciation of the trouble he'd put her to.

Those Kimberley folk spared no effort in keeping us entertained. Dinners, formal lunches, dances, conducted tours of the diamond mines – more about diamond mines in the next chapter – and one or two outlying farms, were crowded into each day. More than one citizen explained that we might well have been his or her guests, as far more of them had wanted to host the Navy than there were officers and men visiting Kimberley from our two ships. We were balloted for apparently, and one woman complained that it wasn't fair for the Palmers to have four while other didn't get any. The reason given by the organising committee was that – like brothers and sisters in an orphanage – messmates from the same ship might prefer not to be separated. (Would have been doubly embarrassing for old Robbo if he hadn't had us around in his hour of need.)

Some six months later *Redoubt* went into dock at Durban for a 'mini-refit', resulting in my getting nine days leave as guest of the owner of a small hotel in Dundee – a country town in Natal about three hours by train from Durban. What I remember most about that was meeting a little schoolteacher who taught me a lot about South Africa, including the words, in Afrikaans, of the country's most popular song – if not actually its national anthem. And in the ensuing years, right until my most recent visit in February 1988, many's the Springbok who's been taken aback by my rendering of 'Sarie Marais' in neat Afrikaans.

I used to write and tell my wife that when the war was over we'd go and live in South Africa, where I'd made so many fine friends (I don't believe I made specific reference to the little schoolteacher) and had the offer of more than one job if I came back to settle. But when I did return to England in May 1945, two years and seven months after leaving it, war-torn England was still far too beautiful a place to consider living anywhere else. And 42 years later I still feel the same.

My younger brother was in the Eighth Army, and had only seen South Africa from the deck of a troopship when it stopped for fuel, food and water while in convoy to Egypt. We didn't meet up again until the war was over.

He could see little future for himself, wife and baby son in England. Both our parents had been killed by the last German V2 rocket to hit London, totally destroying the block of flats that was our home back in 1939, and he had to do the best he could, crowded in among his wife's family. With the result that in 1947 he went to work as a carpenter in South Africa, starting his own building business in Cape Town a couple of years later.

He gave this up on finding his wife's skills at badge-making and embroidery in greater demand and more lucrative than his own building activities. Together they started in business to exploit those skills, training up local labour and buying a couple of second-hand machines from the UK through her old employer. The thing mushroomed whereby they moved from the small old factory rented in the downtown district of Cape Town to a larger one on a new factory estate, into which they installed more and more sophisticated machinery imported from Germany and Switzerland.

He sold out and retired about twelve years ago. Golf, bowls, tending his garden, and the restoration of old and valuable chiming clocks as a hobby, keep him fully occupied at home. He lives in Hermanus, a scenic resort town on the Indian Ocean – about seventy miles from where he first entered the country on the *Winchester Castle*, on an assisted passage and with nothing but hope and a box of carpenter's tools.

And here ends possibly the only chapter that does not warrant closing with the title-phrase of the book. But this is just the opening chapter to the Springbok Connection, intended only as an introduction to the crux of the subject. The next wastes little time in justifying, 'If it wasn't for GOLF . . . !'

"If we hurry we could just about finish"

10

Eccentric Brits in the Transvaal

The clock now goes forward twenty years.
It is August 1965 and I'm taking lunch in the dining room of the Eccentric Club with a couple of business pals. Larry Webb, current Chairman of the Club and Captain of its Golfing Society, comes by and stops to introduce his guest.

'This is John Atkinson, Sam. He's Chairman of the New Club, Johannesburg, with which we Eccentrics have friendly reciprocity arrangements. He wants me to get together a few pals to go to Jo'burg in November and play in a nationwide fund-raising golfing festival. Hundreds of their citizens and business houses are contributing and the proceeds will go to the Widows and Orphans of South African Police. All my little team will have to do is get there, and throughout the two weeks we spend in the country we're the guests of the New Club and its members. Coming, Sam?', he asks.

'Count me in', I tell him, and turn to continue chatting with my pals. They in turn interpret the casual proposals and decision they've just overheard as just another of the 'high-rolling' everyday scenes in our Club. I say nothing to correct the impression.

Lapsing back into the past tense as befits a 22-year old story, it was 14 November 1965 when nine Eccentrics rendezvoused for a champagne send-off by our loved ones in a private lounge at Heathrow. Pausing only for our press photographs on the gangway of his VC10, the BOAC captain took it up and headed quarter of the way round the world in a southerly direction, while we 'scoffed', quaffed and dozed over the next 14 hours, including an hour-and-a-half stop at Nairobi.

It was 6.00 on the morning of 15 November when he landed us in brilliant sunshine at Jan Smuts Airport, Johannesburg. The plane taxied right up to the airport buildings, where a uniformed guard of honour, complete with military band, stood in readiness. Gangways were pushed into position and we stared through portholes in disbelief as Press reporters and photographers, together with what were obviously State and military dignitaries, surged round the foot of the gangway. 'Well', said Larry, 'John Atkinson did say he'd arrange for us to be properly met and escorted through the airport routine, but I never dreamed it'd be anything like this!' And he was right – it wasn't!

Before we could smarten ourselves up and file out among all that pomp and circumstance waiting to greet us, came an announcement over the aircraft's public address. 'There will be a slight delay before passengers in Economy Class can disembark'. So we sat down again.

Through the portholes we watched serried ranks of soldiers come to attention and present arms, while the band struck up an unrecognisable tune with an anthem-ish sound to it. Down the steps from the First Class compartment came a black gentleman with a white lady, followed by a small retinue of followers. We learned later that it was HRH Seretse Khama returning to his home in the British Protectorate of Bechuanaland (to become the independent State of Botswana the following year) from a state visit to Kenya, and changing plane at Jo'burg in the process. With Ruth, his English wife and daughter of Sir Stafford Cripps, it appears that he and his party had boarded our VC10 during that 1.00 a.m. stop at Nairobi.

Our own 'reception committee' was spotted in the background, consisting of John Atkinson and a handsome stranger in a well-tailored buff-coloured uniform with lots of gold braid on his peaked cap. He turned out to be Brigadier Louis Steyn, vice-Chairman of the New Club and Chief of Johannesburg Police. Thanks to his presence, the nine Eccentrics did far better for VIP treatment than HRH, although in a somewhat less ostentatious fashion.

For while Seretse Khama and his entourage were being solemnly led and cleared through the various formalities, Louis by-passed them all and had us whisked straight into a fleet of police cars waiting close at hand. At the same time a squad of his uniformed men transferred our baggage and golf clubs into a waiting 'Black Maria' that had rolled up to the blind side of the plane's hold almost as soon as the engines were switched off.

Then, with sirens blaring, the cavalcade roared up the freeway to the city centre. As the 'sound effects' were mainly for our benefit, they were switched off a few blocks before it rolled to a halt, at 6.45 a.m., at the front door of the New Club in Loveday Street.

A number of members had assembled to greet us by way of a reception committee, and the entrance lounge was like Bedlam as introductions and drinks flew around. Despite protesting that we'd finished a good breakfast on the plane shortly before landing and that most of us wanted nothing more than to catch up on some sleep, we were led straight into the dining room for another full and formal English breakfast – with knobs on! The knobs being pints of beer, bottles of wine, and formal speeches welcoming us to South Africa in general, and the New Club in particular.

In the meantime, our baggage was unloaded by club staff and sent up to the rooms allocated, but not yet seen. The golf clubs stayed on the police truck and, while we breakfasted, were delivered, care of Manager, to Observatory Golf Club.

After breakfast and the welcoming toasts, I was shown to my room on an upper floor and introduced to the Zulu 'boy' (ranging in age from twenty to sixty, they're all 'boys') whose duty it was to look after me. During the ensuing two weeks a doting mother could not have done the job better.

Shirts and underclothes worn one day would be washed, ironed and put away the next, whether I left them out for that purpose or not; suits and shoes were cleaned and brushed meticulously, whether I wanted them done or not; my bed was made each morning when I went down for breakfast and turned back after I left the room to go out for the evening; and a cup of tea and two digestive biscuits, at 6.00 a.m. every morning, placed on the table by the side of the bed whether I'd slept in it or not. I say that because there were at last two mornings when I arrived back at the Club in broad daylight from some Bacchanalian orgy or another, to find my biscuits and tea – now stone cold – in position by the side of an hitherto unslept-in bed.

It wasn't easy staying the course. Golf and social invitations flowed in each day as newspapers continued to publish glowing, inaccurate accounts of our visit. One of their favourite descriptions of our party was that we were a crowd of eccentric millionaires who travelled the world playing golf for charitable purposes, and that we'd chosen the South African Police Widows and Orphans Fund for our current good deed!

The Afrikaans daily paper, *Die Vaderland*, let me have a translation of their three-column, front-page write-up. It appeared beneath a large photograph taken at the airport on the morning of our arrival, and went like this:

> Members of the exclusive Eccentric Golf Club in London, who, on an invitation tour for the benefit of the South African Police Widows and Orphans Fund in Johannesburg, have arrived this morning at Jan Smuts Airport. They were met by Brigadier Louis Steyn, District Commissioner of the Golden City.
>
> On the left stands Mr. Larry Webb, chairman of the Club, which mainly consists of millionaires. In the centre is Brigadier Steyn. The other persons are Messrs. A. F. Trinder, Pat Densham, Ernest Nash, John Atkinson (Chairman of the New Club) and Sam Morley.
>
> The golf competition of the year will take place on Saturday at Observatory Golf Club in Johannesburg. Not only will a few millionaires from the most exclusive golf club in the world, that is the Eccentric Club of London, take part, but also representatives of

more than 50 businesses in the City. Two Ministers of State and also senior police officers will also show of what they are capable.

The Chairman, Larry Webb, said that members of the Eccentric Club take part in golf tournaments throughout the world to raise funds for charity. This however is the first time they have visited South Africa.

The Republic's Ambassador in London, Dr. Carel de Wet, is also a member of the Club there. The Ministers of State who are also taking part in the tournament are John Vorster, Minister of Justice, and Dr. Wilgard Muller, Minister of External Affairs.

Not what I'd call the sort of inspired journalism one would expect from, say, Henry Longhurst – but remember it was an English translation by an Afrikaaner of a write-up in his own language.

The principal English-language newspaper of Jo'burg, *The Star*, printed similar glowingly inaccurate reports of our visit, but played it down a bit by not referring to us as millionaires – just 'wealthy British businessmen, members of London's exclusive Eccentric Club'!

True, all of us were in some sort of business or the other but, if they were anything like me, they lived off the back of their ventures and usually at a faster pace than it could afford! Certainly nobody in our party would ever dream of discussing his wherewithal, and each assumed that the other had to be reasonably well-fixed to be on the trip in the first place. Even if he did happen to be doing it on the firm. There certainly wasn't enough in the Morley family coffers to indulge in that sort of thing. While as for travelling round the world doing charity shows – like the Red Arrows or Bob Hope – I'd classify that as a fine example of fanciful journalism used to colour what might otherwise have been just a bit of prosaic reporting.

Back to that first morning.

Given half an hour in which to say hello to my 'boy', who

had already unpacked my suitcase and stowed everything away before I'd even left the breakfast table, the weary Eccentrics were then whisked away to Observatory Golf Club. There we were introduced to its pro, the immortal Bobby Locke, before going out in fours with our hosts for a quick 18 holes. It was a great course, but Lord knows how I dragged myself around, despite being given a good caddy to do all the heavy work. I'd gladly have made him a present of my clubs just for the opportunity to shove off somewhere and catch up with sleep. But I tried not to let on, and plied my partner, Wally Gunstone, with questions about the course, country, constitution and climate as we strolled round.

The big charity tournament at Observatory was on the first Saturday after our arrival. Played in brilliant sunshine before large crowds of spectators, it was a festival of merriment and colour, with marquees and music providing liquid, solid and aural entertainment to supplement what was taking place on the course.

A uniformed guard-of-honour accompanied the first four-ball to go out and stayed with them around the full 18 holes. Possibly because the Eccentric Club Chairman, Larry Webb, was one of that four – but more probably because another happened to be John Vorster, the South African Minister of Justice and later to become its Prime Minister.

On each of the short holes were a brace of beauty queens with notepads and measuring tapes, stationed there until the last four-ball had played it, and to decide which of the hundred-odd tee shots aimed at the pin that day finished up nearest the flag. Quite a common bit of fun on society and gala days in these gimmickry-laden days, but remember this was 1965 and the first time any of we Eccentrics had come across it. One of our number, Leslie Warren, turned out to be the lucky man on the sixth, and at the prize-giving that evening was presented with a massive automatic washing machine. To avoid possible difficulties with excess baggage in getting it back to England, the South African dealer and donor of the prize arranged for its manufacturers to deliver an identical model from their UK depot to Leslie's home in

Oxted, Surrey, a week or two after he returned.

In order that the 'Eccentric millionaires' could be more easily identified, the organisers had arranged for a Union Jack plaque to be fastened to our golf bags with the name of its owner underneath. Thereby spectators would surge around caddies carrying a plaqued bag, read the name, identify its owner with their programme bought on arrival, and ask for an autograph alongside the entry.

That wasn't too bad, but when they started following the game along to watch the quality of golf we'd brought six thousand miles to enhance their big day, it became a bit embarrassing. With a daily debauching programme to date that would have put an early Roman festival to shame, it's a wonder some of us were able to see the ball – let alone hit it effectively.

With the end of play, a giant carvery and barbecue had been set up in the open air near the clubhouse, including, of course, temporary bars dispensing unlimited free grog. It was quite dark by the time everybody had got through eating, drinking and boasting about the way they had played that afternoon, and had assembled in a large circle to witness the prize-giving and speeches under the starlit African sky above, and a battery of floodlights closer to the scene.

After the prizes came the speeches. John Vorster's was extremely witty, judging by the laughter. Unfortunately, it didn't even raise a smile with me, as it was delivered in neat Afrikaans. He then re-presented it in English for the benefit of those not too familiar with the national tongue, but again it wasn't all that hilarious. When I asked my partner if it was a true translation of what was said earlier he explained it couldn't be done really, as a lot of Afrikaans idiom had been used to have a mild crack at the English guests and some of it didn't translate too well.

However, there was a good closing scene when Larry, after saying his bit on behalf of the Eccentrics and donating our joint cheque to the charity fund, presented John Vorster with an Eccentric Club tie and told him he could now consider himself an honorary member of the Eccentric Club of St.

James's, London. Without hesitation John Vorster then whipped off the tie he was wearing and presented it to Larry, telling him that, as it was the official South African Police Club tie, he could now consider himself an honorary member of the law enforcement ranks of a police state! All good clean fun.

We were invited guests of the Stewards at Germiston on one of their weekend race meetings. At Turfontein the following week, Bell's Whisky were our hosts in their director's marquee, they having sponsored the day's racing. At both places the hospitality was never-ending, with food, wine, cigars and inside information flowing fast and furious throughout the day; which is more than can be said about the horses I backed. Punters are mugs the world over and ready to believe that the other guy, whoever he is, knows it all.

Wally Gunstone, the fellow I played golf with on that first morning, knew a lot about racing. I believe he owned a couple of horses in training and was a Steward at one of the meetings. Before the first race and having carefully studied the card, he warned me to be careful about backing Durban-trained horses.

'They all get so used to running at sea-level, Sam', he confided, 'that when they're sent up here to run in the rarefied air of Jo'burg – six thousand feet above sea-level – they have breathing problems and can't find the wind to finish strongly.'

So I left the Durban-trained horses alone, as so expertly advised, and they proceeded to win six of the eight races that day!

Alex Monteith of the New Club, whose accent and name left little doubt which side of the Tweed was his home before seeking his fortune in South Africa, was also a member of Wanderers – claimed at the time to be the largest sporting complex in the world. I believe he was responsible for the visiting Eccentrics being hosted by Wanderers for a golf match, followed by an impressive formal dinner the same evening.

Helped by the fact that we both played left-handed – although off a handicap of two, Monteith would knock his ball about twice as far off the tee as poor old Morley – we became firm friends. So much so that, when my wife and I were in Jo'burg while on a visit to South Africa eight years later, he picked me up from our hotel early one Sunday morning for a friendly singles round another of his clubs. This time it was the comparatively new Johannesburg Country Club. Whereas he'd laid on for me to have the services of an African caddy, Alex brought along his 11- or 12-year-old son to take care of his 'tools' and needs on the way round, besides giving me a natural history lesson remembered far more vividly than his father's golfing prowess on that beautiful sun-drenched morning.

Graham Monteith, now a qualified doctor, was a healthy-looking youth of above average intelligence and inclined to wander off to explore the surrounding wooded terrain while waiting for his father or me to play our shots. On one of these forays he returned with a chameleon perched on his shoulder. Coming across it in a thicket he'd taken it under his wing, and for the rest of the round continued foraging in search of food for his new-found friend. It continued to sit contentedly on his shoulder, flicking out a 12-inch tongue at the assortment of fare offered it. By cupping hands or holding a large leaf over it, we were shown how it would change colour instantly to blend in with with the amount and quality of light in which it sat.

Before leaving South Africa I saw and bought a terracotta chameleon in a souvenir shop. It was about the same size and colour as young Monteith's – which, incidentally, had been returned to its natural habitat by the time our game was over. That stone chameleon still sits on a shelf in my study, and sight of it never fails to provide an instant flashback to that evocative African morning with the Monteiths.

At his home the previous afternoon Pat and I had met his

wife, Margot, and their two other children. An obvious family photograph on the sideboard showed four children, so I had to open my stupid big mouth and ask about the youngest who, I learned, during the previous summer and aged about three, had wandered down to their swimming pool unnoticed by other members of the family. It was far too late to do anything about resuscitation when the poor little mite was found lying at the bottom of the pool some time later.

This kind of tragedy being all too common, the South African authorities introduced a law requiring all private pools to be fenced in with an unscalable palisade at least 4 feet high, and a locked gate to be the only entrance into the area surrounding the pool.

There wouldn't be any harm in a similar law over here, especially with the number of private pools now in the country. I remember drying off and dressing in the pool-house alongside my own pool one fine morning. My little granddaughter, aged two at the time, had folllowed me down from the house after her Nana had helped her get dressed, and was running round the edge of the pool, tossing her rubber duck in and out and chattering away to it. Half-aware of the succession of splashes as she chucked Duckie in and ran around the pool to retrieve and scold it before chucking it in again, it dawned on me that I hadn't heard her voice after the last splash. Wandering out of the pool-house to see where she'd got to, I could only see her hair streamed out and floating on the surface of the water. Made quite a mess of my nice dry shirt and trousers as I jumped in and fished her out, before carrying her up to the house for drying off.

Standing starkers in the kitchen while getting a final rub-down with the bath towel, she looked up at me with a baleful eye and spluttered, 'You ought to keep that pool of yours covered up when little children are about!' Yes, out of the mouths of babes and sucklings . . . She's 16 now and swims like a fish, but it's so easy for things to go horribly wrong.

Now let's get back to the fêting of those nine Eccentrics in Jo'burg back in November 1965.

101

One day we were taken on a conducted tour of the Premier diamond mine, about 20 miles north of Pretoria, and 45 miles from Jo'burg. It was fascinating to learn that in the final stage of the process they used the same 'homespun' method of sorting the gems from the crushed ore as they did in Kimberley 22 years earlier. The rock-handling and crushing plant was far more sophisticated but the end of the production line was almost identical.

It consisted of a heavily greased vibrating table, slightly inclined, on to which the crushed particles of ore tumbled after passing through a cascade of running water. Being wet, the ore would not stick to the grease and tumbled off the sides as the table vibrated, to be conveyed away to the mountains of slag heaps surrounding the mine. But diamonds, being unwettable, would lovingly cling to the grease until carefully picked off for cleaning and grading by the eagle-eyed harvesting team.

In the assaying room we were shown a miscellaneous handful – and I mean a handful – of tiny stones, most of which would have easily passed through the mesh of an ordinary gardening sieve. We were told they were the total 'catch' of the previous day after Lord knows how many tons of ore had gone through the crushing system. About one ton of ore needs to be processed to obtain one carat of gem stone. The day's takings turned the scale at about 100 carats (a carat is about half a gramme).

That must have been quite a day there when they found the biggest stone ever, way back in 1905. Called the Cullinan diamond – after the boss of the Premier in those days – it weighed 3,250 carats and was sold to the Transvaal government for one million dollars. It was then presented to King Edward VII. Considering it a little too ostentatious to wear in his tie as a stickpin, His Majesty had it cut up into a number of smaller gems, ranging from 50 to 500 carats. Two of the latter were mounted as the principal stones in the Royal Sceptre and the Imperial State Crown, displayed today in the Tower of London with the rest of the Crown Jewels.

Going to the other extreme we were told that 80 per cent of

today's efforts at the mine go into recyclying the 100-year-old slag heaps, in search of the 'tiddlers' once thrown back with contempt. The search is not for decorative gemstones but for little more than diamond dust or chippings, which, due to hardness, are in great demand for tipping rock-boring drills and similar tools.

Talking of diamonds, I remember a fascinating story told by our friendly Police Chief. Standing around the bar of the New Club while waiting for transport to arrive and take us wherever the action was scheduled that evening, one of my Eccentric pals said it would be a shame to have come all the way to South Africa without at least taking one diamond back home. In fact, he gave to understand that he was under orders from the missus to do that very thing. 'So, off the record, is there any chance', he asked Louis, 'of finding somebody slightly dishonest with whom one could get down to a little wheelin'-'n'-dealin'?'

Louis wasted little time in marking his card on that one. Under no circumstances should any of us try to buy a diamond through an unauthorised dealer. Diamonds being a vital part of South African economy, nobody was allowed to trade in them without a Government licence. Illicit diamond dealing or buying, therefore, was one of the most heinous crimes on the country's statute book. He went on:

> Sure, there's any amount of people who can introduce you to an illegal dealer, whereby you'd acquire a questionable bargain in some sleazy back room. But just how long you'd hang on to your acquisition is a debatable point. You see, every one of those shady dealers is known to us, and we allow them to buy the ill-gotten stones – usually stolen by the folk who work the mines – and go on breaking the law by selling them to greedy suckers, on one condition: they must report to us every time they do a deal! That way we always know where the stolen diamonds are being 'fenced' and don't have to ferret around to trace another smart operator after putting the one we know in the 'pokey'.

Once the sale is reported, we make a visit and turn the 'bargain-hunter's' home or hotel room upside down until we find the goods. The usual outcome is confiscation of the illicit purchase, a fine equivalent to three times its value, and a stiff jail sentence as a deterrent to others. The confiscated goods would go into Government stock and one third of the fine into its coffers. Another third would go to Police funds, and the remainder presented as a reward to the 'squealing' dealer. That way he's encouraged to believe it's in his best interests to go on playing ball with the 'Law'.

Then came a juicy tit-bit of case history, but as I've no wish to embarrass anybody we won't bother with names. The Brigadier continued:

We recently had a US evangelist doing a grandstand tour of the country and saving our sinners left, right and centre. The day he was due to fly out with his entourage and save a few more elsewhere, it was reported that he'd been out and done a bit of shady shopping. Not just a single itty-bitty stone as a souvenir, to which we'd normally shut our eyes, but a real king-size purchase of the little pebbles, like he was going into the diamond business.

When he and his party arrived at the airport to check out late that evening, he was asked in the customs if he'd anything to declare. He said he carried the word of the Lord, Jesus Christ, and that was something he was always glad to declare. The customs man said 'I see', and then asked the contents of the Gladstone bag the other carried as hand luggage; but was again not impressed with the reply that it was only a favourite bible to read on the plane and a few personal effects. The evangelist was also beginning to take umbrage over the lack of respect toward his VIP status, and threatened to have the US Ambassador brought to the airport. Ignoring his protests, the customs people took him to an adjoining room and, stripping him down to his socks, thoroughly searched every nook and cranny of his clothes, bags, and body. Nothing untoward was discovered, and it was beginning to look as though somebody had blundered. Then a sharp-eyed official noticed something unusual about the stitching of the lining to the Gladstone bag; so they decided to rip it out. And – lo-and-behold! – there were found a goodly number of little sparklers neatly taped and sandwiched between two flat pieces of cardboard on the bottom of the bag.

Big guns were brought to bear in the airport customs hall that night, with senior members of the South African Department of Justice on the one hand and the US Ambassador, or his second-in-command, on the other. All had been hastily summoned from their beds when told of the individual and the nature of his offence. No publicity at any costs was the order of the day. In the end it was agreed that the Ambassador would go guarantee for a 'gi-normous' fine, and the evangelist would be allowed to leave the country with his Gladstone bag – minus diamonds, of course – and his passport indelibly stamped, 'Persona non grata South Africa'. A polite diplomatic way of saying 'Get out and stay out!'

Louis ended his story with the advice that anybody wanting to buy a diamond to take home should let him know and he'd arrange a visit to a licensed wholesale dealer; but nobody to buy more than one stone. Having been parted from any 'diamond-money' I might have had by those Durban-trained horses at Germiston and Turfontein races, I, for one, never did take up his offer.

While most of our party was taken on a three-day safari into the Kruger National Park, I used the opportunity to escape from the daily round of hedonism and dry out a little – with the help of a thousand-mile trip by 727 to see my brother and his family in Cape Town. Pat Densham, one of my fellow-

Eccentrics, decided to take the plane ride with me as he too preferred the idea of a couple of days' sanity among some friends he had down there, rather than continue the junketing routine midst the wildlife in the Park.

When we got back, the boys said they'd seen just about every wild creature that belonged to Africa; and also some pretty wild nights around the camp fires at the end of each day's trekking. During that time, by contrast, I had rested up and swam in my brother's pool, played golf with him – using left-handed clubs he'd borrowed for me from a friend (mine having stayed in Jo'burg) – and spun yarns or listened to them round the family table in the evening. When we met up again for the plane back to the Golden City, Pat said he had likewise relaxed with his friends and felt a lot better for it. We each reckoned it wasn't a lot different to a short tranquil leave during those wild and wartime days.

But it didn't take long to revert to 'Action Stations' once back at the front. Our battle-weary pals made no secret of their envy of our run to Cape Town, as they told of 'wassailing' till the early hours in the Kruger, before departing at 5.30 a.m. for the three-hundred-mile Range Rover belt back to the New Club. They'd arrived about half an hour before Pat and me, and hardly had time to wash the jungle-dust out their hair before hospitality cars arrived to take us all out to lunch and golf at the Royal Jo'burg Club.

The final party was in John Atkinson's home the day before our return to England. It started with barbecue-style lunch around his pool and just went on. But as there were some far-reaching spin-offs from that party as far as I was concerned, it justifies more than a passing mention.

There were about forty people assembled, most of whom spent the afternoon and early evening under the hot sunshine in or around the pool. The barbecue – or braaivleis, as any form of outdoor cooking is called in South Africa – with all the trimmings, catered for everybody's tastes in food throughout the day. As usual, the amount of liquid consumed could have refloated the *Titanic* – just as the small iceberg John had bought in to cool the drinks might well have sunk it again!

As the light faded and evening breezes freshened up, the action drifted indoors. During a lull in the buzz of party noise, our host, John Atkinson, took the floor, called for hush and then said he had a very special treat for his overseas friends. He opened the cupboard of his radiogram and blew the dust from an old 12 inch 78 rpm record before putting it on the turntable. Everybody went quiet as the wheezy, cracked voice of John Gielgud, or some other great Shakespearean actor, came over. To be fair I'm not sure whether the old actor or the old record was responsible for the wheezy cracked tone. Anyway, the part certainly called for it – as we stood for what seemed an hour, listening to the dying John of Gaunt's speech from *Richard II*.

For the sake of one or two readers who may have forgotten the salient points that old John (Gaunt, that is, not Atkinson) was trying to make, here's the gist of how Shakespeare saw it.

Lying on his deathbed, Gaunt is trying to tell his brother, the Duke of York, what a mess their nephew, Richard II, had gotten the country in. It all happened nearly five hundred years ago but still has an all-too-familiar ring.

After the eight opening lines that sum up his uncle's alleged weaknesses, Gaunt goes on to croak:

This royal throne of kings, this sceptred isle,
This earth of majesty, this seat of Mars,
This other Eden, demi-paradise,
This happy breed of men, this little world,
This precious stone set in silver sea,
Which serves it in the office of a wall,
Or as a moat defensive to a house,
Against the envy of less happier lands;
This blessed plot, this earth, this realm, this England,
This land of such dear souls, this dear, dear land,
Dear for her reputation through the world,
Is now leased out – I die pronouncing it –
Like to a tenement or pelting farm.

England, bound in with the triumphant sea,
Whose rocky shore beats back the envious siege
Of watery Neptune, is now bound in with shame,
With inky blots and rotten parchment bonds;
That England, that was wont to conquer others,
Hath made a shameful conquest of itself.
Ah, would the scandal vanish with my life,
How happy then were my ensuing death!

The wheezing stopped as the record ground to a halt. By this time everybody was cold sober and stood in bewildered silence, wondering where the party went. Then, as if to pour a couple of gallons of four-star over the hot ashes of what was once a carefree 'fire-cracker' of a 'hooley', our host addressed his guests something along these lines:

'We Boers know and enjoy English tradition, history and literature more than 95 per cent of your countrymen who come out here and consider us a load of bad-speaking illiterates. And from what you've just heard it's plain that Will Shakespeare could see what a sorry state your country had got itself into even that long ago.'

And then, out of that spellbound assembly, came an Eccentric Cockney voice – mine!

Well, seeing you're all that keen on Shakespeare, let's shift the action to about twenty years later and see whether he still thought it a mess. Picture the scene:

It's the night before Agincourt and Henry Five, done up in an old civvy suit and a bowler hat, is quietly wandering around among the campfires checking the morale of his troops. They had just marched 260 miles in 17 days and were about to take on 60,000 of the best and freshest that France could put in the field. He puts his head into the GHQ tent just in time to hear the Duke of Westmorland say:

'Oh that we now had here but one ten thousand of those men in England that do no work today!'

By now the John Atkinson assembly – and my fellow-Eccentrics – were beginning to look as fascinated as they were bewildered earlier. I threw myself desperately into the part.

(Before proceeding further, a word of explanation for what follows. Most readers will be familiar with one of the greatest speeches from Shakespeare and may consider it superfluous to see it reproduced here in its entirety. On the other hand, it is a vital part of the story and there may be one or two who don't remember it all and whose copy of the Complete Works of W. S. is with a friend. Or being re-bound. So here goes!)

The King steps into the light of the fire and takes his hat off. Everybody gasps. He looks all around to make sure he has the floor and then, in ringing tones, makes one of the greatest soul-stirring speeches ever credited to an Englishman. It went like this:
'What's he that wishes so?
My cousin Westmoreland? No my fair cousin;
If we are mark'd to die, we are enough
To do our country loss; and if to live,
The fewer men, the greater share of honour.
God's will! I pray thee wish not one man more.
By Jove! I am not covetous for gold,
Nor care I who doth feed upon my cost;
It yearns me not if men my garments wear;
Such outward things dwell not in my desires.
But if it be a sin to covet honour,
I am the most offending soul alive.
No, faith, my coz, wish not a man from England.
God's peace! I would not lose so great an honour
As one man more methinks might share from me
For the best hope I have. O! do not wish one more!
Rather proclaim it, Westmoreland through my host,
That he which hath no stomach to this fight,
Let him depart; his passport shall be made;
And crowns for convoy put into his purse;
We would not die in that man's company
That fears his fellowship to die with us.

This day is called the feast of Crispian.
He that outlives this day, and comes safe home,
Will stand a-tip-toe when this day is named,
And rouse him at the name of Crispian.
He that shall live this day and see old age,
Will yearly, on the vigil, feast his neighbours,
And say, "Tomorrow is Saint Crispian".
Then will he strip his sleeve and show his scars,
And say, "These wounds I had on Crispian's day".
Old men forget; yet all shall be forgot,
But he'll remember, with advantages,
What feats he did that day. Then shall our names,
Familiar in his mouth as household words –
Harry the King, Bedford and Exeter,
Warwick and Talbot, Salisbury and Gloucester –
Be in their flowing cups freshly remembered.
This story shall the good man teach his son;
And Crispin Crispian shall ne'er go by,
From this day to the ending of the world,
But we in it shall be remembered –
We few, we happy few, we band of brothers;
For he today that sheds his blood with me
Shall be my brother; be he ne'er so vile,
This day shall gentle his condition;
And gentlemen in England now a-bed
Shall think themselves accurs'd they were not here,
And hold their manhoods cheap whiles any speaks
That fought with us upon Saint Crispin's day.'

(Well, verse of an epic or heroic nature, both rhyming and blank, has always fascinated, and hundreds of hours have been spent over the years in memorising favourites like 'Horatius', 'Vitae Lampada', 'Gray's Elegy'. But 'Agincourt' always ranked Number One, since I first slogged away at learning it by heart while walking the dog through the woods more than thirty years ago).

Its effect that evening was phenomenal. Modesty prevents me from describing the acclaim, surprise and disbelief, as those final majestic words 'hit the fan' from such an unexpected source. Half-apologising for a long-winded and histrionic outburst, I explained that some chauvinistic come-back seemed necessary after that jibe by our host. Who, I hasten to add, was one of the first to come forward when the cheering had stopped. Putting one arm round my shoulder and thrusting into my still trembling hand another topped-up glass of the tipple – Cane Spirit (like Bacardi) on-the-rocks, half a fresh lime and four fingers of water – that had no doubt given me the Dutch courage to take the floor in the first place, he ordered me to kneel. Then, lifting a decorative Zulu assegai from the wall over his mantelshelf, he touched me on each shoulder with it and bade me, 'Arise, Sir Agincourt!' On went the junketing.

Larry Webb considered I did the Eccentric Club – and possibly the old country itself – a great service by that burst of rhetoric before all those Springboks. With the result that I was invited to join the General Committee of the Club soon after our return from South Africa, honoured with the Captaincy of the Golfing Society three years later, and offered the Chairmanship of the Eccentric Club five years after that.

Now I ask you. Just how much of that could ever have happened – if it wasn't for GOLF ...?

" Throw him your own ball - mine's 2 feet from the pin! "

11

Eccentric Lawmen at Tolworth!

In June 1966, John Atkinson led a party of golfing members of the New Club, Johannesburg, on a reciprocal visit to England as guests at the Eccentric Club. Although we couldn't lay on the Zulu-boy service, nor a game of golf for their leader with Harold Wilson – or any of his Cabinet – it was generally agreed that we gave almost as good as we got the previous year.

For some, like Louis Steyn and Peter Nell, it was their first visit to England. Pat and I had the two of them up at the house for dinner one evening during their stay. Sipping drinks on our back porch – 450 feet above sea level and overlooking five counties – they could not believe that the countryside around could be so scenic and lush. They'd been brought up to think that England was a cold inhospitable place with a cold inhospitable climate, and inhabited by cold inhospitable people.

Peter told how his father had been taken prisoner by the British in the Boer War, and transported to a concentration camp in Bermuda. He spent about three years there before being repatriated some time after the peace treaty was signed. As a result of the ill treatment received, his father's hatred for all things English was so intense that his children were brought up to speak nothing but Afrikaans in the home. They were all taught English at school, but if one word of it was spoken within earshot of their dad, a right old thrashing would result. Peter found it difficult to reconcile all that parental obsession with what he saw and experienced in the country he'd been taught to hate.

Mind you, by the time Peter Nell went back to South Africa it could be said he had at least one good reason of his own to echo his father's feelings about the 'perfidious Brits'. A few days after his visit to Cuffley, he was being taken on a tour of St. Albans and district by Jack Langford and Ernest Nash – two of the nine Eccentrics featured in the last chapter. Jack, being Larry Webb's son-in-law, was driving the old man's Range Rover, or some vehicle of a similar design. They had been out to see Solly Joel's huge estate and thoroughbred stud farm at nearby Childwickbury (pronounced Chilikbury) and the next stop was to be an adjacent village with a pub renowned locally for its extra strong ale.

In his haste to get that first pint down his throat – it being thirsty work looking at stud farms – Ernest scrambled into the motor and slammed the door shut good and hard. Unfortunately Peter's hand was in the way and the poor chap lost half a finger. This meant calling into Casualty at St. Albans Hospital – after emergency dressings in situ – before making for the pub in question. Sadly it also meant no more golf for poor old Peter during the remainder of his stay in this country. A country, he now had every excuse to think, that seemed to go out of its way to antagonise successive generations of the Nell family.

In addition to friendly golfing get-togethers involving miscellaneous Springboks, an official match between the Eccentrics and the New Club was played at Moor Park. A magnificent silver-and-mahogany shield had been put up by the London office of the *Johannesburg Daily Star* through their managing director, Alex Noble. It was to be played for every year in alternate countries to help foster the bond between them, said Alex, when the shield was first displayed at a cocktail party in the sumptuous Haymarket offices of John Dewar, the whisky people. Dr. Carel de Wet, the South African Ambassador in London, made the official presentation to the Captain of the winning side, having himself played in the match that afternoon – left-handed, I might add. He was also a member of the Eccentric Club, but I don't remember on which side he played. Nor do I remember which Captain took the shield back from Dewar's to his Club's trophy room. What I do remember is that the firm of John Dewar was very liberal with both its own product and that of associate companies – and their hospitality that evening helped strengthen the newly-formed 'Springbok Connection' even further.

The climax and end to the South African visit was a grand party in the home of Larry Webb at Redbourn. Or I should say the garden of the home of Larry Webb at Redbourn. Although held out of doors he'd made it formal dress and everyone to be in dinner jacket or evening frock. (I chose the jacket as my wife said it was her turn for the frock.) By midnight there weren't many of the fifty or so present who, whether jacketed or frocked, were not sipping champers while standing immersed up to the neck in Larry's unheated swimming pool. Some party!

Back came the Springboks the following summer. By this time there were many new faces among both Eccentric and New Club members making reciprocal trips throughout the year. But it was the visit in July 1967, led by John Atkinson – for whom it was also an annual business trip – to which I now refer. Preceded by a short digression which becomes relevant as the story unfolds.

On Saturday, 15 July 1967, my daughter Susan was married to Allen Floyd in our village church. For the occasion we had a marquee in the garden and Eccentric Club staff to cater for some one hundred and twenty guests. The sun shone, the bubbly flowed, both the suckling pig and the jellied-eel stall were equally appreciated, and the six-piece Dixieland band played till 2.00 a.m. It wasn't until the sun rose again about 4.30, that I took a final look round the now deserted scene, uttered an audible prayer of thanks for everything going so well, shooed a couple of fieldmice from the crumbs on the table, and went indoors to try and dream up how to pay for it all.

Then came Thursday, 20 July, and the Eccentric Golfing Society had the visiting South Africans joining us at St. George's Hill, Weybridge, for one of our monthly fixtures. My car at that time was a green Healey 3000 and, with the hood folded back, I set off from home about 7.00 a.m. in brilliant sunshine. The country was enjoying one of its rare heatwaves and everything looked set for a great day.

After the usual greetings, coffees, brandies, bets, etc. we went out in threes to play the morning 18-hole Stableford competition. My three-ball consisted of left-handed Frank Pepper – one of the Springbok contingent – and a fellow Eccentric. Whether it was the good company, the morning drive in the sun, or a sense of responsibility as acting-Captain for the day due to the enforced absence of the reigning 'monarch', I don't know – but by the time we finished that morning round, my score-card was a sight for sore eyes. So much so that when it came to prize-giving that evening, I'd won not only a dozen crystal whisky tumblers, but was presented with a magnificent silver punch bowl known as the Upex Cup. Named after Dickie Upex, who'd donated it years earlier for the winner of the annual morning round at St. George's Hill – to be held by the winner until the fixture came round the following year. To give some idea of its size, after I'd tipped six bottles of bubbly into it – to be passed around for all to gulp in the traditonal way – the level of its fizzing contents was still four inches below the ornate and scalloped rim.

Once the gulping was over, sweepstake monies went over the bar and then everybody started buying for everybody else. Just an ordinary Eccentric evening to be sure, only more so now with the help of the Springboks, who would keep 'calling 'em in' long after there was no longer room on the counter for the glasses.

Then Pat Densham invited a number of the party to be his guests for dinner at the Fairmile Restaurant, about ten minutes from the golf club. I drove there and remember getting as far as a couple of pink gins at the bar while the food orders were taken. Then, with a strange weariness overtaking me, the thought of spending the next couple of hours in a hot dining room – loading up still further with unwanted food and drink – did not appeal. Fond farewells were exchanged and I left the scene.

Once in the open car with my trophy safe on the back seat and the sun just beginning to set it looked a beautiful evening for the long drive home; especially as the sooner I made it, the sooner my beloved would learn about my day. There was so much to tell.

But by the time I reached the 'Ace of Spades' on the Kingston Bypass I was fighting a losing battle to keep my eyes open. The obvious thing was to find somewhere safe to close them. Approaching the 'Toby Jug', where the road from Epsom joins the A3, I remembered Tolworth Tower, a high-rise office block on the London-bound side of the road, with a newly built Fine Fare supermarket at ground level. Newly built then, that is. My firm had supplied some of the lighting fixtures for that project, whereby I'd visited the site for a meeting during the building programme. There was a service road by the side of the store, where delivery trucks unloaded and where I had parked my car at the time. It would be the ideal spot for an undisturbed siesta. The area was deserted and as silent as the tomb when the Healey glided to a stop by the loading doors of the building, and I switched the engine off. Sliding the driving seat back as far as it would go, I stretched out with a huge sigh of content and rested the back of my head on its top edge. Lulled by the hum of distant traffic on the busy A3, my eyes closed and I knew no more.

Consciousness returned with a feeling of no longer being alone, and I looked up without moving my head. A lot of dark blue suiting blocked out what little light there was left, and a pair of eyes under a peaked cap looked down into mine.

Before going any further, let me say it is virtually impossible for anybody to quote a word-perfect replay of a conversation ten minutes after it has taken place – let alone twenty years. Sure, we all hear plenty of 'So I said to him' and 'Then he said to me', but in each case the qualifying phrase, 'something like this' immediately after 'said' is taken for granted. But with regard to my Tolworth Tower

Tale, I've told it so many times that I really believe my twenty-year-old conversation with that man in blue went as near to something like this as makes no difference.

'Hello', I said.

'Hello', he replied. 'What are you doing here?'

'Having a sleep.'

'Why here?'

'I got tired driving home and decided to stop.'

'Where's home?'

'Cuffley.'

'Where's that?'

'In Hertfordshire.'

'That's a long way. Where've you been?'

'My daughter's wedding.'

'When was that?'

'Saturday.'

'Sounds like a good party. Today's Thursday.'

'No, it's all coming back. It *was* a good party. But today I played golf with the Eccentric Club and some South Africans. I won the Upex Cup.'

'What's the Upex Cup?'

'It's on the back seat. If there's any bubbly left in it help yourself.'

He picked it up and said:

'There's no bubbly left in it. You sure you didn't get this out of a jeweller's window?'

'No I didn't. I won that fair and square. You're talking to the greatest little left-hander in the business.'

'I think I'll have a word with my mate.'

He walked away to a near-at-hand patrol car that I hadn't noticed so far and in which, by raising my head a little, I could just make out a dim figure at the wheel. He came back.

'My mate's a golfer. He said what's your handicap?'

'Nine. What's his?'

He went away for another chat, but soon came back.

'He said not as good as yours.'

'Tell him to keep practising.'

'He also wondered how you found the turn off into this

cul-de-sac. Seeing you're a stranger round here.'

'My firm do a lot of lighting for Fine Fare. I parked here when I came to a meeting during the building programme. I remembered it as I almost drove past – thought it'd be an ideal spot where I wouldn't be disturbed.'

'You were wrong then, weren't you? I'm going off for another chat.'

He came back after several minutes.

'Right. We've talked it over. You've been having a lovely week and nobody ought to spoil it. You included. We don't think you should be driving again yet. So you're going back to sleep and we're going back on patrol. We'll be back here in about an hour to check you out again. So off you go to bye-byes. Don't move until we get back. If we find you gone we'll put out a call and have you pulled in as unfit to drive.'

'Thanks', I said and, wriggling down to a more comfortable position, was once again happy to close my eyes.

I opened them again and could just make him out in the dark, standing over me.

'Haven't you gone yet?' I asked a bit peevishly.

'Gone yet?' he echoed. 'It's just about an hour and twenty minutes since we left you. We've checked the jewellers' windows in Kingston and Esher. Then my mate said, "Let's go back and see how the greatest little left-hander's getting on". I told him about your Cup and he'd like to have a look at it. Can I show it to him?'

'Of course.' I sat up properly and was now feeling nicely refreshed. He brought it back.

'He said he's going to practise now so he can win one like it. Well,' he went on, 'you look as though you might be fit enough now to drive home. But we're still going to stay behind you for a bit. If we don't like the way you're driving we'll pull you in and make you go back to sleep.'

'Thanks a lot', I replied, 'but I don't think you'll need to. Goodnight and thanks again for everything.'

Switching on the engine and headlamps, I drove out on to the A3 and headed towards Roehampton. My two friends stayed close behind until the last stretch of the bypass before the Robin Hood roundabout. Then they flashed their lights, drew up alongside, paused, gave a cheery wave, took the lead and roared away at the junction in the opposite direction to mine.

Although all this happened about four years before the introduction of breathalysers, there was still plenty of drink-and-drive legislation about whereby they could have thrown the book at me. But, God bless 'em, they did nothing of the kind. When this book's in print I'll contact the Kingston 'nick', see if they can be traced, and send them a couple of copies to liven up their retirement. Especially the golfing one who never did get out of his car.

They were probably on serious crime-prevention patrol and li'l-ole-me down a side-street sleeping off a 'big one' didn't come under that heading, at least not once they'd made sure I hadn't busted a window to pinch that Cup. But, if so inclined, it wouldn't have been a lot of trouble putting out a call for one of their mates to come and pick me up and win himself a medal or two. But the fact that they didn't left me with an ever-fresh true story, complete with happy ending.

One that couldn't have been told – if it wasn't for GOLF . . . !

" Mind you, it's some time since I last played "

—— 12 ——

Stanley Baker and the Zulus

We now come to 1968, the year I became Captain of the Eccentric Club Golfing Society. If nothing else, this chapter again highlights the colourful membership and lifestyle of that grand old club until, five years before its centenary, it was 'put to death' by the duplicity, or stupidity, of those who influenced the sale of its lease to a property company in 1984. The membership was exiled by a trick in 1985, its furniture and furnishings sold off, and the huge building locked up to stand silent and empty until this day – while those who own it 'wheel-and-deal' for its commercial redevelopment.

Back to 1968.

Once again the New Club contingent came in force under John Atkinson, timing their visit to arrive in support of 'ole Agincourt's' big weekend – the 'hooley' held by Eccentrics in June each year at Knokke Le Zout, on the Belgian coast. We always took over the whole hotel for three nights and that year, with the influx from Jo'burg, our numbers must have been well in excess of a hundred. Officially we were there to play a lot of golf at the magnificent course just outside the town – and there were some who did actually get in more than one round during the time they were away. But with so much good food and wine to get through, a magnificent casino that stayed open until long after dawn – providing you still had a few francs they could reckon on taking off you – card schools and singing sessions in and around the hotel bars, some of us got in about as much golf as we did sleep. Nevertheless my wife and I still found time to get out and visit shops or drive out and around for local sightseeing.

The climax of the weekend was the formal dinner held on Sunday night, before all and sundry started making their way back to England. It was usually a carnival atmosphere, ending with a prize-giving to the better golfers, courtesy gifts to a number of people who had helped toward the success of the venture, plus the usual speeches and responses.

While going through the dressing-up routine in readiness for the cocktail party preceding dinner, came a tap on the bedroom door. Without waiting for the invitation, in walked Orrie Orengo – a singular character if ever there was one. Also a great personal pal, acting Hon. Sec. of the Society, and one of the original eight 'Voortrekking' Eccentrics with whom I went to South Africa three years before. He was responsible for organising much of the evening's programme and wanted some last minute words on the subject. My wife's consternation at being found in her dishabille was pooh-poohed with, 'Don't worry, Pat. I'm an old man and with a houseful of women at home. I've seen it all'. Tactfully wanting to change the subject, he went on to ask her if she was all ready with her speech. 'What speech?', she cried. Turning to me in agitation she went on, 'You never said anything to me about a speech!'

I told her that, being preoccupied with all the things the Captain was expected to do and remember, I'd never given a thought to the fact that she might have to stand up and say a few words. Orrie cocked it up further by trying to play it down. He explained to her that the Society usually presented something rather nice and expensive to the Captain's lady towards the end of the evening, to which she would usually get up and say thank-you in her own charming little way. Pat was almost hysterical as she swore I'd deliberately kept it dark in order to embarrass her. Being uncertain whether he'd yet done enough damage to the Morley hitherto-entente cordiale, born-diplomat Orrie departed with a cheerful, 'Well, I'm sure you'll both handle your parts excellently'. A fine thing to say to a self-conscious and shy little lady, who's just been told for the first time that she's expected to stand up and address a hundred people a couple of hours hence!

It would have been much better had Orrie said nothing, as she'd have enjoyed the excitement of being singled out to receive a little 'pretty'. It would then have been just a short step to want to stand up and say thank-you and how nice she felt about being so honoured. But now she wasn't having any and no way did she want to attend the festivities to make a fool of herself in front of all those people – as, she insisted, no doubt I'd planned for her to do.

One or two friends managed to talk her round sufficiently whereby she reluctantly agreed to come down with me into the crowded lounge to what was programmed traditionally as the 'Captain's Cocktail Party'. At which, with a hundred guests and the Belgian franc riding high against the pound, I was too preoccupied with mentally pricing-up the huge trays of champagne cocktails circulating – ad infinitum – among the merry throng, to give much thought to my wife's little hang-ups. But she got plenty of support in her anti-Sam campaign when chatting to wives of past-Captains, who told her how nervous they had been when faced with the same job, and how they'd prepared reams of notes for the occasion – only to leave them in the wrong handbag, or forget to put their reading glasses into the right one. But they were unanimous in commiserating with a 'Fancy Sam not telling you!'

Little wonder she would hardly talk to me throughout dinner, and pretended not to be particularly interested in my performance when I had to stand and deliver. Yet when John Atkinson came over and presented her with a pretty bauble in a velvet box, together with a few well-chosen words, she stood up to her full height of five feet nil, and delivered a charming and witty little speech from the top of her head that had everybody chuckling. Me, especially. But I stayed unpopular for some time to come. In fact, I think she only started speaking to me again last Tuesday!

The scene now shifts back across the Channel a little later the same year. The Springboks have migrated back to their native land and England is beginning to return to normal. It's early autumn and another annual Eccentric golfing event is about to take place. This time it's a match between 12 chosen Eccentrics and a similar number from those who played at the game among the Grand Order of Water Rats.

For those not too familiar with the name, the G.O.W.R. is a form of Freemasonry practised among the élite of the entertainment profession. It started as a fun thing with some vaudeville artistes about a hundred years ago, but as it developed it took itself more seriously and became selective. Recruiting its membership from the theatrical profession generally, it has long been quite an honour among those so engaged to be invited to join its ranks. In addition, people like agents, impressarios, and others considered to have helped the Order in its charity campaigns, are to be found wearing that little silver emblem of a vole, or water rat, in their buttonhole. Our own Larry Webb, for instance, was largely responsible for providing them with one half of one of the upper floors of the Eccentric Club in which to hold their meetings. To show their appreciation they made him a member of their Order, with the title of Companion Rat. Another spin-off was this annual golf match, played at Coombe Hill, where – once play was over – a convivial time was had by all.

Coombe Hill Golf Club is only about a couple of miles from where that police patrol team in the last chapter waved me farewell 14 months earlier.

As the etiquette in golf events such as this required opposing captains to be the first match off the tee – in this case 9.00 a.m. – I thought I'd given myself enough time in allowing one and a half hours for the drive from my home. But the daily commuter stream – or more of a 'log-jam' in this instance – was exceptionally heavy and I arrived late; only by about ten minutes, but by the time I'd changed and arrived on the first tee, with my clubs on the back of the caddy that had been reserved for me, etiquette was under pressure from the twenty or so Eccentrics and Water Rats loosening up and swinging clubs while waiting for the two

Captains to get together and hit off.

Orrie Orengo scolded me for being late, while making hurried introductions to an opponent I did not know. With a quick handshake, the latter wasted no further time in getting his ball into play. I quickly followed suit. Surprisingly enough, they were both pretty good shots, bearing in mind the impatience in evidence around us.

As we walked briskly down the fairway away from our still-murmuring friends, I took a long careful look at my companion. No – the face was unfamiliar and I didn't have a clue who he was. We discussed whether to have a modest wager on our game and, having agreed the sum, I felt the time was ripe for a little friendly candour.

'Look', I said, 'I'm awfully sorry, but in the general panic back there on the tee I didn't catch your name when the introductions were made. And in case you missed mine, it's Sam Morley.'

For some unknown reason he stared at me for quite a long time before deciding to reply, and then said simply, 'It's Baker, Sam. Stanley Baker.'

'Great playing with you, Stan', I said as we broke away to play our second shots to the green. What conversation there was for the rest of that first hole was just golfing talk. You know, 'Good chip!' 'You to go', 'Are these greens fast, caddy?' and 'I don't know how that putt stayed out!' That sort of thing. It was not until we were striding away from the second tee, with the caddies following along about five yards in the rear, that I felt the time had come for further friendly chat.

'What's your association with the Water Rats, Stan? Are you some kind of performer or do you do something in the agency line?'

He stopped walking and looked at me long and hard before he spoke.

'Are you having me on?'

'No, really', I protested, 'I'm not. But I've got to be honest. I don't know your name or your face. That's not your fault, I'm sure. But I watch very little television, and have not seen many films or West End plays over the past dozen years or more. So I know next to nothing about who's who in modern entertainment. Sure, I know all the old performers – like Hoot Gibson or Laura La Plante – but you're far too young to be either of them!'

'Well,' he said, 'such is fame! I happen to be a straight actor, Sam. I don't know how many films or stage productions I've appeared in so far, but there's been quite a few over the years.'

We carried on with our match until, having had time to browse over what he'd said, I sought a little more friendly interchange, having provided him with a rundown on my own background in answer to some of his questions. So I asked him:

'You know those films and plays you've been in? Can you name me one or two, just in case I may have seen, heard, or read of them without ever coupling your name with the title?'

'You *are* having me on!'

'Honestly,' I told him, 'I'd love to be able to tell you that I know you well and remember seeing or reading about your performance in a certain part. But that wouldn't be true.'

'You mean to say you haven't seen *Zulu*?', he asked incredulously.

I think he was still chuckling over my reply as we walked back into the clubhouse at the end of our game. By which time he'd accepted the truthful fact that I was indeed ignorant of that epic film prior to our meeting. I don't know how many times I've seen it since, besides many other of his masterly performances and have nothing but admiration for his patience with me that day. He was a great sportsman and a gentleman. As will be seen.

A couple of years later, I was a guest of Reg Davies – a name that crops up more than somewhat throughout these pages – at the South Herts Men's Invitation meeting. A gala day, when members invite a friend to come and play a day's golf, interspersed with lots of food, wine, good fellowship, and a

babel of voices in and around the clubhouse, lauding or
lamenting bare lies, long putts, near-eagles and lost balls.
Reg and I had played the morning round with another
member and his guest, and were seated on the terrace
overlooking the first tee and 18th green – quaffing
something long and cool in the hot sunshine, and no doubt
adding to the babel from tables around with our own
versions of the afore-mentioned topics.

Suddenly, from a table behind came a cry – with a touch of
'Welsh dressing' to make it all the more piquant.

'I'd know that voice anywhere! It's got to be Sam Morley!'

Spinning round, I saw Stanley Baker. He was seated with
his host, Pat Connolly – an old friend and one-time Captain
of South Herts – plus another couple of chaps with whom
they'd played that morning. Walking over to shake his hand,
I asked if he wasn't something to do with the Grand Order
of Water Rats as I was sure we'd met somewhere before.
Rising to greet me, he threw a playful punch. At least, I
think it was playful.

'This bastard', he said, pointing at me and turning to
his host, and for the benefit of another dozen or so sitting at
adjoining tables who had stoppped their own discussions in
order to listen to what the great Thespian had to say, 'this
bastard had to play against me in a match when I was
Captain of the Water Rats and he was Captain of the
Eccentrics. He turned up late, said he didn't know me after
we'd teed off, asked my name, and when I told him asked
what sort of work I did. He convinced me he wasn't kidding,
and when I said I was an actor with a lifetime of stage and
film appearances behind me, he asked if I could name one
or two, in case he might have heard of or seen them, and
whereby he could then place me. Again he swore he wasn't
having me on. Then I said: "D'you mean you've never seen
Zulu?" He stopped and took a long careful look at me full in
the face. Then told me he'd seen hundreds of them in South
Africa, but they were all a bloody sight darker than me! . . .
I've lived off that story, Sam, since then,' he went on, 'and
now I'm buying us a bottle of bubbly on the strength of it.'

Before that day was out we got through more than that first bottle.

Alas, so many of those about whom I've written in this chapter have now gone on – John Atkinson, Stanley Baker, Pat Connolly, Larry Webb, Orrie Orengo – but it was as great a privilege to know them as it is now to write of them.

Something I could never have done – if it wasn't for GOLF . . . !

"What's the name of the doddery old feller sitting between young Thingammy and Old Whatsisname?"

Sun City Serenade

In September 1987 came a communique from Racegoers Club, of which I'd been a member since it began in 1968, announcing an annual mid-winter trip to summer climes. It read:

In January 1988 the Racegoers Club, in response to numerous requests, returns to South Africa. *(I hadn't gone with them on the two earlier visits.)*

The tour departs on Friday evening, 22 January, when we shall leave the frost and snow behind, arriving in Johannesburg early the following morning. After checking in at the sumptuous new Sun Hotel it will be off to Gosforth Park racecourse for the afternoon. The following day we shall leave for Mala Mala, the privately owned Rattray Game Reserve, where morning and evening game-watching is conducted in Land Rovers, each with its own driver, spotter and game warden. Although it is adjacent to Kruger National Park, Mala Mala offers infinitely better chances of seeing the rarer species – and the accommodation and facilities are superb.

After that it will be down to Cape Town on the world-famous Blue Train, which combines a trip of scenic magnificence with the sort of luxury given on the Orient Express.

In Cape Town the Club will be staying at the Mount Nelson – one of the great hotels of the world which blends old world service with the finest modern accommodation. After four days in Cape Town, with racing at Kenilworth, side trips to studs and the wine growing district, it will be on Durban and the Maharani Hotel overlooking the Indian Ocean. Racing in Durban will be at Clairwood which has established a particular rapport with the Racegoers Club. The Stewards at Clairwood will entertain the group in a style which has been matched by no other racecourse anywhere in the world. Their kindness and hospitality shown on previous visits has been legendary.

To relax at the end of the trip there will be a couple of nights at Sun City, the resort hotel and casino in Bophuthatswana. Swimming pools, a championship golf course, superb restaurants, luxury accommodation are all set in glorious tropical garden setting – and there's a well-run casino to help pay for the trip – or take away any remaining Rands.

Because accommodation at Mala Mala and on the Blue Train is restricted, numbers will be limited to a maximum of forty. As it is unquestionably the best-value major trip the Club has offered it is likely to be oversubscribed quickly. Bookings will be on a first-come, first-served basis and should be made now, accompanied by a deposit of £250 per head.

THE COST

The price, sharing a twin-bedded room £1,575

Single room supplement £250

The price includes:

Air transportation on the scheduled services of South African Airways as per itineraries in the economy class London/Johannesburg/Cape Town/Durban/Johannesburg/London.

Accommodation in twin-bedded rooms with private facilities in de luxe/first-class hotels.

Full board basis (all meals included) at the Mala Mala game reserve and on the Blue Train.

All coach transportation for tours and transfers.

Racecourse admission charges where applicable.

Services of Racegoers Club representatives.

Complimentary champagne reception on departure

at London Heathrow Airport.

I wasted little time in booking for both the Morleys. But when my wife analysed the detailed itinerary that followed a month or two later, she decided that nine changes of sleeping quarters in 16 days, beginning and ending with a 14-hour night flight, were no longer her scene. Like a rare wine, she decided, she did not travel well. So once again I was on my own. Well not quite, because my very good friends Reg and Joan Davies and Kath Barber – also members of Racegoers – had their deposits in the post from the 'off'.

The finished typescript of this book was almost ready for the printers come departure-time, so I took a copy along for final editing during those restless hours to be spent in the air, and those soporific ones around hotel pools.

By the time I returned to Heathrow 16 days later, the book was no longer ready for the printers. There was now the need for a further chapter to round off the Springbok Connection. It took me another ten days to research, write and edit it, but as a result Part Two has been brought out of a time warp and into the present day.

South African Airways are far too popular. Every seat was taken on both our outgoing and return journeys, and they tell me they're booked up solid for months ahead. I can never sleep sitting up – my legs get filled with lead – and despite a sleeping pill, every minute feels like an hour. Too much champers at the cocktail party in the El Al lounge at Heathrow before take-off probably didn't help. (South African Airways and El Al use the same airport facilities.)

Once airborne, the mobile free bar and excellent dinner no doubt increased the problems when it came to seeking sleep. Experts tell us alcohol and big eats are a root cause of discomfort and insomnia during long flights. Must use a little self-discipline next time, besides doubling the Mogadon dosage.

But that's no reflection on S.A.A., who run an excellent airline. As they had contracted with Racegoers to take care of all our air and land movements, together with hotel arrangements, Frank Gurr and Nigel Bottell – from the London office – travelled with us throughout and kept all wheels well oiled. Like organising teams of porters at every arrival point to pluck bags carrying distinctive Racegoers labels off the carousels and take them out to the waiting coaches. Similarly, to transport them from coaches to departure check-in stations; or into hotel lounges where porters would shuttle them up to the allocated rooms. All we had to do was ensure our belongings were among the stack of assembled bags before they were passed into coach, airplane, train or hotel lobby. And nothing went astray throughout the 16 days.

We were an hour late in starting, as that morning had seen the only fall of snow in the South throughout the winter of 87/88 (at least up to mid-February when I'm writing this), because of which the S.A.A. plane on which we were to travel had been diverted to Gatwick on its arrival from Johannesburg at 7.00 a.m., and time was lost getting it back to Heathrow with corresponding servicing and crew problems. But smoked salmon sandwiches and champers in the El Al Lounge – organised by our genial Racegoers Club leaders, Tony Fairbairn and Louise Gold – lasted out nicely until five minutes before we boarded.

It was in the eighties on the Jo'burg tarmac at ten o'clock next morning (they are two hours ahead of London) and a Buck's Fizz reception awaited us at the Johannesburg Sun – a two-year-old fully air-conditioned hotel in the centre of the city, with blue glass curtain-walling cladding all 40 storeys. My spacious double room on the 32nd floor faced west, from which I was to view impressive sunsets over the gold mine slag heaps, and an electric storm during my second night there. The only problem was that the phone was dead in the first room they gave me. When they found they couldn't fix it they gave me another room later that day where the phone worked fine. But the digital illuminated clock on which it stood showed 77 minutes past 77 throughout the next four days.

But first came the scramble to hang crumpled clothes in the wardrobe, shower, and climb into something reasonably formal, before joining the bulk of the party in the hotel lobby. Much as everybody would have loved a bit of leisurely bed or pool-time after that traumatic overnight flight, Racegoer stalwarts were honour-bound to accept the lavish hospitality laid on by the Stewards of Germiston – now Gosforth Park – Racecourse whose invited guests we were. A few succumbed to the call of the flesh but, noblesse-oblige-ing, most of us boarded the waiting coaches and were whisked away to the races – about six miles south-east of City Centre – and welcomed into a private lounge overlooking the winning post.

Racing having started at 11.30, we arrived at the close of the third event on the ten-race card; and even without the experts telling me not to back the Durban-trained horses – as in Chapter 11 – I still managed to find the next four losers in a row, offset by a couple of small 'ticklers' among secondary place bets on outsiders. By this time and with three more races to come everything inside me was crying for a bed. So bidding a quiet, fond and reluctant farewell to friends and hosts – the latter not only having plied us lavishly with food and drink since our arrival, but also a grand cocktail party with more food planned for once racing was over – I left it all behind, called for a taxi, and hugged myself with rapture when finally crawling between the sheets up in room 3217 of the Sun Hotel.

An hour was all I needed, after which a few phone calls were made. One of these was to a book distributor to whom I'd been given an introduction from England, with a view to marketing my books in South Africa. Although it was Saturday evening he thanked me for calling and, being neither a golfer nor a church-goer, arranged to collect and take me back to his office in Randburg, about ten miles away, the following morning to discuss the subject in detail. The second call was to Alex Monteith, of Chapter 11, who invited me to join him for lunch at the New Club on Tuesday;

but surprisingly, made no mention of golf.

Anticipating involvement with book matters and socialising with old friends, I had opted out of the long trek to and from the Mala Mala Game Reserve when booking the trip, in favour of spending all four days in Jo'burg.

Mala Mala was magnificent according to my Racegoer friends. Those who didn't contract tick-fever while camping in the luxury rondavels and swanning about the jungle in Range Rovers with searchlights, seeking and finding lions devouring zebras and the like, spoke highly of the organised barbecue suppers. Some of the semi-indigenous dishes mentioned included: sweet-and-sour warthog with Yorkshire pudding; impala kebabs; kudu steaks with pease pudding; and smoked ostrich with melon balls!

Meetings with book-people on Sunday, Monday and Tuesday mornings, while the 'Wildlife-on-One' mob were away, resulted in firm orders for 150 copies of *Victory on 'Site'!* and 45 *In Search of Eastern Promise*. Also an initial provisional order for 250 *If it wasn't for GOLF . . . !* when published.

Lunch with Alex at the New Club on Tuesday was a nostalgic affair, as so many of the old names and faces were no more. In fact, although I was a guest of the Club's Chairman and vice-Chairman, the 1965 Eccentric visit was a Club legend to all except Alex. Alex had lost interest in golf and was currently engrossed in terminating his job as M.D. of a large engineering business, in search of a better challenge. Anyway, it was far too hot to think about wandering around sun-baked fairways, and we parted with promises to keep in touch.

Instead of golfing, my Sunday, Monday and Tuesday afternoons were spent under sun umbrellas around the hotel pool, editing the typescript of the remaining chapters of this book between frequent plunges into the cooling waters.

The gang got back from the jungle about 7.00 p.m., to be allocated a new set of rooms for the night. My three pals joined me for a Tepanyaki meal in the hotel Japanese restaurant and were full of their experiences at Mala Mala.

Their stories were hilarious and, all in all, what with the range of unfamiliar dishes, showmanship of the diminutive chef and stone jugs galore of hot saki, Japanese eating-out took on a new dimension that night.

The following morning saw us en route for Cape Town on the Blue Train. As somebody volunteered who has travelled in both, the dignified splendour of the Blue Train was far superior to the rococo affectations of the much-vaunted Orient Express. Not having travelled on the latter I can't comment, other than to say it would have to go some to measure up to our Blue Train experiences. Midst air-conditioned splendour we each had a single or double sitting room for the 24-hour journey, and while occupants were away at dinner, the attendant converted them each into a luxury bedroom. Lunch, dinner and breakfast were served in the sumptuous dining-car, with a well-furnished club car adjoining for casual refreshment. And all with an unsurpassed quality of service.

By this time I'd learned that racial or colour segregation in South Africa was a thing of the past. Blacks, browns and whites rode the Blue Train, stayed in the grandest of hotels, ate in the finest restaurants, and thronged the Club enclosures at the races. In mixed groups too. A black man and his wife had the next cabin to me on the Blue Train and ate at the adjoining table, where the white Afrikaans waiter would deferentially 'sir'-or-'madam' them while attending to their needs. Marketing literature for the most prestigious leisure and pleasure amenities showed all creeds and colours enjoying them together – contrary to what the country's enemies are so anxious to have the world believe.

Agreed, only the wealthy can afford what is advertised, but the same might be said about the designer clothes, gold watches, Ferraris and Bentleys in our own Sunday supplements. And I saw plenty of wealth on show when taken on a drive through non-white areas around Cape Town, where many a majestic home was comparable with those around Sunningdale or Moor Park, complete with a shiny Roller standing in its drive.

Sure with a five to one population majority, non-whites can't expect one-man-one-vote legislation for many years to come, but idiotic persecution of little Zola Budd over here won't bring that legislation any nearer. South African radio, T.V. and newspapers delight in quoting adverse and ill-informed comment from the outside world. Nobody pretends they've got it a hundred per cent right down there, but there are conditions a lot worse much nearer home that get nothing like the malevolence heaped on South Africa.

On learning of my impending visit to the country my very good friend, Cawthon Bowen, of Nashville, Tennessee – who earns a lot of mileage in Part Three of this book and the Postscript – sent me a cutting from the *Nashville Banner* of January 1987, bearing his by-line. Here it is:

WHERE WERE THE PICKETS THIS TIME?
by Cawthon A. Bowen, Jr.

Several years ago the South African Davis Cup doubles team played the United States tennis representatives at Vanderbilt. Benjamin Hooks of the National Association of the Advancement of Colored People (NAACP) and the Rev. Joseph E. Lowery (SCLC) and others spent a good bit of money to travel to Nashville to picket and protest these tennis matches. They were joined by a number of Nashvillians who opposed apartheid policies in South Africa.

I attended that match, which the South Africans won handily. Recently I also attended the Vanderbilt-Russian basketball game here. Again, the visiting foreign team was first-rate and won.

But there was not a picket to be seen. It would seem to me that those who take an active public interest in opposing countries with oppressive practices, could discover plenty to inflame their passion for justice from the national Russian basketball team if two South African tennis players could.

One needs to look no further than Afghanistan, where Russian troops have booby-trapped children; and Poland, to discover slaughter of innocent peoples and repression on a grand scale. Or the Berlin Wall. Or the daily repression of freedom for countless Russians, with torture and imprisonment without trial not the least bit unusual.

So I could not help but wonder – where were the pickets?

The article included a photograph of the usual banner-waving slogan-chanting throng outside the stadium when the South African tennis players were there.

There was no shortage of non-whites staying at the rambling four-storey Mount Nelson Hotel, Cape Town, on the slopes of Table Mountain – one of the finest hotels I've known – as well as reclining on gaily-coloured chaises-longues around its magnificent pool. From the verandah of my huge second-floor room I gazed on my favourite mountain, flanked by Devil's Peak and Lion's Head, and had another four days to re-live the memories it all brought back.

With the help of a self-drive car my friends took in the scenic beauty of the area the day after our arrival, while I spent the best part of it with my nephew John, who took me to lunch at his Club and on a grand tour to see some of the many changes and developments since I was last down there 17 years ago. It's comforting being abroad and still be driven on the right side of the road – which is of course the left-hand side of it as far as we Brits are concerned. Pray God that stupid Continental rulings are never extended to the point when the E.E.C. can interfere with the way *He* meant us to travel!

Before John dropped me back at the hotel, we'd arranged for him to bring his wife Diane and daughters Sarah Jane, seven and a half, and Lauren, five and a half, none of whom I'd previously met, to join me for lunch at the poolside restaurant at Mount Nelson on Sunday – two days hence. I then phoned my brother Mark and asked for him and Vera, his wife, to come in from Hermanus, seventy miles away, and join us. Being my brother, with a life-long flair for contrariness, he told me he'd an important game of bowls to play that day and why hadn't I been in touch earlier to come out to his home instead, or make more convenient arrangements than I had? But at the thought of a party with her only son, daughter-in-law, grandchildren, and favourite brother-in-law, I could hear Vera shout in the background, 'I don't play bowls, Sam, I'll be there!' And, of course, having now voiced his token protest, so would he.

A 7.00 a.m. swim next morning, followed by poolside breakfast and a half-hour fry-up under the sun, had me in fine fettle for the day's programme. Coaches were due about 10.30 to take us to Kenilworth races, where once again winners proved awfully hard to find. The Stewards welcomed us lavishly and it was impossible to spend money except by making foolhardy bets on the horses. Drinks and food were all on the house and they never stopped coming. Betting with the Tote was all computerised with a large, ever-changing board in the centre of the track, showing the calculated odds on each runner as the money went on, both on and off the course. And unlike similar tote 'tell-tales' over here, the board stayed on after the race was run, whereby the odds were there for all to read even before dividends were announced officially. Forecasts were called 'Swingers' and to nominate the first three past the post in the correct order was called a 'Trifecta'. As this usually paid a pretty hefty dividend, many tried permutations of three or more horses. And many a heartfelt tale was told after each race, of the Trifecta that almost came up, if only . . . !

Bookmakers, seated under sun umbrellas in front of the stands, marked up prices and laid bets pretty much the same as on a U.K. course, but without all the shouting of odds so typical of domestic scenes. It was too hot and far to walk from the air-conditioned lofty stand in which we wagered and watched, so all my modest betting was with the Tote. As was the case with most of the Racegoer party.

That evening, three of us took a cable-car trip to the top of Table Mountain to watch the sun set in the Atlantic Ocean and the near full moon rise from the Indian one. Still studying the heavens we gazed with awe at our familiar giant constellation, Orion the hunter, standing ludicrously on his head, his belted sword poking up in the air, and his faithful hounds, Canem Minor and Major, ranging away to the right instead of left. Viewing the skies from the Southern hemisphere opens up a brand-new ball game – as my old friend Nicolas Copernicus might have said back in 1530.

Then followed a cracking meal in an Austrian restaurant on Kloof Street recommended by nephew John, where my glazed duck with all the trimmings was served upon a plate about the size and shape of a sailing dinghy.

Although my friends chose well, but differently, they too had the same giant platters. Yet the whole meal, including starters, wines and some delicious pudding that we were too full to eat, but could not refuse when they did a selling job on it, came to something like £12 a head.

Had a great time with the family next day and watched Sarah Jane and Lauren swim like fishes in the hotel pool. John said he hadn't a pool at home yet but was planning to put one in this year. Kath Barber, who had met Mark and Vera more than once when they'd visited the UK, joined us for lunch, followed by a two-car two-hour sightseeing trip around the breathtaking scenery of Chapman's Peak and the coastal roads of Hout and False Bay; followed by fond family farewells and promises to come out again soon.

The day ended with my friends and me dining in the Buccaneer Charcoal Restaurant, a few hundred yards from the hotel, where the chef/proprietor, Joseph Curigor, was so smitten with our praise for the quality and size of the steaks we'd ordered that he sent over a tray of liqueur bottles and glasses with the coffee and his compliments. It is many years since I tasted Van der Hum and we nearly killed his complimentary bottle between us, leaving the port, Cognac and cherry brandy untouched. Must remember to send him a signed copy of the book with a marker on this page – just to show that his kindly gesture was appreciated and the card I asked him for on leaving was kept and put to good use.

Except for the 24 hours on the Blue Train, I'd managed an early morning swim every day so far since arriving in South Africa, and Monday, 1 February, was no exception. However, there was not a lot of time after breakfast to get packed and on parade in the Mount Nelson lobby, ready for the next move.

Bags, as usual, were collected from the rooms, assembled at the hotel entrance for identification, and stowed on the coaches. Driving through the hotel grounds, we took a last look at our panoramic surroundings on the way to board the 11.30 a.m. flight to Durban, with a scheduled stop at East London.

Coaches waited to take us to the 38-storey Maharani Hotel on the Durban ocean front, and all rooms looked down on to the same surf-pounded beaches on which I had been almost swept out to sea 45 years earlier, when *Redoubt* had lain alongside Mayden Wharf between convoys, and I was diving through breakers on a few hours' shore leave.

Mayden Wharf should have nostalgic memories for hundreds of thousands of British and Commonwealth forces, whose troopships would pile into Durban harbour for provisions and fuel before proceeding up to the battle zones of Egypt and Burma. When the time came for them to put to sea again, a lady dressed in white flowing robes would stand at the end of Mayden Wharf. In a rich soprano voice she would sing 'Now Is the Hour' to the silent troops lining the crowded decks, as the ships steamed slowly through the narrow entrance and out into the open sea. Although I must have experienced this half a dozen times or more, it was always a very moving occasion – and in fact still is as I write about it.

I never actually witnessed it close up, as escort ships would stay berthed well down Mayden Wharf, about half a mile from the narrow harbour entrance, until the convoy had assembled outside and was ready to move on. The lady's voice would often be heard from our upper deck and the singer, although just visible in the distance, was a dramatic close-up in the mind's eye.

Talking to some Durban people when at Clairwood races, one or two remembered her well and gave me her name. I didn't know I was going to write about her so didn't make a note of it, but it's probably as well because she was known, and remembered by all who served or passed through those waters at the time, as simply 'The Lady in White'.

(You wouldn't believe it! With a world population of about three billion, I had to pick Helen Wightwick, née de Beer, a mother of three in my village, but born and bred in Cape Town, to convert my sheets of scribbled 'copperplate' calligraphy into a legible typescript – she prefers to call it 'code-cracking'. When working on this bit she phoned me from home to say that Durban's 'Lady in White' was the aunt of one of her best friends at school. The flowing white robes to which I referred never existed, she told me. Whenever somebody said another troopship was leaving, the lady in question, Perla Siedle-Gibson, who did voluntary work in the forces canteen near the harbour entrance, would come out and go through the singing routine – still wearing her white canteen overall-coat! So much for my 45-year-old dramatic close-up in the mind's eye!

Sic transit gloria mundi!)

Another war-time memory – this time with no 'mind's-eye' distortion – was to be seen at Simonstown, where they had recently erected a monument to a Great Dane called Nuisance. When sailors would take the train from Simonstown to the 'big time' in Cape Town during those war years, many would be a little the worse for wear by the time they caught the last train back aboard. Well, with Château brandy five shillings a bottle one can understand why. The approach to Cape Town station and the trains themselves would be haunted at night by vagrants known as 'skolly boys' – coloured youths waiting to pounce on lone drunken matelots – like one of our stokers who was found in the gutter of Adderley Street with a bloodied head and robbed of his boots, money-belt and false teeth!

But Nuisance was the sailor's friend. He'd wander around

the concourse of the station from early evening and attach himself to anybody in blue who looked vulnerable; walking by his side and snarling at non-whites within twenty feet. He'd see him on to the train and then wander up and down throughout the 50-minute run to Simonstown, passing from carriage to carriage at the many stops en route; and woe betide any civilian trying to disturb a sleeping matelot. At Simonstown he'd accompany the lads on their walk in the dark to and through the dockyard gates, and often right up to the ships' gangways, then lope back to the station for the next train to Cape Town and repeat the process. Sounds a bit like Rin Tin Tin or Lassie Come Home, but this is all unvarnished truth. I know – I was there!

During the day he'd feel free to come down to the dockyard and board any ship alongside, to wander around its decks at will. Unfortunately he incurred the wrath of some of us on *Redoubt* when our little mongrel named Fritz (or something like that when christened as a puppy and inclined to foul the mess deck more than somewhat) took exception to Nuisance tucking in at his own food dish and foolishly went for him. Picking Fritz up as a terrier would a rat, the Great Dane administered a couple of quick shakes and our poor little pet was no more. The surprising thing was that the two dogs had often romped together previously when we were in Simonstown, but I suppose poor old Fritz caught the big fellow on one of his bad days.

Nuisance was an institution and a legend in Cape Town throughout the war years and much has been written about him. Now deservedly, there is a monument to his memory. He was a handsome animal and kept in immaculate condition by his unknown owner. Unknown to me, that is, although I believe all is revealed in a recent book. Now, all too late, I wish I'd bought a copy when in South Africa as, having enquired, it is not in the UK book lists. Still, my brother or nephew will probably send me one when I get round to letter-writing again instead of book-writing.

The rate of exchange favoured us immensely throughout our

travels, averaging 3.50 Rand to £1, providing one dealt with a bank. Those simple enough to take their travellers cheques to the hotel desk would get a meagre R3.12. In fact the Indian cashier at the Maharani told one of the innocents who presented some travellers cheques for change not to be a fool but to walk fifty yards round the corner to the Standard Bank and get a 12 per cent better deal.

The early morning swim here was at the roof-top landscaped pool deck on the 38th floor. Trees and flowering shrubs grew in profusion all around, with plate-glass panelled parapet walls overlooking the beaches and the Indian Ocean far below.

Many Racegoers started out at 6.30 a.m. on the day after our arrival in Durban, for a conducted tour and breakfast at the Summerveld Training Centre and Jockey Academy. (Well, a number of them were trainers, owners, breeders, horseflesh connoisseurs, and the like.) Others did their own thing. Reg laid on a self-drive car in which the three of us travelled north up the coast round to Umhlanga Rocks, for a dip in the ocean where the breakers didn't look quite so fearsome. But appearances were deceptive and despite not venturing much further than crotch-high we all got up-ended more than once.

Having 'showered' under a huge concrete pipe jutting out from the rocks, with running water discharging on to the sands below – and hoping it wasn't untreated sewage from the Zulu kraal passed a little later – we got back to the car and headed inland. It was about here I found that the priceless pictures I'd taken so far with my disc camera would never see the light of day. I'd forgotten to put a film in it when leaving England.

Studying the map, we at first were in favour of making for a recommended tourist spot called 'Valley of the Thousand Hills'. But after a few miles decided it might be a bit too far to venture if we were to get back to Durban in daylight.

So instead we followed a sign showing a grinning green crocodile, with an arrow under his arm saying, 'Crocodile Creek – 5 kilometres'. Once we started up the side road, where a similar creature standing on its tail pointed enthusiastically to tell us 'Crocodile Creek – 3 kilometres', we knew why he was grinning. There was no finished surface to this side road after the first fifty yards, just a juddering stretch of reddish brown pebbles that seemed to go on for ever, with another leering croc. waiting to show us the way every time the track forked off to a Zulu kraal or uncharted jungle. Sheer dogged determination kept us from abandoning the mission, until we reached the very middle of darkest Africa, or so it seemed, with a huge empty clearing and a sign that said 'Car Park'.

Entering a circular timber structure with half-walls and a thatched roof, from which a couple of lazily-turning electric fans were suspended, we were greeted warmly by the owner. He first asked us to sign the Visitors' Book, and then for six Rand each. We were then allowed to gaze over a low parapet wall at the meanest bunch of crocodiles, ranging from four to twelve feet in length, ever assembled. There were two stagnant opaque pools around which they wallowed motionless; that is, until our host started throwing them dead chickens in an advanced state of decomposition. The water of the pools boiled with frenzy as those ugly creatures thrashed and snapped at the food, and each other. It was quite easy to see why so many of them had scarred and shortened snouts.

Glass cases around the walkway housed poisonous snakes, scorpions and other unsociable creatures, caught in the lush jungle surrounding the site, and labels on the glass named them in English, Afrikaans and Latin, stating just how deadly or not they each happened to be. We were offered a half mile walk round the complete reserve, but preferred to stay in the reception area and browse around the inevitable gift shop. When asked if we'd like some refreshment both Reg and I voted for a cold beer. The owner apologised. He did not have a Government licence to sell beer but, seeing our cresfallen faces, he told us there was a way of overcoming this. Among the souvenirs in his shop were half-pint glass mugs, each with a grinning croc. and the slogan 'Crocodile Creek', emblazoned on it. They were six Rand each and, in order to ensure that they were 100 per cent leak-proof, each buyer was offered a can of iced lager for free – for test purposes. Will the records please note that neither of the two glasses we bought showed any sign of a leak when so tested!

Thanks to my map-reading prowess Reg had to drive about 73 miles to complete the 30 mile run back to Durban and the Maharani Hotel.

To put the next day's programme into perspective, here's the wording of a note we each had pushed under our door that night:

Racing at Clairwood – Wednesday
The bus will leave the hotel at 11.00 a.m. On the bus you will be handed an envelope with your Stewards Enclosure badge and a card with the name of your particular host. The Stewards there have divided us up into small goups – they had the names well in advance – and they will expect us to stay with them throughout the day – tho' during racing, of course, there will be the usual intermingling. It is a slightly more formal affair than at the other courses – and they are magnificent hosts. Jackets, shirts and ties are required – suits if you have them (gentlement anyway!).

After racing they are holding a cocktail party for us. So the advice is pace yourself!! I think you will find this the racing highlight of the tour – for generosity, friendliness and welcome.

It was signed by Tony Fairbairn. And he was so right – it was a magnificent party. And truly proud we were of our Tony when he spoke some well-chosen words and presented the Club with a large painting of a racing scene that he'd brought along with him from England. The wrapped package must have measured about five feet square and, manhandling that in and out of airports, planes, hotels, trains and coaches until the moment of presentation, was no mean achievement. But it was still all in one piece when Frank Jones, Chairman of Clairwood, unwrapped his gift and held it aloft for all to see.

Host to our little group was Stewart Johnstone, who explained that, as he was one of the duty-Stewards for that day and might have to adjudicate on any racing problem that cropped up, he was under obligation not to bet. For the same reason he withdrew his well-fancied horse, Generous, owned jointly with his brother-in-law, Derek Rock, from the fifth race. But Derek had no such obligation and possessed a profound knowledge of form. At the lunch table he worked out an intricate combination for the last six races – there were eight in all – known as the Pic-Six. It was similar to our Jackpot. He was still in the hunt when the last of them came in on a photo-finish.

Having by this time bought and inserted a film in my camera I have an excellent picture of a very happy Derek Rock holding up his cheque for 30,000 Rand after racing that evening, with his admiring brother-in-law standing by. Once again a copy will be sent as a marker of this page in the book when published.

The next day we were on our way by air to Jo'burg where we transferred to buses for the three and a half hour trip to Sun City, on the border of Bophuthatswana. Not easy to pronounce, I must admit, but its London office just put 'Bot' in their current lobbying-literature for U.N. recognition as an independent State. Although a South African protectorate since the last century (much the same as Botswana was Britain's prior to 1966, see Chapter 11), Bophuthatswana ('The gathering-in of the Tswana people') won complete independence in 1977. It is roughly the size of Denmark, is the second largest producer of platinum in the world, and has one of the highest standards of living in Black Africa.

In the *Spectator* of the 20 February 1988, they took the full back page to advertise: 'While most of Africa is being ravaged by Marxism and its legacy of famine, anarchy and violence, there is one black nation carving out a niche of decency and democracy. That nation is Bophuthatswana.'

The land surrounding Sun City is mountainous with desert-scrub, but lakes, water cascades, lush grass, flowering trees and shrubs, and colourful bird-life, abound in this man-made combination of Las Vegas and Disneyland. It was envisaged by a Johannesburg entrepreneur who flew over the site in a helicopter soon after Independence, found the right backers with the right money, and opened it up in 1979 as a playground for the Springboks – and any others who felt a need for golf, gambling, swimming, sailing, skiing, paragliding, tennis, squash, riding, bowls, eating, drinking, and generally indulging themselves.

The usual (by this time) array of brimming Buck's Fizz glasses were waiting to greet us on arrival in the dimly-lit entrance lounge of Sun City Hotel. Dimly lit, because the spacious hall beyond was alive with flashing lights from gaming machines, creating a Star Wars setting. It was a relief to get to my large, light, and handsomely appointed room on the second floor and look out on the distant vista of lakes and hills, with nearby trees in and around which troops of monkeys tirelessly chased each other. Little time was wasted in unpacking and getting down into the largest and bluest pool yet seen on the trip. The air temperature being somewhere around ninety degrees that afternoon, the only place to be was in the water or under an umbrella shading a sun-lounger close to it.

Come the evening, Reg, Joan, Kath, Sam and one or two others were the invited guests of Tony and Louise to dinner in the Silver Forest Restaurant. They did us proud. Especially as Tony decreed smart casual wear to be the rig-of-the-day. One fully-suited gentleman considered it de rigueur to be coatless and tieless in the presence of elegantly-groomed females, but none of the e.g.f's seemed to mind being surrounded by comfortably-clad menfolk.

All along Reg and I had promised ourselves a little golf once we reached Sun City, on the world-renowned Gary Player million-dollar course. We would hire clubs and a run-around caddy cart. But having reached it, we now felt that to leave the pool and succession of cooling colourful drinks delivered by dusky handmaidens in fetching straw hats, in favour of bashing a golf ball around distant mountain slopes under a broiling Phoebus, one had to be some kind of a super-masochistic nut. Not that the opportunity to start a game was so distant. The golf shop and first tee were only about 75 yards from our favourite water's-edge loungers but even to walk that far under a firecracker of a sun seemed the height of foolishness.

True, I did walk that far and further to look around a tree-shaded watery grotto at the foot of the Cascades and had to pass the golf shop to do so. But the shop was closed at the time. When explaining to somebody the need to return there and shop the following day, if only to get myself a souvenir hat – as once was my wont at famous golfing venues – I was told they all bore the words 'The Million-Dollar Golf Course' or some such blatant slogan. I couldn't see myself ever wanting to flaunt that around my old familiar haunts so didn't bother to call back. At least not for a hat or other golf paraphernalia. Not when another couple of dozen steps would take me into the Cascade wonderland. But it would take a far better pen than mine to do justice to the bosky grotto, caves, swaying rope bridge over water tumbling into rock-strewn rapids below, the brilliant plumage of the wide variety of tropical birds all around, and a boulder-lined basin filled by natural hot springs, with jacuzzi-like jets half-hidden in the rock crevices above and below the water surface. It was sensually stimulating to swim around in and under those waters and those of us who found it must have returned two or three times for yet another session of self-indulgence. Even met a coach-driver taking his lunch-break in it before driving his bus back to Jo'burg.

Not being much of a casino-addict I spent most of my surplus Rands in the course of an hour at the wheel of fortune on our last night, while Reg did about four between the wheel and blackjack – and didn't come out too badly, I believe. Others reckoned they played almost through to dawn – with the usual good, bad or indifferent results.

Earlier that evening, a grand Racegoers cocktail party was held in one of the private meeting rooms of the hotel. A thoughtful member had quietly collected from us all, whereby a tasteful purchase by 'sister' Kate at the ever-open gift shop next door resulted in a token presentation to Louise, preceded by a few words from yours truly in appreciation of the masterful (mistressful?) way she and Tony had organised everything.

The various gift shops were the final ports-of-call to spend surplus Rands on Saturday morning.

Although we had to be out of our rooms by 11.00 – when the hotel would start filling rapidly with the usual influx of weekend visitors – the pool remained tops in popularity until our coaches arrived for departure to Johannesburg at 3.00 p.m. Two rooms in the hotel had been allocated to the party where belongings could be deposited and clothes changed before leaving.

The plane to London was chock-a-block, and the less said about sitting upright or semi-upright for what seemed an eternity the better.

But I'd gladly go through it all again for another such Springbok Connection!

" For your information, Madam Captain, the place for
  Fairy Liquid is the bloody kitchen not the ball cleaner"

PART THREE

THE
NASHVILLE
CONFECTION

— 14 —

Enter Skinny Huggins

History books tell us that Mary Tudor was so obsessed with having lost England's last stronghold in France, she reckoned that on her death they'd find 'Calais' engraved on her heart. With me I think it'll be 'Nashville'. Nothing to do with possessing or losing the place – just that, since the spring of '68, it's added a lot of colour to what I like to think is my 'rich tapestry of life'!

Some of what follows in this chapter is paraphrased from the opening one in *Start-Off-Smashed!* But with 16 years since publication, and believing that – judging by royalties received to date – parts of the English-speaking world have not yet got round to reading that initial venture into literature, I still don't know a better way of illustrating what goes into weaving one of the afore-mentioned 'tapestries'.

It all goes back to a Belfast pub in March 1964; in those lovely pre-Ian-Paisley days when everybody in the North and South of Ireland was reasonably nice to each other, and 'no-go' areas in places like Belfast or Londonderry were simply licensed premises without toilet facilities.

Idly discussing current affairs and mutual interests over a jar of the national brew, an Englishman and an Irishman discovered they had a mutual interest in left-handed golf; to the extent that each was a member of his national left-handed golfing society. Flushed with emotion and half-way through their fourth Guinness, they agreed that something should be done to bring the two groups together – thereby forging a bond between afflicted minorities of two great countries.

Once the news got back to the respective bases, little time was lost in circulating membership on both sides of the

Irish Sea – in the form of an invitation to attend the first Anglo-Irish Left-handed Golfing Convention, to be held at Southport, Lancashire, in June that year. Close by the hotel at which we were due to stay were the magnificent links of the Southport and Ainsdale Club; they in turn adjoined those of the Royal Birkdale, where the Dunlop Masters Tournament was to be played over the same weekend as the left-handed English were to meet the left-handed Irish. And by Irish I mean the whole of Ireland. Both the North and the South ran separate societies then, as they do now, but in those days made no bones about working or playing together when the occasion arose.

It was on Friday, 22 June 1964 (exactly 23 years to the day prior to my typing this draft – only today's Tuesday) that 12 left-handers from each country arrived at that Southport hotel. One or two with their wives, and others – like myself – with but a friendly thirst, a bag of clubs, and a handsome range of choruses, ancient and modern.

My first meeting with the opposition resulted in at least five of us failing to get to bed at all on that Friday night; there just didn't seem to be enough time before breakfast on Saturday to spin half the yarns or sing half enough songs, to the accompaniment of Jack Campbell's guitar. Jack was a G.P. from Belfast, where he shared a practice with his wife, Mona, also a qualified doctor. He was the hon. organiser of the Irish party. Once a two-bottles-a-day man, Jack had been in hospital with his drink problem; but on discharge about six months before Southport forswore all forms of alcohol – for life. Yet he still insisted on being first up at the bar getting them in for all and sundry, but with just tonic, dry ginger or Coke for himself and taking great care a kindly soul didn't slip a vodka or gin in his when reciprocating. With his melodic guitar (no electronic gimmickry) and a repertoire of over 2,000 ballads, he was the life and soul of any party – singing and strumming away long after most of the booze-laden songsters had passed into oblivion.

I remember a full breakfast, swilled down with half a dozen cups of black coffee, before driving down to the course and playing some kind of golf game with Jack. After lunch in Southport and Ainsdale's clubhouse we went walkabout to watch some of the 'greats' of the day competing for the Masters at Birkdale. By about 4.00 p.m. a strange weariness overcame me; I just made it back to the hotel and knew no more, until a telehone call from reception said they were waiting for me so dinner could start and would I try to get down in the next 15 minutes.

After dinner it was back to the lounge bar where, in no time at all, the singing was bouncing off the walls as Jack led us through some of the choruses we hadn't got round to the previous night. But it couldn't go on for ever, because (a) we were running out of songs and (b) I was due on the tee in a four-ball at Crew's Hill at 8.30 on Sunday morning. There was something like two hundred miles between me and Crews Hill when I said farewell to my Irish friends a little after 4.00 a.m.

I came off the motorway at Hatfield just as the nearside tyre burst on my Healey. Had it happened while hitting 120 m.p.h. a few minutes earlier, somebody else would have had to write this book. Phoning from a call box after changing the wheel, to say I was running about 15 minutes late, I took a quick cold shower on reaching the clubhouse, went out to spray the ball in every direction except the right one, had a quick half a bitter in the bar after 18 holes, drove home, kissed the wife, asked her to put my lunch on the back burner, fell into bed, and knew no more. Until she woke me to say she'd run me a bath and did I want a nice freshly-boiled egg or my reheated 'gunged-up' lunch for supper?

There ended my first Left-handed International Golfing Convention.

The following year we reconvened with the Irish at Drogheda, about thirty miles north of Dublin. The year after that at Ilford, Essex; and in May 1967, my wife and I, accompanied by a mixed party of some thirty intrepid souls, spent a mad week at Lahinch, on the West Coast of Ireland. By this time it had become a great annual event, with each side putting out its best in left-handed golfers and ambidextrous bon viveurs.

I particularly remember a party scene in the 'Aberdeen Arms', close to Lahinch Golf Club, and run by the Vaughan brothers. It was well after midnight, with a grand circle of us sitting and standing around, taking it in turns to sing or tell a story. When called upon, a petite and demure young lady from Dublin, where she worked as a hospital nurse, pulled a 'penny-whistle' from her handbag and had us all enthralled as she went through a repertoire of James-Galway-type traditional airs.

When the self-appointed Irish master of ceremonies decided it was my wife's turn to perform, she gracefully declined, claiming to be neither a storyteller nor a singer. But your man wasn't having that: 'Nonsense. Everybody can sing. It's just that some people like to show off more than others. You just start off any old thing you know, Pat, and we'll all come on in and help you'. And they did. While they were at it I stepped up to the bar to replenish empties and near-empties in our segment of the circle. As the elder Vaughan levered away at the Guinness pump handle, I commented on the fine time everybody seemed to be having in his warm and hospitable tavern and asked casually:

'What time d'you reckon on closing, Eamon?'

To which he replied, conspiratorily, in his soft County Clare brogue:

'October!!'

A left-handed Texan, touring and playing the picture-book courses of Ireland while on holiday with his wife, was playing Lahinch during the time we were there. Intrigued by the number of golfers he could see hitting the ball in a similar fashion to himself – and left-handers look just as weird to their own kind as they do to conventional right-handers – he got talking to one or two in the bar. With the result that he and his wife were invited to be guests for dinner on the final evening of the Anglo-Irish convention. However, he was made to 'sing for his supper', in the form of saying a few words when the meal had reached the coffee-and-brandy stage. Although not everybody could follow his John-Wayne-style of delivery, he gave us to understand that every State in the U.S. had its own left-handed society. In fact, there were about ten such societies in Texas alone. He, as it happened, was not only a member of his county Left-handed Golf Association, but also of the State and the all-American one. And wouldn't it be a great idea, he enthused, if he could arrange for a fun-loving crowd of his folks to come over next year for a big tripartite clambake with the English and the Irish?

Of course, enthusiastic support resounded from all sides in the euphoria around that dinner table, but in the cold light of days to come nobody gave it a lot more thought; let alone believe that an ambitious spontaneous idea of that nature would ever come to pass.

So life went on, until early in 1967 came a communique from John Turner, Hon. Sec. of the English left-handers, confirming that the annual Anglo-Irish left-handed assembly would take place at Southport in May; with the hope that all would attend to help make it even better than the first Southport and Ainsdale meeting three years earlier. About a month before it was to take place I had a letter from Pat Collins, Dublin-based Secretary of the Irish left-handers. Proudly he announced that after much correspondence with all parties concerned, a five-day Golfing Convention had been organised for left-handers and their guests from England, Ireland and the United States. It would take place at Killarney, Co. Kerry. The date given was about ten days before the Southport meeting. Exhorting all and sundry to be there and ensure lots of entente cordiale with our American cousins, the letter – quite rightly – stressed the top priority of the fixture. But it ignored the fact that not many would find it easy to stay away from both domestic and business responsibilities for several days at a time and twice within the space of two weeks.

But in my case, I felt it would seem churlish not to travel a few hundred miles and rendezvous with a number of folks who had winged several thousand miles just to be with me.

That decision was not reached until after I'd opened the post at the office on the morning the Killarney convention was due to start; but, having once made it, little time was wasted in driving home for golf clubs and a hastily-packed bag, from whence – to the usual 'You-must-be-mad!' from my dearly beloved ringing in my ears – I drove to London Airport for the next Aer Lingus flight to Shannon. On arrival I hired a self-drive car, having left mine in the long-term park at Heathrow, and set off on a leisurely ninety-mile drive through the Kelly-green countryside, on empty, winding roads. With the City of Limerick a bare twenty miles off my route, it was a golden opportunity to call on an old friend who had worked for several years as general handyman and truck driver in my Holloway factory. He had also done a lot of paving and landscaping around my home where, even today, the thirty-year-old humped-back bridge of random stone across the fish-pond is known in the family as the 'Eugene McMeel Fish-Bridge'. And nobody will ever appreciate the quantity and range of fine Irish epithets that went into the shaping of that hump!

He had always said that one day he would retire and end his days back in the Ould Country. About three years after that bridge he finally shook the dust of North London off his feet to take his wife Josie, and the eight children they'd begat since coming to England, to run a little general store he had bought in Limerick. We'd kept in touch with Christmas cards and the odd letter, but with this trip to Killarney some six years later, it now seemed an ideal opportunity to call in and pay my respects to the lovable old rascal.

Writer or not, I could never conjure up words to describe his face when – after I'd entered his shop and stood quietly by while he served a little girl with three bottles of Guinness, four pounds of potatoes, and a penn'orth of jelly babies – he looked past her, stared for a full couple of seconds and bellowed, 'Holy Mary, Mother of Jesus, it's Sam Morley!' Then followed a call to Josie, somewhere out of sight in the back of the shop, to drop everything and come at once

In less time than it takes to tell I was in the back parlour, clutching a half-pint tumbler filled with neat Scotch and tucking into a huge plate of sausages, bacon and fried eggs, despite half-hearted protests that I'd been wined and dined well on the plane only a couple of hours earlier.

Old Mac has now been dead twelve years or so – fell out of a tree while helping a friend to cut it down – and Josie survived him by about six years.

Sentimental curiosity brought on when editing this episode of bygone days a few days after writing it, had me calling Breda, Mac's eldest daughter, at her home in Cleggan, Co. Galway. I hadn't seen her since that visit to Limerick, but she sends a Christmas card and a long letter every year, with news about her husband, her home and her ever-expanding family. Five girls, she told me, at the last count – once she'd got over the shock of my call – with the oldest currently ten years and the youngest ten months. Her opening words once she knew who it was on the line at 10.00 p.m. on a July Saturday, weren't all that different to her father's when I walked into his shop twenty years earlier. She told me she'd not long sat down after spending the full day helping to get the hay in on their farm, and had cursed at having to struggle out of the chair to answer what she thought was just a neighbour calling. But she made no secret of her delight once she'd got over the shock and made me promise to come and see her family with a copy of this book once published. To do that I'd better get us back on the road to Killarney.

This wasn't my first visit to that renowned golfing and tourist centre. There had been a previous occasion when, touring Ireland with my wife, we'd stayed at the Europa Hotel, Killarney. One of the highlights of that trip was when, leaving her to her own devices one morning, I looked into the clubhouse hoping to find somebody wanting a game of golf. It was early Spring and visitors, as yet, were thin on the ground. Over a bottle of Guinness in the upstairs lounge, the barman said that Father Baker, a parish priest and golfing fanatic on holiday from Dublin, was staying at a local hotel and would probably be in shortly looking for a partner. While awaiting his arrival I was more than happy to gaze at the colourful scenes visible on all sides through the panoramic windows. Blue skies with creamy cumulus clouds drifting across them; Kelly-green fairways of the nearby course; and the mauves and browns of the towering McGillycuddys Reeks, with the bright blue lakes of Killarney nestling at their feet. My barman friend went into the origin of the place as a de luxe golfing resort, devised by Lord Castlerosse in the 1930s, and some of the innovations, regardless of expense, that went into creating it.

Noticing a flash of bright blue and white through the trees and not too far from the clubhouse, I asked if it happened to be a swimming pool – being rather keen on a plunge when the opportunity presented itself and having not yet reached the stage of owning my own.

'Sure', said yer man, 'an' isn't it the darlingest little pool you ever did see?'

He went on to describe in detail some of its colourful features, but when asked if it was available for use by visiting golfers, he replied:

'Why, an' you're free to use it as much as you want. But I don't know about swimming in it. It cracked right across the middle about twenty years ago and it's never had any water in it since. If you go across and take a look you'll find it's more of a little peat bog or a natural sunken garden in there.'

Father Baker then arrived, a genial, soft-spoken addict with a handicap of 12 – as was mine at the time. We had a couple of local boys to caddy for us, of whom there were always a number hanging around the caddy shed. My partner explained the poverty and lack of opportunity in the area, other than for those employed catering for tourism between May and September each year. Any attempt to organise the rustic population toward some kind of gainful employment, he reckoned, was inevitably doomed and gave the following example:

At a large modern factory opposite the entrance to the Europa Hotel, a German-owned business manufactured earth-moving equipment, training and using local labour as much as possible for the unskilled and semi-skilled tasks. Even the kindly old caddy-master at Killarney Golf Club was found a simple job to keep him occupied during the months when golfers stopped coming. He was stationed at the main gate and, taking his instructions from the credential-scrutineer in the gate security office, would raise the counter-weighted barrier pole for a vehicle to enter or leave, and drop it back across the roadway after the vehicle passed. On his second day he dropped it squarely on the roof of his managing director's Mercedes! The M.D. 'vas not amused' and next day it was back to the caddy-sheds for 'your man'.

But there was no crunched-up Mercedes lying under the barrier this time, as I drove past the German factory up to the Three Lakes Hotel at the end of Killarney High Street.

It was about 7.00 p.m., and most of the afternoon golfers and early evening pleasure-seekers filled the entrance lounge with movement and sound as I struggled through their ranks to the check-in desk. They had been pouring into the place throughout the week from all parts of the United States. Husbands and wives, golfers and non-golfers, right- and left-handers, East and West Coasters, Confederates and Unionists, Democrats and Republicans, Alcoholics and Abstainers (though I don't remember many of the latter).

On accepting a welcoming draught at the bar from a couple of familiar Irish faces who'd seen me arrive, I learned that the hotel was almost chock-a-block with all those attending this great international golf-orientated assembly. The actual numbers were 86 Americans, five from Northern Ireland, four from Southern Ireland, and two from England – me and John Turner.

But our American cousins weren't in the least bothered

over the paucity of attendance from the British Isles and, having travelled all those thousands of miles, were determined to suck the bones of traditional tourism dry while staying in the area. So while some went on organised coach trips to kiss the Blarney Stone, others toured the Ring of Kerry, swilled Irish coffee at Kate Kearney's cottage in the Gap of Dunloe, conversed unintelligibly with the equally unintelligible 'Jarvies' on the 'Jaunty Cars' (drivers of the horse-drawn sight-seeing carts), bought Lord-knows-how-many shillelaghs, Waterford pitchers, head scarves, clay pipes, and bile-green water-colours in the souvenir shops lining both sides of the High Street along its entire length, strode the emerald-green fairways surrounded by Killarney's celebrated lakes and mountains, and ruined the linings of their delicate stomachs at mediaeval banquets in commercialised Irish castles.

The following morning after breakfast I was scheduled to play with Skinny Huggins, a left-handed extrovert from Nashville, Tennessee, against a left- and right-hander from Oregon and Indiana respectively. For some inexplicable reason, except perhaps a telepathic salt-water affinity when we discovered, a year or two later, that the U.S. destroyer in which he served during World War Two was at one time or another during 1944 tied up alongside *Redoubt* in the Allied naval base at Trincomalee, Ceylon, Skinny and I hit it off together from the off. His real name was Harold, but wherever golf was played in the 49 States Skinny Huggins was his recognised 'handle'. It was no misnomer either, as he must have turned the scale at something like nine stone – sopping wet!

We played together again on the following morning, and of the incessant stream of 'you-all', 'cotton-pickin'' wit with which he enlivened those two rounds, I shall never forget his shout of 'Fire Two, General Custer!' in a stentorian voice, when one of our opponents put too much into a practice swing and 'let one go' that echoed off the mountain side!

Six months later I sent him a Christmas card on the approach of the festive season. My card had a coloured photograph on its front of Brickendon Grange Golf and Country Club, Herts., a newly-formed enterprise by some friends, and of which I'd recently become a life member. As a result, Skinny wrote to me from his insurance-broking office in Nashville to say that a party of 16 friends, husbands and wives, were planning a trip to the Old Country in May 1969 – about four months hence – during which they would visit London, Stratford-on-Avon, and one or two well-known golf resorts in Scotland. Would it be at all possible for the golfers among them to play a round on the beautiful course pictured on my Christmas card? No problem, was the reply, and I started roping in those of my pals and their wives most suitable for coping with the hospitality duties that would arise.

The Nashvillians arrived in England on Wednesday, 14 May 1969. My wife and I took Skinny and his wife, Juanita, to dinner at Stone's Chop House that evening, during which they were told of the plans for Friday 16th. The day started with a coach laid on to pick his party up from their Bayswater hotel, and bring them back in time for an informal cocktail and reception party at my home. This was followed by a light lunch and golf at Brickendon.

A conducted tour and tea at historic old Hatfield House were arranged for those who didn't golf. During the afternoon Skinny and I played for the 'left-handed championship of the free-and-civilised world', in which he beat me by bringing off a miraculous putt on the last green. It all ended with a grand dinner, prize-giving, speeches, cheers and counter-cheers in the clubhouse lasting until long after midnight, when the weary travellers climbed back on the coach to be taken back to their Bayswater hotel. There were only a few hours to go before they were due to climb on another one and be whisked up to Stratford-on-Avon; followed by yet another coach trip to Gleneagles, after having spent a couple of nights in the Bard-country.

Before leaving Brickendon, they'd extracted a promise that I'd bring a party over to Nashville the following year for some return hospitality.

By the time that came round, and with all the build-up of correspondence and planning, the whole thing had become so obsessive that I started to diarise it while our party of 16 winged its way across the Atlantic in May 1970. We were heading for Tennessee, via San Francisco, Pebble Beach, Grand Canyon, Las Vegas, Prescott and Dallas.

Then after five hedonistic days in Nashville – with hospitality showered upon us from all sides – we came home via three days in Miami Beach, one in New York and, for some, a morning in Paris.

After much editing and rewriting, those notes became my first book, published in 1972 as *Start-Off-Smashed!* The title, while being in itself an almost true description of our travelling style, was made up from the initial letters of 'Super Trans Atlantic Reciprocal Trips Organised For Friends of Sam Morley and Skinny Huggins – Eccentric Diplomats!'

But no common-or-garden diplomat could ever have forged as strong a bond between two countries as did those trips and that book. A friend of mine, Paul McGrath, saw a copy on the book shelves of the St. Andrews Golf Museum while browsing around one morning when it was too wet and windy to go out and play. The curator, on learning the author was a personal pal of Paul's, told him that, at a recent meeting of the Golf Writers Association, it was spoken of as the funniest book of the year (or was it the century?) on golf! Paul wrote from St. Andrews to tell me as much. A truly handsome accolade.

Having mentioned playing Pebble Beach, a 1988 spin-off – 16 years after the book was published – is worth including here. It was at the Publishers Golfing Society annual dinner when Alex Hay, B.B.C. golf commentator and managing director of Woburn Golf Club, was guest speaker. Incidentally, one of the best after-dinner raconteurs in the game.

During his masterly delivery, he told of a 1987 fact-finding tour of U.S. clubs in search of ideas for further enhancement of Woburn, and his arrival at Pebble Beach. At this point he stopped and addressed me across the heads of intervening diners. 'You wrote about Pebble Beach, Sam, in your book. Do you remember when you were there and what you paid for green fees and cart hire?' I told him, '1970, ten dollars green fee, ten dollars cart'.

He beamed, nodded, and went on to speak of his wife's anxiety to play the celebrated course. Presenting himself at the pro's shop – now about the size of a Tesco hypermarket, he reckoned, with about a dozen liveried assistants in attendance – he asked one if perchance he might qualify for a courtesy round on presenting his British P.G.A. card. He was told it had no recognition there and he'd have to pay the going rate – 120 dollars green fee each, and 50 dollars to hire the cart. And as the course was permanently full, the first starting time they could give him was two days hence. In vain he explained his mission, standing and expectation of at least a little favoured treatment, until somebody associated him with the name on one of his books currently on sale in the shop.

When admitting he was the self-same Alex Hay, he was asked if he'd mind autographing their stock of about twenty. And as fast as he did so he found that customers browsing around the shop would halt, gaze over his shoulder, and cry excitedly, 'Hey, Frank, here's this author-guy signing his books – now we've just gotta buy one to take back and show the folks! And while you're at it, better get one for Uncle Charlie!' With the result that all twenty were sold by the time he'd finished signing them.

Then along came the manager to thank Alex for boosting his sales figures for the day, and said it was understood he'd asked for a complimentary round at Pebble Beach on the strength of his British P.G.A. card. 'In all the circumstances', went on the manager graciously, 'you have the courtesy of the course and I've slotted you in for a starting time at 2.30 this afternoon'. As Alex started to express his thanks on behalf of his wife and himself, the manager cut him short by explaining that the gesture was meant for him alone. Whereas his wife would be allowed to join him and play at 2.30, he would be expected to pay 120 dollars for her to do so and 50 dollars for their hire of a cart to ride around in.

I've visited Nashville many times since 1970, and don't believe our popular Royals could ever expect a more magnificent welcome than has been meted out to us each time by those ole Nashvillians. We try to do much the same for any of its citizens who come our way. Some highlights from those reciprocal visits are featured in the ensuing chapters of Part Three.

15

How Not to Plan a Banquet

Having spread myself on the story of that first Nashville visit in *Start-Off-Smashed!*, I'm not anxious to do it all again for the sake of these pages – albeit with possible update in writing style that the original needs. Instead I'll go on from there to throw further light on how the capital of the State of Tennessee got its name on the author's heart.

The Nashville Connection is by no means a one-way link. Hardly a year goes by without one of the original Tennessee cast, or a family member or friend, getting restless and deciding its high time to cross the Atlantic and 'do' Europe. If the 'doing' is to include Merrie England, I'll probably get a letter from somebody back there advising who is coming, when, and at what hotel they plan to stay.

Charlie and Lu Cornelius have been two of our most frequent visitors. Charlie is senior partner in one of Nashville's top legal firms and the Tennessee Medical Association is one of its clients. Astronomical claims for alleged negligence and malpractice on the part of doctors are a way of life over there, necessitating mind-boggling insurance cover. To help minimise the burden of pay-outs when the boggle-claim goes against them, American insurers need to cross the water and seek reinsurance with the daddy of 'em all – Lloyds of London. They are usually accompanied by leading members of the State Medical Association and, of course, its 'legal-eagle', Charlie Cornelius. And where Charlie goes, so usually does his petite and delightfully droll wife.

Based at the Waldorf in Aldwych, and with his working week packed with meetings at Lloyds, Charlie welcomed the suggestion one year that he and Lu spend Friday to Monday midst the green and rolling hills of Hertfordshire; whereby Charlie and I could golf together, while Pat and Lu shopped around and boasted of their respective grandchildren. And as I met two of their special friends when joining some of the party for dinner at the Waldorf one evening, they, too, were invited to come for the weekend – Tom Cummings of the State Volunteers Insurance Company and his five-foot ball-of-fun of a wife, Putt. I don't remember how she came by that name, but I gave up trying to understand the origin of American Christian names years ago.

But the name, Putt Cummings, and the circumstances of our first meeting, remind me of the doctor from Knoxville, Tennessee, who sat beside me at that Waldorf dinner. An avid golfer, he told of a fellow he played with back home.

This person had never been known to concede a putt. Even with the ball just a few inches from the hole he'd say 'Spike it!' meaning, mark it. And out would have to come a dime to be placed on the green while the ball was lifted.

Playing with this fellow a few days before coming away on this trip, my friend's ball came to rest almost on the very edge of the hole they were playing. He look enquiringly at his partner, waiting for it to be conceded.

'Spike it!' he was told and he put his dime down with a sigh.

On the next hole he put his approach putt even closer, if that were at all possible.

'Spike it!' said his partner remorselessly.

'You've got to be joking!' exclaimed the medico, with disbelief.

'No way, I've seen little ones like that fluffed under pressure', insisted the other.

'O.K., if that's the way you want it,' said the doctor, 'lend me a dime to spike it with.'

On the point of fishing for the coin in his pocket his

partner stopped to ask, 'Where's the dime you've been using?'

'It overbalanced and fell in the last hole!' came the withering reply.

Our visitors were booked into the West Lodge Hotel, about ten minutes drive from my home and set in about 150 acres of rich woodland. West Lodge is a stately manor-house with the proud boast that' Queen Elizabeth I slept there back in 1577. Whether it now boasts just as proudly that the Cornelii* and Cummingses did the self-same thing exactly 400 years later is a debatable point. In fact they slept there three nights in all, during which time we fed and watered them chez nous and at one or two of our favourite hostelries.

But throughout the time they were with us never a blade of grass did anybody see, never a leafy lane did the ladies tread, and never a wood or iron club did we fellows wield. You see, it was February 1977, when there was more snow on the ground here than on the Alpine ski resorts, with temperatures that never rose above freezing for weeks. From the panoramic windows of the West Lodge bedrooms or our hillside bungalow, the world was an unbroken, undulating sheet of frozen white as far as the eye could see, with roads and footpaths so iced-up as to make driving or walking extremely hazardous. But not hazardous enough to prevent us meeting up for the customary prolonged bonhomie sessions until it was time for our friends to leave.

But the first Nashvillians to visit after our party returned from the States at the end of May 1970 were Miller and Mary Kimbrough. They had been in Skinny's group that visited us in '69 and had also played a big part in the hospitality laid on for us over there.

I never did find out exactly what kind of business Miller was in, but well remember his gravelly voice, laconic wit and impressive house just visible through the trees from

*Well, Corneliuses does sound a bit clumsy!

the seventh green at Nashville's Belle Meade Country Club. During our stay in Nashville that May, I remember him calling at the hotel to take a couple of us to golf. As we hadn't yet seen the city centre I asked if it were possible to be driven in that direction en route to the country club. 'No problem', said Miller. Travelling on what was obviously one of the main downtown thoroughfares, with high-rise office buildings lining both sides of the road, he pointed to one as we approached and drawled, 'That's my office there, Sam'.

I looked at its imposing façade and said, 'That's a fine-looking building, Miller. What floor are you on?' He turned to give me a deadpan look through his thick lenses and growled, 'To hell with what floor!' Putting his left hand through the open window he pointed at the entrance lobby, slowly let his arm travel up until he was pointing at the roof, brought it back to street level and repeated, 'That's my office there, Sam!'

Reg Davies, Captain of South Herts Golf Club at the time of Miller's visit to England, laid on a four-ball, consisting of we three plus Chris Henry. It was preceded by a champagne lunch to which our ladies were also invited. The quality of golf that followed is lost in the mists of time and, no doubt, the alcoholic haze in which it was played. Except I remember that, as Miller hadn't brought the necessary bits and pieces with him, Reg fixed him up with clubs, shoes, socks and the customary casual wear. Including a pair of his own snugfit trousers.

Now although Miller was quite a well set-up fellow in his own right, he hadn't quite reached the ample proportions of my genial and somewhat bulky dental friend. Nevertheless, with the the help of a couple of hand-tucks in his waistband and a good strong belt, Miller looked every inch the sartorial golfer as we strode off down the first fairway, despite the width of trouser hips, legs and bottoms being a little on the full side.

Once Miller had played his second shot Reg asked how he was getting on with his borrowed plumes. 'Just fine', was the reply, 'now I've gotten used to the pants setting off 'bout three paces after the shoes start walkin'!'

That evening Chris and Mary Henry played host to all 16 of the Start-Off-Smashed party, with Miller and Mary Kimbrough as guests of honour. It was at the Terenure Country Club, the owner of which, Kath Barber, gets a lead part in the next chapter but one.

In November 1970, just six months after Start-Off-Smashed, the Racegoers Club ran its annual trip to Washington D.C. for its members to witness the running of the prestigious Laurel Park International at the nearby Maryland track. I'd done the same thing in November of the previous year, but this time, instead of staying with the crowd and heading for our Washington hotel, I took the bus transfer to the domestic airport and boarded a plane to Nashville soon after our international flight got in.

I'd written from England to the Nashville hotel at which I was to stay, in order to arrange for a dinner on Friday, 13 November 1970, two days after my arrival, in one of their private banqueting rooms. It was to be a touch of reciprocity in appreciation of those five days of Southern hospitality they'd given my friends and me back in May.

'Skinny' Huggins and a couple of his pals were at the airport to greet and run me to the hotel, from which it was arranged they'd pick me up the following morning for golf. Once they left, I called Reception from my room and asked to speak to the banqueting manager. Time had come to tackle the 'nuts and bolts' of the morrow's big thrash! Fun-worded gilt-edged invitations to it had been sent out from England, and I was told in the drive from the airport that everybody was looking forward to a really big night with ole Sam. And ole Sam was anxious to ensure it would be a memorable one.

Reception said they didn't run to a banqueting manager, but 'Mz.' Peters did all the catering and she'd be pleased to talk whenever it suited me. Mz. Peters turned out to be a nice motherly soul as she came shuffling across in carpet slippers to greet me in the lounge and invited me to share her crowded desk in a nearby office. As the bones of the ensuing conversation are engraved indelibly on my memory I'm going to try and tell it just the way it was. Except that, although it's a conversation with a lady from the deep South – whose name, incidentally, I decided to change – with a drawlin' you-all turn of speech straight out of *Gone with the Wind*, I've set most of it down in prosaically-correct English – leaving you-all to transpose it into 'Southern-style' as best suits the imagination.

I open with:

'Well, Mz. Peters, I've got this party laid on tomorrow, and as I said in my letter from England we'd discuss the menus and other matters when I arrived.'

'That's right, Mr. Morley. You just tell me what you want and I'll tell you if we can do it.'

'The idea is to try not to give the conventional party food you'd expect to find in Tennessee. Instead, something after the style of a traditional English banquet if it were held somewhere like the Guildhall, or in the 350-year-old Wig and Pen Club in the Strand. But before talking of anything specific I don't mean to ask for anything beyond the scope of your kitchen staff. So what kind of chef do you have here and has he done much travel internationally – whereby he'd be acquainted with non-American dishes and might even suggest one or two novel ideas?'

She looked at me long and hard through her horn-rimmed spectacles while weighing up just how to phrase her reply. Then:

'Well, Mr. Morley, if you've got to have a true answer to that, we ain't got nothing but a no-account nigger cook; and I guess the only travellin' he's ever done is on the freight trains between here and South Georgia. But you just tell me what you got in mind and I'll tell you whether we can do it.'

It was my turn to pause long and hard while tucking that priceless riposte into the memory bank. Then:

'Right. So how about starting with a Charantais melon?'

'We don't have Charantais melon but we can give you cantaloupe.'

'Well, I didn't want anything too big. It needs to be small, soft and sweet. How about a scooped-out half-melon each, with the fruit partially mashed and port poured over it in the bottom of the bowl formed by the shell?'

'You mean port-wine?'

'Yes. Can we follow that with a consommé, say turtle soup?'

'Sure, we can give you turtle soup.'

'O.K. Serve it good and hot and have your people ladle warmed sherry into each plate of soup once it's served.'

'You mean sherry-wine?'

'That's right.'

'You mean you want port-wine poured into your melon and then sherry-wine poured into your soup?'

'That's right.'

'Is that the way you do it in England?'

'Well, I believe there are some parts north of Watford where they prefer it on their mushy peas, but that's how it's often done in our better restaurants and at prestigious banquets.'

'What are you all over there – a nation of lushes? But O.K., if that's how you want it, we'll see you have it. What next?'

'Well, I know you're land-locked in Nashville with the nearest salt water about six hundred miles away. But a little poached deep-sea fish-dish would often follow back in England.'

'Mr. Morley, here in Tennessee we've got the finest lake trout in the United States. Why don't you let me fix you some trout the way I'm sure your guests are just gonna love it.'

'O.K., please do that, Mz. Peters.'

'Oh, and just what kind of wine were you wanting poured over your fish, Mr. Morley?'

'No, Mz. Peters, we've done with marinating the food. From here on in folks will take their wine in a glass as they wish from the many bottles you'll have spread around on the tables. But we'll discuss wines after we've done the main course. I can't think of anything more traditional than the roast beef of old England. But can you do it?'

'Well, Mr. Morley, here in Tennessee we breed the finest beef cattle in the United States. We'd be delighted to serve you with succulent beef the likes of which you've never known in England.'

'All very well, Mz. Peters, but the glorious roast beef of old England is always complemented by our equally glorious Yorkshire pudding. I don't believe your man will be able to tackle our celebrated Yorkshire pudding.'

'Why, Mr. Morley, they ain't nothing but buckwheat cakes – we'll have no difficulty there.'

I sat in shocked silence while she scribbled busily on her pad. We went on to discuss vegetables, which I asked to be of a hot green and leaf variety, rather than a side salad; but accepted with good grace the baked Idaho in jacket with sour-cream dressing that she insisted was a house speciality and much loved by the locals. I had to insist that we finished with coffee whereas over there many would start their meal with it.

Having dealt with the food we talked of what wines were to be on the table and the need for more than one glass at each place-setting for those preferring white with fish, red with beef, and all that 'jazz'. Then came plans for providing a welcoming drink for guests as they arrived. I suggested trays of glasses – some filled with straight champers, others Buck's Fizz – at the entrance door.

'No problem, Mr. Morley,' said Mz. Peters, scribbling

away.

'While we're on the subject, what sort of champagne can we have?'

'Well, if you want a real good champagne we would give you Taylors.'

'Taylors? I don't think I've heard of that on a bubbly label. Although there's quite a good range of port called Taylors.'

'Why, Mr. Morley, Taylors is one of the finest New York champagnes you can buy!'

'Well, I wasn't quite thinking of New York, Mz. Peters. Back in England when we talk of champagne we mean a sparkling wine from the Champagne district of France.'

'Oh you mean French champagne, Mr. Morley. Why, we can get you any French champagne you want.'

To my pleasure and surprise she named one or two well-known labels. I chose pink Taittinger and with that bade her farewell and best of luck for the morrow.

The following morning Skinny picked me up from the hotel, furnished me with a set of left-handed clubs, and with Bob Walker and Miller Kimbrough we played a four-ball around Belle Meade, the Nashville country club featured so prominently in *Start-Off-Smashed*! Come the evening and I was down in the private dining room a good hour before the party was due to begin. A big oval table was laid up for the requisite number and I spent the first ten minutes shuffling round it with the place cards in an effort to get everybody seated right. Near the door was a table stacked with champers and orange juice in tubs of ice with three black waiters in smart livery waiting to serve it.

'You'd better get some of those bottles open so that we have a trayful of loaded glasses at the ready when the first guests arrive', I suggested.

'We've been told not to open anything until your folks are in the room,' said their leader.

'Nonsense, I don't want bubbly gushing everywhere in a panic to cope with a dozen or more people arriving at near enough the same time. Get a few opened up, as I certainly need one now, and there are voices and footsteps coming down the corridor.'

The leader grabbed a bottle, twisted off the wire and was hit squarely between the eyes as the cork flew out with a report like a pistol shot. He sagged against the wall, but I managed to catch the foaming bottle by the neck as it slid from his palsied fingers. There was just time enough to bend over his prostrate body, gaze into the bloodshot left optic, and tell him he'd probably wake with the mummy and daddy of a white eye in the morning, before the place started filling up. The other lads had opened a few more bottles without further disaster, and the management sent in a new man to replace the injured one who was sent home to rest clutching a sympathetic five-dollar bill slipped him before he left.

Before long the room was a hubbub of excited sounds as folks greeted friends they didn't see too often, or wandered around clutching a glass while checking the gaily decorated table and place settings. I say clutching glasses, but when a photographer plus a reporter from the *Nashville Banner* appeared, those glass-clutching fists would vanish from sight whenever a camera pointed in their general direction. Well, most of the Nashville citizenry present were respected pillars of their respective churches, with no desire to be seen taking part in a bacchanalian orgy. Which, even if it hadn't yet reached that stage, was certainly not far short of it when the time came to sit round the table a good hour or more after the dramatic opening of that first bottle.

I'll touch quickly, from what I can still remember, on cantaloupe half-melons overlapping the sides of the dinner plates on which they were served. But despite all that preamble with Mz. Peters not a drop of port lay in the bottom of those melons. I took up the matter quickly and quietly with the maître d', and he hurried away, brought back a couple of bottles, and walked round the table asking each diner if he wanted port. Many said no; some, bewildered, pushed an empty wine glass forward, while others having watched me nonchalantly have it slurped into my melon, and into that of my immediate neighbours, did likewise.

Some were already calling impatiently for their coffee as starters; or eating the side salads that had been set out, despite my agreement with Mz. Peters that they'd only be provided with the main course and only for those who asked for them specifically.

The turtle soup was served about five degrees above room temperature, and when I asked for the tureen of smoking-hot sherry-wine that was to be elegantly ladled into each plate of soup, I was shown bottles of chilled sherry among the array of red and white wines along the length of the table. 'Oh, what the hell', I thought, 'if you can't beat 'em, join 'em!', as I poured cold sherry into my cold soup. In my support, stalwarts round that table did likewise without question.

By this time the tumult and hilarity were akin to a Mad Hatter's Tea Party – or a Marx Brothers version of the 'Last Supper'!

Passing quickly over the fish course, we came to the roast beef of Olde England, with all the trimmings. The diners were first served with a cold plate on which rested an oval slice of luke-warm underdone beef about the size, texture and thickness of the sole of a Wellington boot. Then came two waiters solemnly wheeling a silver trolley on which rested what looked like a large yellow paving slab. When they got nearer, you could see that the slab had been dissected into a number of identical rectangular blocks.

As the trolley stopped by each diner one of the waiters would lift a block with a pair of silver tongs and place it on the plate alongside the aforementioned 'sole' of beef.

It was Mz. Peters' version of our glorious Yorkshire pudding. The prongs of my fork twanged musically as I tried to puncture the crust of a buckwheat 'brick' with the consistency of close-mesh foam polystyrene. The first and only mouthful confirmed it had a taste to match, as all round the table folks pushed uneaten beef and 'cake' to one side of their plate and tucked into the vegetables.

But the wine flowed while the room echoed with excited speculation on what other traditional English fare ole Sam'd laid on that evening.

Amid the general hubbub the meal ended with a huge soufflé. The day was in fact Skinny's birthday and his wife, Juanita, had had one made and sent in specially to be served for dessert.

Everybody, and I mean everybody, around that table was hyped into a state of euphoria. Then came a succession of impromptu speeches with lots of comment on the singular nature of the food set before us that evening. It was summed up by one with, 'I've never enjoyed an evening's festivity more than I have tonight's, despite being in the presence of one of the greatest catering disasters on record. If Sam wants us to believe that we've just experienced the way they prepare and present American food in England today, then thank God with all my heart that this country decided to go it alone two hundred years ago!'

'Horses for courses' is a well known racing maxim. Keeping to the racing idiom, but sticking to the culinary theme, that Nashville hotel cook – when he wasn't riding the freight cars to South Georgia – was no doubt a good performer on the local 'favourites'. But it was a mistake to saddle him with an unknown ride and expect it to win because it had finished well with another jockey on a different track 4,000 miles away – if you get my drift. Despite Mz. Peters' glib assurances.

On the other hand had he performed successfully, then that evening would long since have gone to join the oblivion of countless other grand and immaculately-run fiestas, of which very little, if anything, can be remembered to talk about a month or two after the event. As it is, those Nashvillians who shared that cataclysmic evening with me and still walk this earth, re-live it in glorious technicolour each time we write or meet, to the eternal chagrin of their fellow citizens who never made it.

After the last of the departing 'Roast-Beef-of-Olde-England' guests had hugged me to his or her bosom and said, 'What a swell party it was!' I took a final look around the now deserted and darkened banqueting chamber and silently agreed, before wending my way to bed.

Saturday morning was spent in a brain-washing four-ball out on Belle Meade, with no prizes for guessing the main topic of conversation as we staggered around those 18 beautifully manicured golf holes. Well, 'staggered' is a bit of an exaggeration, seeing we travelled in state in motorised golf carts, plus a caddy each to hand out the selected club, clean the ball and move the cart while putting out so that we didn't have to walk too far off the green when getting back into it. Yes, golfing at Belle Meade sure was hell!

With a well-earned sleep back at the hotel after a light lunch in the clubhouse, came a final small dinner party hosted by some of my guests from the previous evening.

When it came to checking out to leave for home the next morning, they told me at the desk that – what with the cost of Friday night's party – the bill was far too large for them to accept the American Express card offered in settlement. But the genial manager solved the problem by rewriting it as two bills and applying a separate American Express counterfoil to each of them.

Skinny then drove me to Nashville airport so that I could rejoin my Racegoer friends before the flight back to London.

. . .

In November 1971, my wife Pat came along on the annual Racegoers pilgrimage to Washington. The journey involved a change of planes at New York, from whence we left for Nashville. We'd planned to spend three days there in the same hotel as on my last visit, but Lu and Charlie Cornelius would not hear of us staying anywhere but with them on their 500-acre farm just outside Nashville. They laid on a grand dinner party for ten just a couple of hours after our arrival. The following day I played in a four-ball at Belle Meade while Pat was given a welcoming lunch by a number of the wives. The four-ball became a five-ball at somewhere around the 14th, when Cawthon Bowen drove up in a caddy cart to join us. He'd said on the previous evening that we'd have to golf without him as he was to be in court all day on a business action. He explained his presence now by telling us how he asked the judge if he'd mind speeding things up a little as Sam Morley was back in town! 'The judge', he went on, 'duly obliged and sent his best wishes'.

'Bo', as he is known by everybody who is anybody in and around Tennessee, had a chain of cold-storage warehouses and ice-making depots in the Nashville area. He reckoned his busiest time was midsummer. With the temperature in the mid-nineties, the phone never stopped ringing with frantic calls from the overheated citizenry, ordering truckloads of ice to be delivered and tipped into their lukewarm swimming pools.

We were driven out to Rock Island, a secluded area of great natural beauty up in the mountains, about ninety miles east of Nashville. There the Cornelius family had a lakeside holiday home, right next door to that owned by Jimmy Hofstead – another of our Nashville hosts and general organiser of most of the hosting parties. It was at Jimmy's place we spent the next two nights.

One of his all-time-great organising feats was a seven-hour cross-country jeep-trail, the day after our arrival, bouncing through the rock-strewn canyons and undergrowth of Caney Fork Gulch. Pat's spinal system still jangles in protest at the mention of Jeep, Rock Island or Jimmy Hofstead.

On our return we all were taken by Jimmy to the Rock Island monthly mountain-community supper, with home-made victuals spread to overflowing on tables in the barn-sized hall. There was hardly time to wash up after that nightmare Jeep survival course before facing a series of introductions to dignitaries among the local mountain folk. Scarcely a spoken word could we understand, and when out of the blue their leading citizen announced they were honoured to have with them some special guests of Mr. Hofstead, who happened to be distinguished visitors from England, I was told it was now expected for me to rise to say something in defence. Lu Cornelius whispered there was nothing to worry about as nobody there would understand a word I said anyway. I do remember, however, getting a big hand when I sat down. Or probably because I sat down.

Strolling down the moonlit lakeside path on the way back from the community supper, strains of rhythmic mountain music could be heard close by. Tracing the source, we finished up in the kitchen of a retired parson's home – close by Charlie's place – and sat there, clapping hands and tapping feet to four fiddle and banjo players with a combined age of some three hundred years. After relating a long and bloodthirsty story about the defence of nearby Murfreesboro against those 'damned Yankees' in the Civil War, the old man of God turned-to with his pals and played a souped-up version of 'Red Wing' that had us bouncing in our seats.

And just to be sure I wasn't missing out on the great outdoor mountain-life, Charlie and Jimmy took me on a canoe trip over that silvery silent lake just a little after midnight. Long before which, Pat had opted out of the action-packed day and taken her weary and Jeep-wracked body to bed.

On getting back to Nashville our plan was to take a plane to Richmond, Virginia, hire a self-drive car, and motor up through the State of Virginia until we reached the airport at Baltimore, Maryland; from whence our Racegoers' return flight was due to leave the following night. But Jimmy, with his profound knowledge of American history, said that instead of heading north out of Richmond it would be akin to sacrilege if we didn't first drive east fifty miles and visit Colonial Williamsburg. And am I glad we did. Since then, I can never watch or think of the TV series, *Hawaii Five-O*, without recalling Virginia and that spacious Information Centre at Williamsburg. Or read of the epic speeches of the 1770s at Williamsburg, by people like Patrick Henry or Thomas

Jefferson, without thinking of *Hawaii Five-O*. (It'll all come clear in a minute.)

This is no place for a history lesson, especially as hardly a week goes by without another TV series featuring what went on between George III and the wild colonial boys of Virginia. But as, in my opinion, the restored city of Colonial Williamsburg takes precedence over Las Vegas or Disneyland when visiting the States, let's see if I can explain why.

The area in question was first settled by British colonists in 1633. Being situated between the York and James rivers, it was called Middle Plantation.

By 1699 Middle Plantation was still only a few scattered houses, farms, one inn, two mills, a small church and the College of William and Mary – opened in 1693 and named after the ruling British monarchs.

In 1699 the State leaders decided to move the capital of Virginia to this site, after the original capital, Jamestown, was half-destroyed by fire. The new capital was renamed Williamsburg, after William III, the reigning British King. (Mary had died four years earlier.)

In 1780, during the Revolutionary War, the capital was shifted again, this time to Richmond, fifty miles further inland and less vulnerable to attack from the sea. At that time Williamsburg was prosperous and bustling with self-importance. After all, it had been the capital city of the young State of Virginia since the Declaration of Independence in 1776. It had wide, straight streets, parks, imposing public buildings, a grand college, a court house, noble dwelling houses, a theatre, shops, inns, a public gaol and, of course, a Capitol. The first to be so called among the State meeting-houses of America.

But once it lost the role of State capital, Williamsburg faded into obscurity; until, by 1926, it was a forgotten small college town with its once proud buildings destroyed or derelict.

Then John D. Rockefeller led a 30-year project to restore the old city centre to its former glory, and spent Lord knows how many millions of his personal and family fortune in so doing.

Motivated by patriotic pride, he financed and masterminded the restoration of existing buildings and reconstructed – from old records, drawings and paintings – many of those that had been destroyed. No motor vehicles are allowed through the sanded roads of Colonial Williamsburg, except the tour buses operating from the Information Centre, just outside the Restored Area. Inside that area everything has been lovingly reinstated as it was two hundred years ago. Houses, some of which are fully furnished and decorated down to the minutest detail as they were in 1780, while others are just façades, line both sides of the three main streets running parallel to each other for almost a mile. The mock Capitol graces one end of that mile, and the original College of William and Mary the other. In all, 83 original structures have been faithfully restored and 48 major public buildings authentically reconstructed on their original foundations. The Williamsburg Inn, at which we stayed the night, was meticulously fitted out as it might have been then. The printers, apothecary, harness-making, wig-making, clock-making and gunsmith shops were at work, staffed mostly by college students wearing traditional dress, and using the tools and machines of two hundred years ago. Everything was geared to that two-hundred-year-old time warp.

A constant stream of tourists pour into Williamsburg throughout the day, but driving out of sight and sound of the Restored Area, on clearly marked routes encircling it. Signs advise all to make first for the Information Centre with its free parking for 1,500 cars. Free buses and horse-drawn landaus with liveried coachmen run continuously on a circular tour of the restored city, dropping and collecting passengers at speci-fied places of interest. But before boarding one, a visit to the Red or Blue cinema in the Information Centre is essential. Admission is free and they both run the same 35-minute film continuously. While the Red is showing it, the Blue is filling up, and starts to run as soon as the other finishes.

The film is *Williamsburg – the Story of a Patriot* shown in colour on wide screen with stereophonic sound. It's a dramatic presentation of life in Virginia generally – and Williamsburg specifically – in the years just prior to the Declaration, with a young farmer as the principal character. A most familiar character, I might add. When the film opens, we see farming life of the day, before our hero sets out for the capital on market day and shows interest in the political views being hotly bandied about in the King's Arms Tavern. It ends with him leaving his farm to take up arms against 'those perfidious Brits'.

Having thus been thoroughly brainwashed and indoctrinated, we poured out of the dark cinema into the brilliant sunshine, boarded a bus and went to see for ourselves how faithfully and how lovingly it has all been re-presented. Even the King's Arms Tavern. And although the young 'patriot' was nowhere to be seen, I'd have recognised him immediately, had he been one of those round the bar. Despite his three-cornered hat, velvet breeches, white stockings and silver-buckled shoes in the film, there was no mistaking Jack Lord – alias Steve McGarrett – the 'Book him, Danno' of *Hawaii Five-O*!

And to think I might have known nothing of all this – if it wasn't for GOLF . . . !

" At this hole it's customary to tee up
on a pinch of Past Captains "

16

Over the Sticks in S. Carolina

In November 1972, Racegoers enhanced and lengthened the party's annual stay in the United States. This was done by introducing an adventurous train journey – after the Laurel Park International on Veterans Day – down to Columbia, the capital city of South Carolina. Two or three days were spent in the deep and sunny South, terminating in being taken by coach to Camden, about thirty miles from Columbia, to witness the running of what was then the most valuable steeplechase race in the world – the Colonial Cup. In a field of more than twenty horses, three or four top chasers from the U.K. and their British jockeys had been invited to take part. Immediately after racing at Camden, all would be transported back to Columbia airport to board the chartered 707 for the journey back to England. Of which more later.

My personal plans were to leave Washington after the running of the Laurel and head for Nashville. Then to make my way from there to Camden, in time to rejoin the group for the big race at the jump meeting and subsequent journey home.

I know things went every bit as well this time as they usually did at Nashville, but without specific highlights to dwell on, my story of the good times could be a little repetitive and boring – if it's not that already. So let's just skip talking about Nashville this once, and head east to S. Carolina.

Arriving at Columbia from Nashville, I checked in my suitcase at the desk for the flight home, and hired a cab to take me out to Camden. The driver said he knew the place, but had heard nothing of any racing there. Entering the city limits after a 40-minute drive through flat and uninteresting country, he must have stopped to ask his way three or four times before somebody could point him in the general direction of where there might be some horse-action.

Everything about Camden was the way an unspoiled U.S. country town might be expected to look based on impressions left, say, by the Judge Hardy films of the fifties. A wide dusty main street with a few vehicles; two or three small knots of people idly chatting under what shade they could find from the hot sun; and timber-framed houses and shops, each with a deep shady front porch and a couple of old rocking chairs. But there was not the slightest sign that the town, that day, was staging the most valuable steeplechase race in the world. No posters, no hurrying crowds, no coaches, no traffic control, no traffic needing control, no street vendors touting burgers, hot dogs or ice cream, or offering insider racing information to the gullible.

True, it was early afternoon and, wherever the action was taking place, racing, no doubt, had already started; but in my experience there's usually a bit more hubbub and bustle around a rural point-to-point back home than there was to be heard or seen in the neighbourhood of Camden's prestigious event that day.

I remember asking the cab driver if there was possibly another Camden in South Carolina, but he didn't know of one. When he did finally track down the racing scene, it was at the end of not much more than a bridle path on the outskirts of town. An open five-bar gate gave access to a make-shift reception point, where entrance tickets were being sold from an old wooden table – for all the world like a local church fête or pony club event. No Silver Ring, Tattersalls, Grandstand or Members' enclosures, whereby one could pay more for a better view or better facilities – you just paid your dollar (or was it two dollars?) and you were in.

There was no shortage of people now – which probably accounted for the town looking so empty and quiet, but the crowd scene was like Hampstead Heath. Toddlers, prams and picnics abounded on all sides, around the wide-open doors of large cars and estate wagons, parked anyhow and each with its own favourite radio programme blaring out. Children scampered in and out among numerous side shows and fast food, ice-cream and Coca Cola stalls. I felt like one of the 'bit' players during the making of that old film, *State Fair*, and took a double-take at every pretty girl in case it might be Doris Day. But among that bumper crop of deep-tanned, deep-Southern pulchritude gracing the scene in every direction, I doubt if the delectable Doris would have been noticed.

But the familiar trappings of a top-flight racing event, as I knew it, were nowhere to be seen. No covered stands – grand or otherwise; no sloped or banked ground to form an amphitheatre for spectators; no rows of Tote windows besieged by queues of grim-faced speculators studying race-cards and clutching betting money; no crowded bars besieged by hordes of grim-faced punters studying race-cards and clutching glasses; no twin curve of white-painted running-rail sweeping away into the distance between which the cream of international steeplechasing would strive for rich pickings – nothing but a galaxy of brightly-clad family folk having a day out in the country.

Wandering on toward where the crowds had thickened up even further, and peering in all directions for a familiar face – Doris's or a Racegoer's – I came to the focal point of it all . . . a raised concrete platform about half the size of a cricket pitch and reached by half-a-dozen broad steps from where roamed the common human herd. A couple of rows of chairs or benches on the platform indicated that this area was reserved for officials and local dignitaries, thus providing a tiny privileged proportion of the 'gate' with the only uncluttered view of what went on around that strange-looking left-handed track.

Yes, there was a race-track there after all; but a pretty makeshift affair compared to Sandown or Cheltenham. From what I could see from the far end of the home straight – where I finally found a spot to stand and watch the rear-ends of galloping horses coming into view for a moment as they rounded the near bend, before disappearing from sight again around the far one – it consisted of slalom-like poles pushed into the ground at about 20-foot intervals to form a sharply-curved ellipse. Although I never did see the home straight, back straight, or other end of the ellipse, I'd say its total perimeter was hardly three quarters of a mile, judging by the amount of circuits it took those 'rear-ends' to complete a race.

That line of poles formed the inside running rail of the track. There was no outside rail – just a long slack rope looped between posts on the straight; over which the male, female and infant population of the Carolinas wandered around at will. I believe there were two or three jump fences along each of the straights but I never did see one, let alone watch any of those 'rear-ends' rising majestically over it.

Occasionally there would be a call over the public address system politely asking folks to get back to the other side of the ropes as horses and jockeys were getting restless waiting to start the next race. Starting time, or post time as they call it over there, was very flexible – depending, as it did, on how long it took to encourage the last few toddlers away from the path of the ensuing cavalry charge.

Members of Racegoers were easily distinguished from the shirt-sleeved locals in psychedelic shorts or jeans, being almost the only male members of that ever-milling crowd wearing conventional suits. Understandable, as it was straight on to a plane and back to the U.K. for the Racegoers after the races; and as bags were collected and checked in on leaving the hotel that morning, their South Carolina day had to start clad as would best befit the raw November morning at Heathrow 24 hours later.

A couple of Racegoers to whom I spoke told of horrendous facts that had come to light, with resultant ruination of their day, on arrival at the races. In the first place, as South Carolina was a 'dry' State, there was no alcoholic beverage of any sort on sale in any part of that sporting assembly. In the second, as South Carolina was also a God-fearing State that frowned on any form of gambling, there were no facilities provided for a modest wager on the horses. No bookmakers, no Tote, no pari-mutuel – nothing!

But in order to show some good old Southern hospitality to the decadent British contingent with its sinful gambling habits, there was a clearing behind some trees where illegal bookmakers were allowed to accept illegal bets from folks who didn't live around those parts – plus a fair number that did! And in an effort to ensure that only bona fide travellers used that concession, each of the two paths leading into that clearing was guarded by a uniformed State trooper! There was, however, little need for those bookies or law enforcement officers as far as Racegoers were concerned. Of the 26 runners in the Colonial Cup, the generous Southern bookmakers made no less than five of them odds-on! And five to one against was their best offer for any of the remainder. Including the 'three-and-a-half-legged donkeys' taking part in the big one. So the boys organised a tote among themselves, with calculations and payment to the winners made on the plane during the flight home.

Before the start of the Colonial Cup, Tony Fairbairn – director of Racegoers Club since its inception – was chatting to a big Texan near the rails. Came an announcement over the public address that one 'Michael O'Hehir, the top racing commentator from Europe, was among those present, and had been persuaded to come to the microphone and enhance the big event for all with his phenomenal race-reading powers'. The big Texan turned to Tony and enthused on the good fortune of being present to witness an international maestro doing his stuff.

'Have you ever heard him do a race before?' asked Tony, puzzled by the enthusiasm.

'No, never', answered the Texan.

'Well, I don't know what you're all so het up about', said Tony. 'He's one of the nicest men in the world, but with his broad Irish accent we English can never understand what he's talking about when he's covering a race on radio or television, especially once he gets all worked up over the closing stages. So Lord knows how anybody here will follow him.'

'By God', said the Texan once the race was over, 'how right you were. Who won?'

Watching the Colonial Cup from my own vantage point, close to the rope and nowhere within sight of the winning post, I didn't know – or care – who won. The cavalry charge passed me three or maybe four times in completing the two and a half mile race, but without a drink or a bet I had little interest in the outcome, other than a chauvinistic wish for a horse from the old country to pull off that £75,000 purse. That doesn't mean I was bored by it all. Far from it. So much was novel and oh, so different. The people were delightful and full of friendly interest in our presence. They just couldn't believe anybody would travel 5,000 miles just to see one of their li'l ole horse races. Did we have horse races back in England – and come to think of it, just where was England, anyway? A sweet-looking peacherino said she remembered it cropping up once or twice in geography or history lessons back at High School, and if her memory served her right wasn't it some place the other side of Baltimore?

Yes, sitting on the grass sipping Coca Cola and munching at a big wedge of blueberry pie, with the banter flying back and forth, I remember thinking that boozeless and betless racing in the Carolinas was every bit as pleasurable as some of the good times at sinful Ascot.

While putting this story together 15 years after it all happened, I spoke to Tony Fairbairn to check some of my facts. He gave me a few more worth recording. When planning the trip with Club colleagues and travel agents, the idea of taking the train from Washington to Columbia struck them as a novel idea. As he said, 'We were very naive in those days and didn't realise why everybody in the States travelled by air, car or Greyhound bus. What few trains still ran were red with rust and mainly carried freight.'

When the party was in Washington, the President (of the

railway line, not the White House) came to see Tony in his hotel to check whether this one-way booking for 182 Englishmen was not just a send-up by one of his pals.

On learning the facts he bacame wildly enthusiastic and promised to get his best rolling stock and dining cars out of mothballs. 'Do you English like oysters?', he asked. 'Well I do', said the mystified Tony, 'and I'm sure many others do, but I can't speak for everybody'. 'Great,' said the President of the railroad, 'down in Carolina we've got the best oysters in the world (*shades of Mz. Peters!*). I'm coming with you folks, on my train, and we're all going to eat the finest oysters you've ever tasted!'

True to his word, there were four barrels of oysters among the magnificent array of food provided for Racegoers in the dining cars of that train, which never travelled more than 35 miles an hour in the ten and a half hour journey to Columbia. The food was served by liveried attendants complete with white cotton gloves and wearing expansive grins on black, shining faces that never faltered – even when one or two of the less 'couth' among the debauching Racegoers would call out something like, 'Hey, Sambo, how about more bread!' or, 'Another couple of bottles on this table, Rastus!'*

The sun had set by the time we completed the coach ride from Camden back to Columbia airport. Our lone Boeing 707 was silhouetted on the tarmac against the darkening sky and parked close to the airport buildings. No other flights in or out were scheduled for that evening and ours was the only plane with any activity around it. But Columbia was purely a domestic airport and international flights had never flown from there before; which meant there wasn't anybody around to take charge of our exit formalities. But Tony Fairbairn and David Smith, the travel agent, had pressured TWA, the charter operators, that for a full planeload charter booking, they expected all the stops

*There were no sinister racial overtones to the remarks – it was all one big party, every bit as much enjoyed by the dusky attendants as by the passengers and the President himself.

pulled out to provide maximum facilities for the intrepid Brits. Like the concession allowing us to leave for home from Columbia, instead of having to endure the wearisome business of checking self and possessions on and off domestic flights before formal departure procedures at a recognised international airport. And no doubt TWA had pressured bureaucrats into allowing rules to be bent, on the strength of the U.S. firm getting trade that might otherwise have gone to a British or European airline.

Tony and David collected passports, took them into the deserted departure lounge, and franked all 180 of them with an exit stamp they'd begged, borrowed or stolen for that purpose. No customs barriers, no solicitous requests to have a nice day or to come back soon, no hanging about waiting for flight calls, as – without let or hindrance – we walked straight from the coaches on to the aircraft. Cases of liquor were stashed around the gangways and no time was wasted in getting cabin staff to start opening bottles. After all, it had been a long and unexpectedly dry day. As on the outward trip, all refreshments were 'on the house'.

But when the plane put down at Boston, Mass. one hour later for topping up with fuel before crossing the Atlantic, a completely new crew came aboard, and the plane restocked from scratch with a fresh consignment of food, drink, cigs, and other duty-free goods. The departing crew said they were not interested in handling and checking in the vast stocks placed in their care earlier that day. It was a lot easier just to make a 'nil' return. So the steward in charge just asked Tony to share the stuff out among the passengers. Whereby not only did all have 'freebie' fags and bottles from the original Columbian stock to take away, but throughout the overnight flight home those who wanted it by the glass were kept permanently topped-up by those friendly Boston folk – far friendlier than were their home-town ancestors, we're told, when they threw that historic 'Tea Party' for our ancestors a couple of centuries earlier!

Yes, all in all, a highly memorable trip, on which I'd never have travelled – if it wasn't for GOLF . . . !

"By the way, if you hear a loud klaxon blast at any time it'll be my anti-rape device"

17

New York, Washington and the Vanderbilt Gridiron

In the summer of '75, somebody's birthday, anniversary or cremation brought a few old friends together for dinner at the Terenure Country Club. Seated in our midst, Kath Barber, the Club owner, asked if I still kept in touch with Skinny Huggins and the Nashville folk, and did I visualise ever going there again? That set the old nostalgic adrenalin flowing – it being three years since the last visit. The thought of one more reunion before my arteries fossilised prompted: 'What a great idea. I can do it via the Racegoers trip to the States in the autumn. But I'm not going on my own – who's with me?' Starry-eyed with goodwill and grapejuice, there were five enthusiastic volunteers round the table that evening. By the time Racegoers started calling for the up-front money to Washington and the Laurel Park International, there were just two left. Kath Barber and you-know-who. Pat, my wife, was one of the five original enthusiasts, but once away from the evening's euphoria, decided she could live contentedly for the rest of her days if she never again had to step over an airport threshold. She welcomed the idea of my being out of her hair for a week and taking sister Kate along for the ride.

Kate, or Kath Barber, is not my sister. But her husband, Leo, was a good friend who died tragically about seven years before this story and some three years after they'd bought the Club. Kath was grief-striken over her loss and looked pretty near going the same way with a broken heart – or, more likely, an overdose of something or other. After a fortnight or so with little improvement on her part, I tried shaking her out of it with a 'tongue-lashing', exhorting her to do all her crying in bed at night and devote the day to picking up the reins and running the Club the way Leo would have wanted it. My apparent callousness worked and ever since I've been 'big brother' in her eyes.

Approaching take-off day, Hugh Donald was prevailed upon to join us. Elsewhere in this book I tell of my very first game as a new member of Crews Hill Golf Club – a friendly singles with Ted Ray. Hugh Donald was my first four-ball partner at Crews Hill. In the ensuing 15 years we must have walked a thousand miles together, fished the Channel for turbot, conger and skate in both winter and summer, and pursued hedonism in various forms both in this country and abroad – including participation in the nocturnal Esso Open at Finchley Road as described in Chapter 4. He had an estate agency in New Southgate, and when I needed a desk and a phone from which to start a new business after selling out in 1967, offered me half his back office until I could sort myself out more permanently.

His younger brother, Reginald, lived and worked in Bermuda. I visited the island in 1966 at the end of a business trip to Montreal, getting my wife to fly out and meet me in New York. Our onward flight to the sub-tropical island coincided with the final cruise of the *Queen of Bermuda* from New York. Its arrival on Front Street, Hamilton, three days later turned the capital into carnival city. Reg hosted me at his golf club and on a deep-water tunny-fishing jaunt aboard a luxury cruiser owned by a friend. Didn't catch any tunny, but always remember reeling in one of the many smaller fish caught that day. As it neared the surface, still threshing about on the end of my line, there was a sudden swirl of water and a five-foot shark had it with one sharp 'chomp' of its jaws. Not all of it, because I was left still reeling-in a surprised-looking fish-head with a hook in its mouth.

Reg had lived on my favourite island ever since following up a post advertised in the *Daily Telegraph* back in the 1950s. Although he and his wife holidayed in England almost every year, Hugh had never yet got round to visiting his brother in Bermuda. Well, by arranging for him to join us on the Racegoers flight as far as New York, with a connecting flight to Bermuda the next morning, that was about to be rectified. And to keep him company between flights Kath and I, too, would leave Racegoers at New York, stay the night, and get an early plane to Washington about the same time as his to Bermuda. Accommodation had been booked at the Holiday Inn, close to La Guardia airport, from which we were due to fly out next morning.

A crescent rising moon and a top-magnitude Venus were hanging perilously low over Manhattan, as our cab drove us into the 'Big Apple' a couple of hours after we'd checked in, snoozed and cleaned up. I could not think of a better way of introducing my friends to the great city on such a beautiful clear evening than from the top of the Empire State Building on Fifth Avenue – having done the same thing with my wife one clear Sunday morning nine years earlier.

When the cab-driver was asked if he could stop and wait while we shot up the lifts to the 86th floor, took a quick look round, and then came down again, he seemed a bit taken aback but said, 'No problem'. In those days the cabbies were garrulous Brooklyn boys with a laconic wit à la Allen Jenkins or Broderick Crawford. Now, I understand, they're all dour Puerto Ricans with little or no English.

Our man parked about fifty yards from the entrance to the Empire State on West 34th Street but on the opposite side of the road. As he was on a double-yellow line – or the US equivalent of one – he switched on his warning lights. We got out, threaded our way on foot through six lanes of traffic and paid the entrance fee at the turnstiles. It needed two of the building's 72 express lifts to reach the Observation deck on the 86th floor, where there's a complex of souvenir shops, snack bars, postal franking booths, and similar 'touristophalia' to cater for the 35,000 visitors they average every day of the year – most of whom seemed to be milling about up there when we stepped out into the balmy night air. There was another observatory on the 102nd floor, but 1,050 feet above street level was quite high enough for our needs.

Having taken in the different scene from each of the four sides of the Observation platform, we hurried back to the patiently waiting taxi below. Switching off his flashers, the driver drily commented that nobody but a crazy Englishman would tell a cab to wait with the meter running while he went on a sightseeing trip up the Empire State Building. I had to tell him that nobody but a crazy New Yorker would drive three people for forty minutes from La Guardia to the downtown end of the City, and let them mingle with the crowds entering and leaving the world's largest building without asking for payment, in part or in full, for what was already on the clock.

When asked if he could recommend a good place to eat he said, naturally, that New York was full of them, but went on to name one or two specialising in sea-food, or Chinese, Jewish, Italian or English cuisine. He'd heard a lot of people speak highly of the English one – Glockister House. Wasn't until he was asked to spell it that he could be told how to pronounce 'Gloucester'! 'Crazy!' he said.

Anyway, we hadn't come 3,000 miles to eat what they probably did more naturally at any of half-a-dozen places up the Finchley Road, so settled on one of the top restaurants providing live entertainment – the Waldorf-Astoria. And the live entertainer was to be that all-time favourite, Miss Peggy Lee.

'No room!', said the Mad Ha-, sorry, the Maître d', as we entered the crowded restaurant from the sumptuous foyer of the hotel. Remembering how suave screen heroes handled that situation in the man-about-town films of yesterday, I pressed a carefully-folded five-dollar bill into the other's warm and receptive hand. Without deigning to look at it – but no doubt checking denomination and serial number with sensitive finger tips – he snapped the five on the other hand. A nearby pair of waiters sprang into action: one to pick up a small pedestal table with a round marble top from a stack near the door, and ask us to follow as he carried it upside down over his head; the other to bring up the rear carrying three gilded basketware chairs in a similar fashion.

When our leader had threaded his way across the crowded restaurant to within about thirty feet of the stage and the twenty-piece band, he set down the table and persuaded all around to tuck in chairs, feet and tummies so his colleague could space our chairs around it. Nobody seemed to mind having to make room for the newcomers. In fact, even as we went to sit down, a fellow leaned across from the next table, put out his hand and said:

'Hi! You're English, ain't you?'

'How'd you know that?', I asked, taking the proffered hand in mine.

'Easy', he replied. 'Ain't nobody from New York'd thank a crummy waiter just for putting down a chair. God knows they screw enough out of you before you ever get a favour out of 'em!'

Throughout the evening diners were herded closer and closer together to make room for yet more groups to be seated. But nobody really minded.

The band played lively big-band music while people got up to dance on the bit of uncluttered floor in front of the stage. By now our marble table-top was awash with 'freebies' – salted nuts, cocktail onions, gherkins, pretzels, crackers, and glasses of iced water – while the waiter took the order for such food and drink as we'd be expected to pay for.

Came a break in the music, followed by a prolonged fanfare from the brass section. This led to the announcement that Miss Peggy Lee was about to entertain us. And that she certainly did – from the moment she swooped on stage swathed in a substantial yardage of diaphanous garments that billowed around her, for all the world like a spinnaker-rigged yacht running before the wind. Tumultuous applause echoed around the vast restaurant for the next hour and a half as she sang any number of old and new favourites, many of them in response to requests from her wildly enthusiastic audience. She even kindly obliged with one of the titles called from our little table.

Yes, it was a night to remember.

The following morning the courtesy bus from the hotel took us across to La Guardia airport – Hugh for his connection to Bermuda, Kath and me to Racegoers in Washington.

When planning the trip back in the U.K. I'd incorporated some business calls into my travels, whereby I could put it all down to the firm. This involved correspondence and meetings with the British Overseas Trade Board in London, and a call on the Commercial Secretary of the British Embassy in Washington. I'd planned that for late morning on the day of our arrival from New York and once up in my room phoned to confirm. Yes, I was expected and sure, it was O.K. to bring my 'sister' along for the ride. It was grand to gaze at the array of Union Jacks fluttering proudly above our palatial British Embassy in Massachusetts Avenue, after the number of 'Old Glorys' we'd seen dominating the skyline of the capital. Setting up in business to make Stars-and-Stripes flags in the U.S. must be like a licence to print money. They're everywhere.

November 1968 was my first trip to Washington with Racegoers, and to justify paying for it from company funds, I'd written to our Trade Board and to the Embassy in search of potential business in the States. I wanted some names and introductions to firms planning expansion into Europe, and employing British consultants and/or contractors for their building programmes. Getting the ear of the latter in search of some of the action would be made easier if I could say that the U.S. VIP employing them had recommended that I make contact.

Our folks at the Embassy proved both knowledgeable and helpful. They had not only done their homework by the time I called, whereby I was able to speak to one or two top executives from distant States on the telephone, but had opened the door for me to visit two firms within a 25-mile radius of Washington.

But it was the meeting they arranged while I was in their office that proved of more than passing interest. Not that the firm in question was planning anything in the U.K., but because it was the bright and breezy success story of a couple of enterprising Englishmen. They were the McAteer Brothers, of Falls Church, Virginia – about twenty miles south of Washington – but originally out of Liverpool. Billy, the elder, had made front page news 11 years before I met him by entering the United States through stowing away in a packing case aboard the liner *Queen Mary*. Determined but broke, he wanted to be with his younger brother, Johnny, then British and European middleweight boxing champion, fighting around the States in pursuit of the world title.

Billy was allowed to stay in the States and was soon working for himself as an electrician. Once Johnny hung up his gloves, he joined his brother and set up a Heat and Vent. side to the enterprise, having previously served his time as a plumber and fitter around Merseyside. The brothers prospered to the extent that, when I got to know them over a take-away lunch at their offices, and later over dinner at Billy's home, I found they each ran around in a custom-built Cadillac, each had four children, each lived in a palatial country house near Falls Church, and that Billy's sailboat anchored on the Chesapeake was slightly longer than Johnny's 40-foot motor cruiser moored nearby. Yet they were just as unmistakenly 'Scouse' in their accent, idiom and humour as any latter-day Tarbuck or Beatle.

While at the Embassy on the day of arrival I'd asked if there was any chance of getting a bit of golf on the morrow, when the bulk of the Racegoers party were on a conducted tour of somebody's stables. It was suggested that I ring Burning Tree Golf Club, where only members and male guests were allowed – no green fees, no societies, and certainly no females. Even bar, cleaning, and secretarial staff were all male. With half the country's politicians as its members, grass-widowed senators and representatives in Washington from remote States could not be exposed to temptation when known to be at the Burning Tree, thus allowing suspicious loved ones to sleep easier in distant and lonely beds.

The Club Manager said they didn't allow visitors when I phoned – other than well-vetted guests of members – but felt he could hardly deny my request to come and gaze upon the hallowed course on which their famous President played. Especially as I'd travelled some 4,000 miles to do so. So he said to take a cab and come on out, where no doubt something would be done, both for me and another member of the group who, on learning of my quest, wondered if it was O.K. to join me. And something was most certainly – and most handsomely – done.

We were entered up as guests of a member of the British Embassy, known to be currently out of town. The Club pro. Max Elbin, then-President of the American P.G.A., fitted us out with shoes, rented clubs and a caddy cart. Also asked if we'd like to make up a four with Spiro Agnew and another senator, who were about to go off on the first. That seemed like pushing it a bit, so we demurely declined – contented to play a 27-hole round and a half of singles play in the autumn sunshine and on an almost deserted course. Twenty-seven holes, because the battery on the cart gave up the ghost halfway round the second circuit. So we carried the clubs back to the shop and duly rewarded the assistant awaiting our return once we'd explained just where the abandoned cart needed collecting from on the morrow.

The sun had set and the bar was completely empty by the time we'd said all our thank-yous, downed a couple of drinks, and asked the barman to ring for a taxi.

The souvenir Burning Tree hat and the dozen branded golf clubs, bought in Max Elbin's shop on that memorable day in 1968, have long since gone the way of all souvenirs. But the events of that day all came back again six years later when Kath and I entered the Embassy and were escorted up to the Commercial Officer's room. After telling him of successful business dealings in the U.K. thanks to introductions from the previous visit, we went on to talk of more general things. He was a young all-American ex-Harvard or Yale type, and appreciated the signed copy of *Start-Off-Smashed!* I brought him. In answer to my question he said he'd love to join us for lunch, but his day was filled up with meetings and there was hardly time for a coffee and sandwich at his desk; but went on to recommend the Horse and Groom, Georgetown, as a better-burger establishment in a picturesque part of the city's residential suburb. With regard to what to do after lunch, he suggested a visit to the Arlington Memorial Cemetery and the Custis Lee House, once the home of Confederate leader, General Robert E. Lee.

The mansion with its 500-acre plantation was built for George Washington Parke Custis – adopted son of George Washington. Through marriage, it became the family home of Robert E. Lee until his native state, Virginia, seceded from the Union and he felt obliged to go along with it. Branding him a traitor, the Government got its own back by confiscating the estate, turning his house into a hospital for the war wounded and the plantation into a graveyard for its dead. After the Civil War, the Supreme Court ruled that the house belonged to Custis Lee, son of Robert, who in turn sold it to the Federal Government. The burial ground became the renowned Arlington National Cemetery, with currently about 100,000 graves of U.S. forces killed in battle or on active service from 1861 until the present day; each marked by an engraved marble block about 24 inches high, and identical in size irrespective of the rank, race, colour or creed of whoever lies beneath it.

In 1926, about the same time as John D. Rockefeller was resurrecting Williamsburg, the house was completely restored and refurbished to its original antebellum* design. It'is recognised today as one of the finest examples of Colonial architecture in the country. We spent a memorable afternoon on a conducted tour of the house, followed by one over the vast cemetery, stretching right down to the walls of the Pentagon, where sit the military decision-makers, many of whose decisions, no doubt, played a large part in helping to fill the cemetery in the first place. Passing among the white headstones and reading inscriptions, we witnessed

*Americanese for pre-Civil War

the hourly changing of the guard at the tomb of the Unknown Warrior and gazed with awe at the dramatic settings in which John Kennedy and Robert Kennedy had been laid to rest.

After crossing the Potomac on the drive back to the Sheraton, we had the cab stop and wait more than once along the two-mile stretch of tailored green sward between the Lincoln Memorial and the Capitol, in order to enter and take a closer look at some of the impressive monuments to those who had helped shape the nation's history.

That evening our culture-filled day ended with a Chinese meal at a restaurant specialising in Peking cuisine and recommended in the hotel guide book. Our only mistake. We had to wait for well over an hour while they prepared their precious duck – and when it was brought to the table midst much pomp and ceremony, sat watching in silence while they pared-off bits of skin and gristle to place on our plates, before wheeling the rest of the bird away, no doubt for the staff supper!

Bidding farewell to our Racegoer friends until the next reunion in New York three days hence for the homeward flight, we departed on American Airlines for Nashville on a bright sunny morning. But at Nashville we ran into a 'can of worms'.

I'd written to explain to Skinny how it was that Kath Barber was on the trip with me – he'd met her more than once when partying at her place during his visits to the U.K. – and had given him a brief run-down of the 'big-brother' relationship. Skinny and a couple of others were at the airport to greet us and said that when my letter told them I'd booked into the airport Hilton Hotel, they decided to cancel it over the phone and put us into one a bit nearer to their neck of the woods. It was a Travel-Lodge to which we were now taken where, on checking in, the desk clerk gave me but one room key and looked mystified when I asked for the second room. One room for Morley and another for Barber had been booked at the airport hotel, but in deciding to move us, our friends were unaware that adult brothers and sisters in England were not in the habit of sharing a double bed.

Despite their infatuation with religion – they were almost all devout 'Bible punchers' – my impending visit with another woman could only have had one meaning for them, and to hell with 'blessed are the pure in heart'! But being kindly Southerners, hospitality was the name of the game, and if that's the way ole Sam wanted to play it then it was all right with them. They must have thought me pretty thick or insensitive to believe I'd want to embarrass good friends who knew my wife so well by bringing an alleged 'playmate' into their midst.

Travel Lodge found us that second room; although, despite my righteous indignation, I felt some Nashvillians still preferred to believe the second one to be something of a 'blind.' Like in case divorce lawyers came snooping around at some later date. But Kathy was made welcome by all throughout our three-day stay. On the other hand, I don't know how many times she'd hear me asked in her presence, loud and clear, 'How's your sweet wife Pat, Sam?'

We'd hardly had time to put our cases down and wash up, than the boys were back to take us to Belle Meade Golf Club. Me, to play in a four-ball with Skinny, Bob Walker and Cawthon Bowen. Pat Walker, Bob's wife, took Kath under her wing and kindly found her some left-handed clubs with which to play nine holes. Yes, my 'sister' was just as much of a wrong-way-rounder as her big brother. Must run in the family. But Pat Walker played off a handicap of seven – or some such magical figure – while Kath Barber had only once before ever been on a golf course. True, they rode around in a cart, but it was a hot, tired and dispirited Kath who eventually went to sit out on a deserted terrace overlooking the tennis courts at the back of the clubhouse and watch the sun go down. Meanwhile, Pat had taken her leave to go home and get tarted-up for the big 'Welcome Sam Morley' party back at Belle Meade that evening. But I knew nothing about their afternoon until much later.

Once our four-ball had showered, downed a drink and paid our bets, we went in search of the ladies in the now almost deserted clubhouse. They were not to be seen. Bob Walker said Pat wouldn't have wanted to hang around, so she'd probably ran Kath back to the hotel before going home herself.

We split up and night had fallen by the time Bo dropped me at the Travel Lodge. But Kath's room key was still hanging in Reception. Bo phoned Pat Walker who confirmed she'd offered to run her partner back to the hotel but Kath had said not to bother as she'd prefer to wander about the rambling clubhouse and wait to go back to the hotel with me. A phone call to the night porter confirmed there was nobody left at Belle Meade.

I asked Bo if Belle Meade happened to run a white-slaving venture on the side and whether at that moment my poor 'sister' might be trussed up in the hold of a clapped-out old banana boat, on her way to end her days dancing on the tables in some Central American waterfront café. But he didn't think so. She wasn't quite the right shape and to the best of his knowledge there hadn't been a banana boat in for at least a week.

Time passed and we were good and worried. Then came a phone call from Belle Meade. It was the furnace attendant who'd been checking all was well with the central heating for the evening's festivities, and had just had the bejasus scared out of him when coming face to face with a white English lady wandering around the subterranean corridors. She in turn suffered a similar trauma when waking, cold and alone, on the outside terrace of a strange and deserted building. It didn't take long for Bo to collect and bring her back to start preparing for the dinner party, the preliminaries for which had already commenced with folks gathering for drinks in the homes of their friends.

In our case the pre-party cocktails were at the home of Jimmy Hofstead, to which we were chauffeured again by Bo and his wife Martha, once he'd gone back to get her and complete a lightning change of clothes. At the 'Welcome Sam Morley and ?' party at Belle Meade, almost everybody with whom I'd rubbed shoulders on the four previous visits to Nashville was present. Had I been President of the United States, they could not have shown greater warmth and hospitality. Mind you, nobody concealed an avid curiosity about my consort – which probably accounted for the number of enquiries about the health of 'my sweet wife, Pat' echoing round that room.

The next afternoon we were taken to our first American football game. Vanderbilt University, alma mater to so many of our Nashville hosts, was to play the State University of California. It was a magnificent spectacle on a hot and sunny November afternoon. Having the mysteries of the game explained to me by Skinny during the match still comes to mind every week when I watch it now on Channel 4 twelve years later. The rules of college football vary slightly from those of the professional game, but certainly not enough for me to notice, let alone care. But it's a pity British TV doesn't show more of the cheer-leading and general razzamatazz that liven up every game in the United States – especially the pulchritude-laden, high-stepping strutters providing Barnum-like entertainment at half-time.

Kath sat a couple of rows behind with some of the wives from the previous night's party. They were just as enthusiastic and vociferous as the menfolk, and tried hard to explain to her what all the noise and fuss were about. Yet with about 40,000 demonstrative supporters from both camps in that packed auditorium sitting cheek by jowl with each other, partisan differences were good humoured and violence among spectators almost unknown.

Morley popularity in Nashville waxed even greater thanks to our presence at that football game. Vanderbilt were up against a far stronger side and had not been doing too well of late. But they still managed to pull it off and win by a very small margin in the dying seconds of the game. All our friends reckoned it was the added support of the two-strong English contingent that did the trick. I wrote and presented Bo with a three-stanza 'Paean of Victory' that evening to commemorate the day. (Well, more doggerel-ish than paean-ish.)

After the game Bo quickly wove us through the departing crowds to where his car was strategically parked. Just as quickly he then wove it strategically through the traffic to his home. We were puzzled about all the hurry until he switched on the television and bade us sit in front of the set. Just in time to watch the start of the Laurel Park International, with Lester Piggott riding an English horse on which we'd left a modest wager. But it was a Canadian team, Nobiliary ridden by Sandy Hawley, that finished first – proving you can't win 'em all.

That night we were taken to dinner at a popular downtown sea-food restaurant, staffed, as we were to learn, mainly by visiting songsters and the like, looking for the big chance in the City of Song – just as stores and soda fountains around Los Angeles in the Thirties were staffed by would-be starlets looking for their big break in Hollywood. And, as everybody knows today, the capital city of Tennessee is the Mecca for those trying to make it with music. The proud boast on a free entertainment booklet in Nashville hotel bedrooms proclaims: 'We didn't get the name of Music City of the World just by Whistlin' "DIXIE!"'

Sitting eight-handed in the crowded restaurant, we were browsing through the impressive range of fish in the menu when a pretty uniformed waitress passed by carrying a laden tray. Catching my admiring eye she stopped, put the tray down on an adjacent table, parked herself on my knee, put one arm loosely round my neck and, looking me straight between the eyes, broke into full Judy-Garland-like voice with 'You Made Me Love You!' – accompanied by whoops of joy from all my party and most other diners in the place. The song over, she rose, kissed me lightly on the cheek, demurely straightened her skirt, picked up her tray and delivered its contents to the table of diners patiently awaiting its arrival.

During the evening other waitresses would suddenly burst into song while going about their duties, but I don't remember another customer receiving a personal service to match mine. Skinny said it was probably due to my being mistaken for a prosperous show-business impresario. The girl must have gambled, he believed, on my being the means of her getting that one big break she was after. I told him if they hadn't all been there with me, ole Sam might well have offered her one, too!

The following day it was farewell to Nashville again after a morning four-ball and a bit of lunch. By this time my friends had taken Kath to their hearts, to the extent that their womenfolk were even passing her messages to give to 'Sam's sweet wife, Pat'.

Hugh Donald was scheduled to fly in from Bermuda and meet us at Kennedy Airport about two hours before the Racegoers UK flight was due to leave. But Kennedy was getting all misted over when we landed from Nashville and a thick fog built up as the evening wore on. We sat up at the bar in the TWA terminal, quaffing dry martinis and watching replays of the afternoon's professional football matches on a TV set at the back of the bar. This gave an opportunity to acquire yet more knowledge of the game through heated exchanges between other customers at the bar over referee decisions and action replays of the alleged incidents.

Incoming flights were now being diverted to Newark, New Jersey, and it was anybody's guess whether planes would get out of Kennedy that night. With or without Hugh Donald. Ours did go eventually – without him, albeit two hours after the scheduled time of departure. But we were lucky. Soon after take-off and setting a course east above all the rubbish, the captain announced ours to be the last plane out of Kennedy that evening. The fog had rolled in again with our departure and the airport had decided to close officially till the morning.

The airline put Hugh Donald into a local hotel for the night and it was another 24 hours or so before they found him a flight to Heathrow. When we did meet up again he was still all starry-eyed about his Bermuda experience, sandwiched between our joint taste of New York at the beginning of the trip and his lone one at the end of it.

None of which could ever have happened – if it wasn't for GOLF . . . !

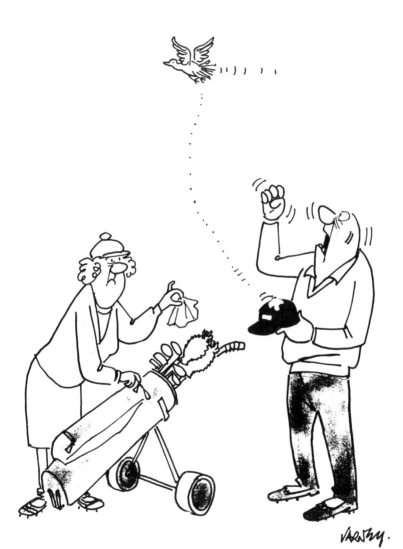

" For the rich you SING!"

18

Way Down Yonder in
New Orleans

In the autumn of 1982 Reg Davies retraced the 'Start-Off-Smashed' expedition with a lone nostalgic visit to San Francisco, Las Vegas and Nashville, no doubt accumulating enough impressions to do his own book but to the best of my knowledge still to start on it.

On his return he said there were still people up and about in the fair city of Nashville who knew of Sam Morley. Vaguely, and not too many of them, but I felt flattered. Skinny, he said, was in a bad way with Alzheimer's disease, but Cawthon Bowen, Skinny's best pal, masterminded the familiar pattern of Nashville hospitality with which Reg was swamped during his stay. Well, it always was 'Bo' pulling the strings behind the scenes for that sort of thing and he still hadn't lost his enthusiasm or touch. Reg Davies was given a great welcome and a farewell dinner at Belle Meade on his departure. 'Bring Sam back with you next time,' they cried when he left.

That's how it came about that two years later we decided another visit was about due. As neither of us had yet seen the birthplace of jazz, we'd do it the pretty way, via New Orleans. Our plan was to leave in September '84 via a British Airways flight to Atlanta, Georgia; from whence we'd take turns in driving a rented car five hundred miles down to New Orleans, with an overnight stop somewhere en route. After four nights in New Orleans we'd drive another five hundred miles up to Nashville and stay three nights, followed by two hundred miles to Chattanooga for two nights, and finally one hundred or so miles to Atlanta for the evening flight home. That way we'd have taken in five Southern states – Georgia, Alabama, Mississippi,

Louisiana and Tennessee.

Reg was getting somewhat fulsome and looked upon long-distance 747 flights in Economy class seating as a form of punishment or penance for past indulgences. So we indulged a bit further by digging into the 'piggy bank' and treating ourselves to first-class travel on this trip.

When I wrote to pass the word around Nashville about the impending visit there were at least three heartwarming letters from different friends inviting us to stay at their homes instead of booking into hotels. They were sent replies appreciating the offer but diplomatically explaining a preference for the privacy of a hotel. Cawthon Bowen then phoned from Nashville to insist we accept his offer, as we would each have one of the four hospitality suites on the second floor of the 12-storey condominium block in which he lived. They were a feature of the development intended for residents to accommodate visiting guests without having them round their necks all day. How civilized, we thought, accepting graciously.

It was late afternoon when our luxury flight arrived at Atlanta. By the time formalities were completed for the rented car, what little daylight remained was swallowed up in the mummy and daddy of a thunderstorm, complete with torrential raindrops the size of silver dollars. Fortunately Reg won the toss for first drive of our 'Herbie', the hired Granada coupé – once we'd located it in the rented-car compound – and in so doing earned a citation for the Duke of Edinburgh Award, perhaps even the Congressional Medal of Honour. No way could I have coped so masterfully in that murky tempest with a strange steamed-up car having all its controls on the wrong side, and needing to be driven on the wrong side of an almost invisible and unknown road. And in addition, having to peer between windscreen wipers, crashing to and fro at top speed, in search of the route number we wanted among the countless directional signs at each intersection. More than once we pulled into the side to study maps, hazarding conflicting guesses on our position and what lay ahead in the rain-sodden gloom, and then decide on whose opinion to follow. And we still had hardly left the rented-car compound.

The original plan was to head south-west out of Atlanta and get about a hundred miles down the road before pulling in somewhere for the night. But what with having to negotiate this filthy weather after a tiring ten-hour plane journey, it was proving traumatic just looking for where to start on our travels without two and a half hours of hurtling through dark wet space once we'd found the jump-off point.

Then we saw it. A brilliantly-lit building bespattered with neon signs reading, 'Century Inn – Vacancies'. To us it was like the mirage of a soda fountain to a thirst-crazed legionnaire in the desert. In our case the mirage was on a service road. And the service road ran parallel to the airport perimeter road on which we travelled, with no visible means through the driving rain of crossing the grassed banks separating them. It took three U-turns to the accompaniment of full beam-flashing and horn-playing from irate motorists before we finally located a shy little slip road that allowed access into the hotel car park.

We knew it was a good decision immediately after scampering through the deluge into the dry, well-lit entrance lobby. Right opposite the Reception desk – where we had no difficulty in getting a couple of well-appointed rooms for the night – was a doorway into the bar, with a brilliant neon sign beaming its name, 'Sam's Place'!

After a quick trip to our rooms for a clean up and change of shirt we rendezvoused on a couple of bar stools in 'my place' where, while supping a few beers and a little food to the music of a lively five-piece band, we agreed on an early start in an effort to make the five hundred miles to New Orleans in one day. But Reg hadn't reckoned on my ringing and waking him at 4.30 a.m. to say I couldn't sleep and how about hitting the road in 20 minutes. I think he'd have preferred to hit me, but once showered and dressed, thought it a good idea when we met in the lobby and checked out.

It was still belting down heavens-hard as we hurried

across to the car and set forth on our travels in the Stygian gloom. But we were fresh, traffic was almost non-existent, and with friendly guidance from the desk staff there was little trouble finding that elusive Interstate 85 road we wanted. Reg was still at the wheel as he reckoned the previous evening's stint didn't count.

He earned a bar to that 'gong' of yesterday in pushing that car for the next two and a half hours down what could only be likened to an unlit Channel Tunnel with a perforated roof. Except for the 'cat's eyes' in the road reflecting our headlights, we were in a black cocoon with no way of knowing where the skyline began or ended. It was only when the black started to fade into dark grey and the deluge into heavy rain as we approached Montgomery, Alabama, that our first glimpse of the tree-lined Southlands through which we'd been travelling came into view.

With breakfast in mind we turned off into a commercial complex on the outskirts of town and parked opposite a Shoney diner. It was almost 8.00 a.m. but, although lights and bustle were to be seen on all sides through the windows, the doors of the restaurant remained locked from within. When I rattled them another prospective customer waiting on the step said they never opened up until 7.00 on the dot. 'But it's nearly eight', I told him, holding out my wrist for him to see.

'That's either a lousy watch', he replied laconically, 'or else you've driven from Georgia, which is Eastern Time, and didn't switch to Central Time when crossing the Alabama State border about 80 miles back'. He was right on the second count.

After eggs, bacon, sausage, pancakes, grits and hashed browns, plus cinnamon toast and coffee galore, we were ready for phase two of the voyage with me at the helm. That was the easy bit, once I stopped tending to hang to the right in the fast lane as one does on our own roads. It had stopped raining and patches of blue were beginning to show in the sky ahead.

It didn't take long before Reg was nodding off, as I'd done

216

during his long nightmare stint, but there was now plenty of traffic around for company. Although the U.S. speed limit is 55 m.p.h. I found difficulty in keeping down to 70, but often had to ease into an inside lane to allow a 28-wheeler giant coming up behind to roar past. And if it wasn't done fast enough to please the Rambo at the wheel, the blast from his ear-piercing set of horns would almost blow us into it.

The tyres on those juggernauts were never designed to operate at the speeds they were driven and the sides of the carriageways were littered with lumps of burnt rubber. In fact at one time I was stuck behind a truck while one of his back tyres disintegrated slowly as I watched it. Chunks of rubber came flying off at me as he thundered along, some of which hit the windscreen and woke up Reg!

Stopping for petrol, I noticed the garage hand carefully washing and polishing the windscreen of a car filling up alongside. How accommodating these people still are, I thought, and politely asked if he'd do ours. Contemptuously he pointed to a bucket of dirty water with a dirty rag hanging over its edge and told me to help myself! I, apparently, was on the cheaper self-service row of pumps, while the adjoining row charged more for its gas and threw in attendant-service for the price. Something that was carefully borne in mind after that. With the amount of insects and other rubbish making a beeline for windscreen and lamp-lenses as we ploughed along the highway, those few extra cents were well spent in opting for the gas-plus-service pumps.

At Mobile, on the Gulf of Mexico and close to the Mississippi State line, we stopped for a couple of beers and a snack lunch, having clocked about 250 miles since leaving Montgomery. Reg now took her on the last hundred or so into New Orleans, the final twenty of which involved traversing a motorway built on stilts above the waters of Lake Pontchartrain. It was along the stretch from Mobile that we ran into swarms of what we learned later were called love-bugs, spreading their flattened carcasses all over the screen and front of the car; also noticed many armadillo corpses, about the size of a squirrel, by the side of the road. Two kinds of wild life not often seen around Hertfordshire.

Driving down Canal Street toward the waterfront, the old, or French, quarter of New Orleans was on the left. With the help of a town map acquired from the U.S. Tourist Centre in London we were able to weave our way through its narrow one-way streets in search of somewhere to stay.

Twice we stopped at unobtrusive hotels from a bygone age; hotels with secluded courtyards and friendly barmen, but the rooms were in keeping with the wrought iron architecture that abounded all around. A bit heavy and dated. So we settled on a new Holiday Inn on the corner of Canal Street and Royal. Because of traffic congestion it was built with the first six floors as public car park and the next two for residents. When booking our accommodation at the ground floor office we were told to park the car on the sixth and take our gear up in the lift to register at Reception on the ninth.

Having done that, the love-bug-encrusted car was left where it was and not touched again until we checked out and left New Orleans four days later. The swimming pool was on the roof and with the ever-present heat and humidity little time was wasted in getting up there and into it once I'd unpacked.

Our hotel was only two blocks from Bourbon Street, the traffic-free walkabout centre of the Vieux Carré thoroughfare – thronged year-round with visitors and lined on both sides with gift shops, bars, eating houses, prostitutes, girlie and all-male shows advertising topless and bottomless 'entertainment' – in fact all the tawdry paraphernalia of Soho, Blackpool and the Costa Brava rolled into one. But nowhere else could match the music. Every bar had its own five- to seven-piece band blaring out traditional New Orleans jazz. Not a sheet of music between them, nobody waved a stick, all invited requests from their audiences, and every number was given an individual version by each instrumentalist in turn before the final ensemble treatment. It was magic.

Cleaned up after 13 hours on the road, we took a glass in the air-con 'coolth' of the hotel bar before going in search of the music-makers. Outside the first bar in Bourbon Street a small crowd were gathered round the open door, watching and listening to the six-piece band inside playing 'South Rampart Street Parade'. As though in a trance we entered and sat at a table. It all seemed like something out of a film and we didn't move from that table for the next couple of hours.

The house rules were simple. The first beer, coffee, or what-have-you, was charged at seven to ten dollars and sit as long as you like. If you wanted more to drink or took a meal from the wide-ranging menu you paid regular competitive prices for all you had after that first one – which, of course, went to pay for the main attraction. But, except for requests, they ran through the same sequence of numbers after a couple of sessions, each session lasting about thirty minutes with a fifteen-minute break between. We got to know when the break was due, as the final number at the end of each session would be 'When the Saints Come Marching In'. This was the case with each group we saw while in New Orleans. And we saw plenty. I think we did four bars that first evening.

Menus in the bars and restaurants were rich in local dishes and each claimed that their particular speciality – be it Creole Jambalaya, Gumbo, Oyster Rockefeller, Crawfish Etouffée or Pecan Pie – was the one gourmets crossed oceans to enjoy. Being firm plats-du-jour and vin-du-pays adherents we tried them all – plats, that is, but sticking to local beer usually as far as vin was concerned – and made a point of never eating, drinking or listening to the band in the same place twice.

One night Reg had a dodgy leg and didn't fancy too much walkabout. When he limped back to the hotel I wandered along on my own and found Preservation Hall, where jazz was first played at the turn of the century. And I swear nobody's put a paint-brush to its walls or woodwork since. Not much bigger than the width and depth of a terrace house, it was a picture of carefully maintained dilapidation. Even the fly specks on the bare electric bulbs – 40 watt , I'd say – hanging from the cracked old ceiling looked as though they too had a preservation order on them. The clarinet player of the seven-piece band was Willie Humphrey, born 1900 in New Orleans. His kid brother was five years younger and played the trumpet. Jo Frazier on the drums was born in 1904, Marvin Kimball, on the banjo, in 1909, and James Miller, piano, in 1913. The two white 'youths', Frank Demond, trombone, and Allan Jaffe, tuba, were of 1933 and 1935 vintage respectively. They sat on a miscellaneous assortment of old chairs facing the tiny auditorium, with the stripped-down old honky-tonk piano at an angle, and folks threw a dollar into a straw basket to come and sit in, if lucky, on about half a dozen wooden forms. Those not so lucky would just stand behind the lucky ones in the dark. No food. No drink. Just music.

I must have stayed through three sessions before they closed up for the night, and was still in an ecstatic daze as I strolled through the now almost deserted Bourbon Street back to the hotel. So much so that when a black lady came toward me from the shadows and asked if I'd like to go home with her, I murmured without thinking, 'What, all the way to Africa!' – and had to hurry to escape her peevish stream of abuse.

The following morning I gave a detailed account of it all to Reg and couldn't wait to have him see it for himself that evening. But unfortunately it was a different band playing. An excellent group, mind, but not the original Preservation Hall Jazz Band that I was so fortunate to have found. Since then we've seen them at the Barbican Hall and on TV at home. I understand they go on a world tour every year. But I couldn't image two greater extremes of venue. The pristine decor of the huge concert hall at the Barbican in the City of London with its massive stage and armchair luxury-seating for about 2,500, and Preservation Hall, New Orleans, with its built-in decay, stained walls and wooden forms for 30. Yet those wonderful old musicians seemed equally at ease performing in either place.

One morning Reg and I went on an all-day coach tour of the area. Our driver/guide, Bob Wilson, a university history graduate, had a profound knowledge of his subject, with a dry and flippant line of patter to go with it. He taught us a lot about his home town. One of my most vivid recollections is of the above-ground cemeteries of New Orleans, about the existence of which we knew nothing until a large sign advertising one had us puzzled on the initial drive into the city. Incidentally, one of the first things the passengers were told by Bob Wilson on his conducted tour was how to pronounce 'New Orleans'. Four syllables were condensed into two and by airily referring to 'Norlenes' one would be recognised and envied as having learned to speak correctly in the 'Birthplace of Jazz.'

New Orleans is built on the delta of the Mississippi River and many parts of the city and surrounding parts are below sea-level. The water-table is so high that coffins or caskets containing the remains of loved ones, when placed six feet underground, float to the surface before long due to the frequent flooding that takes place, despite all attempts to weight them down. The predominantly Catholic community overcame this with typically-French ingenuity. They built stone or concrete tombs in horizontal cubicle formation – like filing cabinets with non-pull-out drawers. The front of each multiple tomb would present a solid dignified appearance, but the back entrance to each 'drawer' was open. A laden coffin would be ceremoniously slid into the cubicle or 'drawer' and the aperture crudely bricked up once the mourners had departed. One year and one day later the bricks were chipped out and, humidity and heat having done their work, there would be just a little heap of dust and ashes to be raked out before the cubicle was ready for the next occupant. Coffin makers therefore were obliged to use only the cheap, less durable timbers, and metal handles – whether cast brass or solid gold – were forbidden.

As the sites were very expensive, there were a number of

simple multiple units for the none-too-wealthy. One 12-cubicle unit had an engraved facia reading 'Young Men's Benevolent Association' – no doubt presented by that body for community use. Others, more ornate, belonged to wealthy, old-established New Orleans families and had but two or three cubicles; although engraved 'In Memoriam' plaques on the ornamental wrought-ironwork surrounding the tomb named dozens of kinfolk and the dates they'd gone to rest there for a year and a day.

Well, that was just one of the 41 above-ground cemeteries of New Orleans. According to a guide book there also happened to be 516 churches, of which I'm ashamed to say we didn't enter any – and 3,700 licensed bars, of which we did.

The horse-drawn caleches – open carriages conveying tourists around the Old Quarter, with each nag wearing a 'gladbag' – were another sight unique to New Orleans. The gladbag was attached to the end of the horse farthest from the end that carried the feedbag, whereby the animal's unsavoury deposits, while trotting or standing around the narrow streets, were neatly retained out of sight for subsequent disposal by the driver – no doubt, at a price, to local rose or rhubarb cultivators. The road surfaces thereby remained unsullied. When Bob Wilson was asked why they were called 'gladbags', he said it was because the folks of New Orleans were sure glad they wore 'em!

Our coach tour of the city and surrounding parts included the ten-mile-long St. Charles Avenue, lined with impressive houses of yesterday and featuring single-decker streetcars running down the central reservation. At one point a number of long thin houses were pointed out, only six to eight feet wide, but with a total depth of a hundred feet or more. They were a relic of ingenuity, going back to the last century, when householders were taxed according to the amount of street frontage their building took up. So they built 'em long and thin to cut down on the outgoings and the end products were known as 'shotgun houses'. And when they built these long, thin dwellings in pairs, as side-by-side semi-detached units, they, of course, became 'double-barrelled shotguns'!

Near the end of that entertaining six-hour run-around, we passed a newly built concrete structure that tapered down and disappeared into the surrounding grassland. 'There', said Bob proudly, 'is New Orleans' only anti-nuclear fallout shelter. It goes down Lord knows how many feet below the surface and there's just about every form of computerised monitoring equipment installed for keeping tabs on all that's happening above ground. Sufficient provisions, and health and recreational facilities, are stored down there to keep 240 people safe and well for up to two years if necessary.'

'Mind you', he went on reflectively, 'if ever the need arose, I don't think it's going to be much help to the million-odd who live in and around New Orleans. But I have heard it said that 240 is about right for the number of elected members on the City Council – including their immediate families – who voted for it to be built, and they each have a key!'

The parking lot for the horse-drawn caleches was on the wide sweep of Decatur Street, fronting Jackson Square and the magnificent St. Louis Cathedral. On the other side was the Mississippi River and the levee where stern-wheel passenger-carrying river-boats would berth. Each would herald its approach with 'Waiting for the Robert E. Lee' at full blast on its steam-fired organ, or calliope. In consequence, a goodly proportion of the tourists strolling around the waterfront shopping arcades would stop whatever they were doing, grab their best gal or pal, and shuffle-on down to the levee. Which is how Reg and I came to board the *Natchez* for a river-trip link-up with those ole cotton-pickin' 'Showboat' days!

But there wasn't an awful lot to see, except some rusty cargo ships moored in mid-stream, and the mudflats of the river banks with a vast acreage of dirty brown water stretching between them. Mark Twain was pilot on one of those river-boats in his early days, before travel and a prolific pen brought him immortality as a warm and witty writer who could 'debunk' established 'holy cows' without malice. He once described the Mississippi as being 'too thin to plough and too thick to drink!'

Came the final morning when we piled our belongings into the love-bug-encrusted car, and headed back up Canal Street in search of the Interstate motorway up to Nashville. About the same distance to cover as it was from Atlanta to New Orleans, but this time we didn't intend 'busting a gut' trying to do it in one day again. Just wanted to get near enough for a couple of hours' easy driving next morning, stopping over where convenient for a relaxing board, bottle and bed before doing so.

As this deep-Southern odyssey still has a way to go, it merits running into another chapter – ending this one with our departure from New Orleans.

The next can be introduced with the reminder that Part Three began with the belief that 'Nashville' might one day be found engraved on my heart. If it was anguish made Mary Tudor feel that way about Calais, then it's 15 to 8 that, when the time comes, Reg Davies will have 'Decatur' on his!

Within a couple of pages all will be revealed, but first a potted history of the name.

Stephen Decatur (pronounced Dee-*kate*-er) was a U.S. naval commander who did rather well against Tripolitans and Brits during the early 1800s. He was killed in a duel with a fellow officer in 1820, and subsequently immortalised by having any amount of streets and towns around the United States named after him.

"Well, we've talked enough about my prostate — how about your prostate?"

19

The High – and Dry – Road to Chattanooga

Forty miles out of New Orleans, we left Louisiana for the State of Mississippi, and speculated on the functions of a Weigh Station – a clearly signposted building reached by a slipway from the main road. There was a Weigh Station at the side of the road every time we crossed a border between States. Subsequent enquiries confirmed them to be somewhat similar to custom's posts between foreign countries.

Commercial vehicles crossing State boundaries are obliged to stop and complete questionnaires about the nature of load, weight, destination and other relevant matters that might concern the laid-down traffic, revenue, agricultural, and commercial laws of that particular State, and a charge made toward wear and tear on its roads. Taking oranges into Florida, tobacco into Virginia, gambling machines into Nevada, potatoes into Idaho, and so on – in competition with the major home product – would probably qualify for some kind of levy. I am told they even dip a vehicle's tank and charge tax on the quantity of fuel in it.

And whereas there's not a Weigh Station on every secondary road running between States, the driver of a commercial vehicle is expected to find and report to one when entering another State, and is held to be violating its laws until he's done so. And they call it the land of the free!

Heading north, we turned off into Poplarville in search of a garage with car-wash facilities. Old 'Herbie' certainly needed a bath, and some melodramatic citizen at a filling station, getting his car topped up at the same time as we called in there, had thrown his hands up in horror at seeing its frontage festooned with battered love-bugs. 'Those critters are full of acid', he had cried. 'They'll strip every last drop of paint off your auto!' It didn't seem right to tell him it wasn't our auto, but we did want the paint to stay on – at least until we checked it back in at Atlanta.

Poplarville was a sleepy, High-Noon-type small town about eighty miles north of New Orleans. It didn't rate a mention in the excellent *Mobil Southern States Travel Guide* – our motoring bible and far superior to the A.A. or R.A.C. equivalents – but nobody seemed to care very much.

'You-all thinkin' of settlin' here?', the lady in the small diner enquired when we stopped for coffee and asked if there was a garage in town with car-wash. Reg told her we weren't sure yet, once we learned the car-wash facilities consisted of a hose and a D.I.Y. brush. I didn't fancy it much either when, asking whether there happened to be a toilet in the place she hesitated, fished a key out of the till drawer, and handed it to me with instructions to lock the door afterwards and bring the key back. Especially as it meant walking out the front door, round the back and over heaped-up debris of empty boxes, cartons, milk crates and the like to get to it. On learning that we came from England she said she had a nephew currently over there on a ship in Northampton. Reg pointed out that, as Northampton was landlocked about 75 miles from the nearest ocean, she possibly meant the deep-sea port of Southampton. She said, 'With 75 miles between North and South, sounds like your Hampton's got to be as big as all outdoors!'

Unlike the usual scene on lesser highways and freeways in the U.S., Interstate roads were not cluttered with rows of garish hoardings featuring commodity advertisements. The only signs on the side of the road were either the usual directional and traffic control kind, or informative ones regarding facilities ahead. Like those advertising the petrol, hotels, garages, entertainment and other amenities available by turning off into the next township.

Approaching Birmingham, Alabama, there was a large pictorial sign above the trees bordering the road, announcing that greyhound racing took place there every

Tuesday and Friday evening. It seemed incongruous to find the 'way-down-south-in-Dixie' world suddenly linked up with Harringay dogs, where Reg had so often spent an evening after he'd finished surgery. Musing as we sped along, he wondered on the reaction of his friend and fellow-member at South Herts Golf Club, Gordon Dennis – who ran a chain of betting shops – if he were to phone a forecast bet on traps three and five in the first race that evening at Birmingham, Alabama. And would reversing the charge for the phone-call be accepted – bearing in mind that Gordon Dennis made a point of offering that facility to all customers placing bets with him? But as it was now something like two o'clock in the afternoon in Alabama – 8.00 p.m. in London – and Gordon's office usually closed at 5.30, he didn't think it worth turning off the Interstate in search of a phone box.

We kept motoring until it started getting dark at about 6.00 p.m. and with another hundred miles or so to Nashville decided to stay the night at the next town. That way we'd be good and fresh for knocking off the final stretch in the morning. The next town on the map was Decatur, with signs on the Interstate as we approached it that Best Western, Ramada and Holiday Inn each had a hotel in the place just 'busting' to look after us. But the turn-off to Decatur was on me before I was really ready for it – yes, ole Sam was at the wheel at the time and his rheumy old eyes weren't working too well in the gathering gloom – so we just had to go sailing on, hoping there'd be another chance to leave the Interstate further along the road. It was another three miles or so before that was possible, by which time Reg was looking at the map and wondering if we should go on to the next turn-off to Huntsville. (If only we had!)

But the option of returning to Decatur loomed up in the shape of the junction with Highway 31, which took us across the picturesque Wheeler Lake, in the waters of which the distant but rapidly approaching lights of Decatur were prettily reflected.

Soon after entering the town the familiar forecourt sign of

a Holiday Inn brought the day's run to a welcome close and no difficulty was encountered in getting a couple of adjoining rooms close to the swimming pool.

I wasted little time diving into it, but found its water murky and heavily chemicalised. While I showered it off back in the room, Reg – who'd got himself cleaned up in the meantime without a swim – put his head round the door and said he was off to the bar and what should he order up for me. Licking my lips I decided on a Jack Daniels on-the-rocks as the best antidote for a chlorinated mouth.

But he was back, ashen-faced, before I'd finished knotting my tie.

'Sam', he said, 'they haven't got a bar!'

'Well, that's all right', I told him. 'Ask at the desk and they'll probably bring 'em out to the lounge.'

'You don't understand,' he said hoarsely, 'I've done all that – and more. But they tell me this is a dry county and no liquor of any description can be bought anywhere in Decatur.'

We returned together to the lobby and restaurant. No, there was no way a resident or traveller could call for an alcoholic drink. No beer. No wines at the table. Nothing.

'But surely,' I asked as we ordered from the menu, 'we can have a drink of some sort with our food?'

'Sure,' said the accommodating lady, 'I could bring you coffee or iced water. Or perhaps you'd like me to get you a Coke from the machine?'

'What do people do round here,' asked Reg, 'if they want to have a dinner to celebrate something? Like a wedding, birthday or business convention.'

'Oh,' she said, 'in those cases they often go over to Huntsville in the next county where there's no restrictions, buy and bring back what they want, and we serve it.'

'How far's Huntsville?', we asked in unison, half rising from our chairs, but sinking back into them when she said about twenty miles. (The bracketed cry from the heart a couple of pages back has by now become clear).

While sipping our iced water we learned quite a lot about

how the local folks coped with the unsocial conditions. She said most people who travelled around usually had a well-stocked car, from which they'd provide for their needs when stopping for food and rest. Also the people and Town Council of Decatur vote heavily every year in favour of switching from 'dry' to 'wet', and every year the decision is nullified by the all-powerful Church Council – many of whose members, she believed, had connections with those running bootleg liquor into Decatur and surrounding parts and didn't want their faithful flocks buying the stuff elsewhere.

With no bar to lean on or chat over we decided to call it a day after the meal was over and were in bed by nine o'clock.

As the pool was an unhealthy-looking green in the early light I forwent my morning swim and had a word of commiseration with the worried-looking maintenance-man. He said he was waiting for the pool experts to arrive. On impulse I told him my own pool went sour on me once or twice a year and that adding one bottle of Johnny Walker to every 10,000 gallons usually cleared it up in a couple of hours. Did he happen to know if the pool men carried a stock of Scotch in their kit, because if they didn't he'd better waste no time in getting it in from Huntsville? He said he'd never heard of that before. I've often wondered since if he passed it on and if anybody ever tried it. Who knows, in my still simmering pique I may have invented the answer to many a pool owner's dilemma.

It was somewhere around 1.00 p.m. when we drove into Nashville and found the tall condominium block in which Cawthon Bowen lived. We'd phoned from Decatur the previous evening to give some idea of our progress, including the empty 'waterhole' at which we'd chosen to camp overnight. We were greeted with brimming glasses and shown up to the two hospitality suites made ready for us. They were magnificent, with bowls of fresh fruit and welcome cards on the sideboard. Once we'd cleaned up Bo ran us down to Belle Meade for lunch and to show us the new million-dollar (give or take the odd hundred grand) locker room, built somewhat on the lines of a university chapel.

As with all golf clubs, members are usually hypercritical over building decisions thought up by their committees and the new locker room was no exception. Entering it one felt a sense of awe and reverence. Oak-panelled walls, highly polished leather tub chairs and hardwood tables, stained glass windows and what looked suspiciously like a high altar near the far wall. Even the bowls of salted nuts spread around might well have been incense holders or collection plates. 'It's not quite finished yet', said Bo apologetically. 'We're waiting for Michelangelo to do the ceiling!'

He took us to see Skinny whose condition had got steadily worse. Walking and speech were limited and communication difficult. His eyes lit up when Bo said, 'Here's ole Sam come to see you'. Mine were pretty misted when we came away, after talking to him lightly about the good times of yore. Caring for him during his deterioration over the previous seven years had been a full-time dedicated task for Juanita, his wife, who so successfully concealed all signs of strain when bidding me welcome into the house.

When we got back Reg took our car out, found a real car-wash and got a grand job done on what was left of the love-bugs on the car frontage.

That evening we were hosted by Bo at the Vanderbilt v. Iowa University match, starting with a 'tailgate' picnic supper around the 'back door' of his pal's shooting brake. Bob McGaw was the retired secretary of Vanderbilt University, and with his wife 'Libbo', had laid on a succulent alfresco meal for the six of us before we entered the stadium for the game. All four were long-established season-ticket holders, but to accommodate his guests, Bo had given up his accustomed seat to Reg, and bought a couple of seats for himself and me, a few rows behind, among the hoi polloi. Generous thoughts and deeds like that abounded and there was very little we could do to reciprocate.

Vanderbilt were once again facing a superior side and the

mood among its supporters was sombre as the game drew to its close some three hours after we first entered the stadium. But all was not yet over. The situation was summed up and included in a letter I sent Bo shortly after returning to England, with a promise that if ever I wrote another book about these later visits to Nashville I might cover this particular occasion with the following:

Vows, vespers, and votive offerings at the High Altar of Belle Meade's multi-denominational Locker Room had proved of no avail. With only seven seconds of playing time left on the clock, Nashville's Vanderbilt University trailed Iowa State University by 22 points to 26. It was now 10.00 p.m. under the stadium floodlights on a sultry Saturday night in mid-September 1984.

The gangways and stairs to the exits were thronged with hundreds of scurrying figures, faces streaming with tears of mortification – and de-hydrated Coca-Cola – each supporter anxious to expunge the odium of a home defeat with a quick bout of boozing, wife-beating or self-flagellation, and before the final whistle set the seal on their night of shame.

But the two ageing Englishmen, calm and dry-eyed, remained seated midst those who were left of the 30,000 weeping fans, their rheumy eyes glued to the helmeted 'Michelin Men' clustered round the oval ball on Iowa's 45-yard line.

'It is not yet over', they reminded their four sobbing hosts, each busily engaged in pouring sackcloth and ashes over the other three.

'The situation is not unknown to us', mused one of the two Anglo-Saxons, nostalgically. 'We had it like this at Dunkirk.'

'Nil desperandum', pontificated the other. 'Take courage and be of good cheer. Have faith in the powerful magic we have brought you from our Great White Queen across the waters. True, much of it was used raising the score when Vanderbilt were trailing 3 to

17 at the end of the first quarter. But there might yet still be a drop or two of the potion in the bottom of the bucket.'

And that there most certainly was – resulting in a forty-yard pass for a touchdown followed by a conversion, with the ball passing between the posts as the final whistle blew. Result: Vanderbilt 29, Iowa 26!

In answer to my request in a letter to know more about the background of the game in general and the colourful bowl matches in particular, Cawthon Bowen sent me the following:

There now are some 20-odd post-season bowl games that scramble mightily near the end of each season to scoop up the best teams still available. Some bowls are set; the Rose Bowl, for example, always has the winner of the Pacific Eight Conference playing against the winner of the Big Ten Conference (a Mid-West group of schools). Most of the others, however, try to get the most attractive match-up they can arrange in order to attract full crowds, which most of them do, but more importantly the TV sponsor money that can amount to very large sums. These bowls are, in no particular order of importance, Orange, Tangerine, Citrus, Peach, Sugar, Hall of Fame, Liberty, Cotton, Sun Bowl and on and on. They become civic endeavours with monstrously large and sometimes quite beautiful parades, lots of fireworks and other spectacular attractions.

The Rose Bowl, the first and still most prestigious of the Bowls, began all this around 1910 as a civic promotion for Southern California, and more particularly Pasadena, near Los Angeles. This was before radio, of course, and attracted little attention except locally and in the city from whence each visiting team came.

The Rose Parade, which is held the morning of the game, is one of the most spectacular shows anywhere. All the designs of the floats, and there are hundreds, are brought into living color by the fact it is required that all figures, houses, vehicles, whatever, be covered in living flowers or fresh flower petals. It really is something to see. And nowadays, since television, up to a hundred million view this absolutely beautiful spectacle. In order that the full color of the flowers be maintained, teams of helpers from the various towns, cities, clubs, and national sponsors such as Coca Cola and other corporate giants, stay up all night putting the finishing touches on the unbelievable floats that are displayed this once before half a million spectators lining the routes, and then discarded forever. I've seen three in person, seen them in preparation from behind the scenes, and the freshness and excitement never dies.

The other bowl celebrations try, to varying degrees, to match this magnificent spectacle, using their native lore and products for special emphasis. Although fun to attend, it's a whole lot easier these days to get with a group, gather around the bar and television, and not worry about weather, crowds, traffic and the difficulties of travel. I say that in retrospect after having seen a number of these things.

College football, in quite a few instances, is used as a promotion for the schools; a rallying point for alumni and local communities; and relaxation and pleasure-breaks for the student bodies. Some schools, the minority of those engaged in this sport, have gone to the edge of professionalism and allowed the academics to suffer. These few – fortunately they are decreasing – have 'student' athletes who, after four years of attendance, have still not learned anything except how to run with a football or toss a ball into a basket. But all in all I still would argue that football produces more good than evil, especially for those young men with athletic ability who could not attend school if there were no athletic sponsorships. Vanderbilt, for example, has about ninety scholarships for football players and ten for basketball. They cover all expenses except spending money and travel.

You and Reg saw a typical example of a school community that is quite batty over its team. This is duplicated in hundreds of schools throughout the country each Saturday and, to a lesser degree in followers – but not less in enthusiasm – in thousands of high schools. The games are taken seriously but are not life and death matters, except in a few cases where the sidewalk-alumni become overly enthusiastic.

I sent the above copy with a covering note to Channel 4 asking if they could show us some of these pre-bowl parades. Time will tell if they ever read my letter.

The following day we came across many who had been to the match, left early in despair and gone home to bed mourning the result as they thought it to be. One told of almost coming to blows with his golfing partner who, having heard the result on radio, congratulated the other on having witnessed an exciting victory the previous evening.

We played some golf on Sunday afternoon and in the evening got spruced up for the traditional 'Welcome Sam and Reg' party at Belle Meade, with about thirty of our Nashville friends, and their friends, present. What made it really special was that Juanita had been prevailed upon to bring Skinny. I sat with him for quite a while during the cocktail session in the lounge prior to dinner being served. They went early but I like to think our meeting gave him pleasure. Being confined to home, only a few of his friends had seen him in recent times, but they reckoned he looked as happy and relaxed at this reunion as they'd seen him for a long time.

Dinner ended with the usual round of fun speeches and nice things said. Fortunately Reg and I had anticipated the need for a little gifting and had bought up half the novelty-shop stock of New Orleans in readiness for the Nashville occasion.

The following morning we breakfasted with Bo at a Shoney restaurant before the usual handshakes, farewells and promises to come back next year. Or the year after. Or the one after that.

But now we were off on the last-but-one leg to Chattanooga, in the south-east corner of Tennessee and about 150 miles from Nashville. Two thirds of the way along the road we passed through Sewanee – made famous by songwriters who couldn't spell – but couldn't see anything about the place to have made Jolson sing about it with such feeling. Looked for all the world like any of the other small dusty townships we passed through during our travels.

Deciding to stop for a beer and a lunch-time snack we found a suitable roadside diner. Having been badly 'bruised' in Decatur and warned by Bo there were many more 'dry holes' in those parts, we asked first whether they could serve a drink if we ordered a burger or banger salad.

'Well,' said the girl, 'it so happens that you're in a dry part of Tennessee. But we're right on the edge of it, with those railroad tracks you can see through the window forming the border with the next county. A wet one. And if you look just across the tracks you'll see a building with the sign "Liquor Store" over it. Now you just tell me what you'd like and I'll order your food from the kitchen. While they're fixing it I'll go across and get whatever you want to drink!'

'But isn't that a lot of trouble we're putting you to?', asked Reg anxiously.

'Hell, no!', said the young lady. 'I'm doing it all day. If ever I stopped, both this diner and that liquor store would have to close down!'

Approaching Chattanooga the countryside began getting both historic and mountainous. Lookout Mountain was 2,100 feet high and dominated the city. We made a point of taking a tortuous road to its top for a bird's-eye view of the place before entering it. It was first settled by the Cherokee

Indians who named the city Tsatanugi, meaning 'rock coming to a point'.

The nearby river is Chickamauga (river of blood), a name twice justified by (a) the Indian population of three states being herded here by Federal troops for a forced march through a freezing winter to Oklahoma, about 800 miles away, and (b) the Battle of Chickamauga in the Civil War in which there were over 34,000 casualties. The Confederate forces were overrun and it was from this success that General Sherman set out on his march through Scarlett O'Hara country, devastating the city of Atlanta en route.

On a lighter note, the town is immortalised with two world-renowned songs, 'Chattanooga Choo Choo' and 'Chattanooga Shoe Shine Boy'. It is also the birthplace of Coca Cola.

We decided on a Best Western hotel about two miles outside the city – once Reg had looked in to check that it had a bar – and booked in for a couple of nights. Looking through a local guide book on where to eat that evening it was decided that the Choo Choo Hilton Hotel looked worth a visit, where, according to the book, 'a turn-of-the-century atmosphere is provided in the restored 1905 station yard. The bar is an authentic Wabush Cannonball club car hitched on to an 1880 Chattanooga Choo Choo engine'.

With painstaking American thoroughness Hilton had converted that old disused station (the modern one was the other side of town) into a living piece of history. The old rolling-stock sleeping cars were luxury bedrooms and uniformed porters kept watch at the entrance to each coach. We took a drink in the club car of one of the trains and had an excellent dinner in the converted old station house. The various waiters and waitresses took turns in climbing on to the stage and performing, with a four-piece live band providing a wide range of foot-tapping music.

The following morning I checked through the phone book and found Valley Brook Golf Club. Calling the secretary/ manager, I explained that Cawthon Bowen, ex-President of Belle Meade Golf Club, had suggested that we ought to see

Valley Brook if we stopped at Chattanooga on our way back to England. It was explained that we didn't have any clubs with us but would gladly rent them and a buggy if allowed to pay a green fee and play the course. 'No problem', he said, 'come right on over', and explained how to find it from our hotel. He even said there'd be no problem when told that one set of clubs would need to be left-handed, but proved a bit over-optimistic on that one.

When we arrived and had shaken hands all round, the pro apologised and said he'd been unable to raise any left-handed clubs. That was catastrophic! However, while we changed, he and his assistants searched and searched until they found me an old No. 1 wood, a slightly rusted No. 1 iron, a very rusted No. 8 iron with a flattened kink half-way down the shaft, and quite a reasonable ambidextrous putter. He kindly said there'd be no charge for renting those four clubs as he popped them in a bag big enough to take a full set and a kitchen sink, and strapped it on to the back of the cart alongside the pristine set of 14 provided for lucky ole Reg. We bought some balls and agreed on the drive down to the first tee that I'd have a shot a hole off Reg in view of my limited and peculiar range of tools, and the loser should buy the lunch. Well, we had to call it off at the 18th, when a torrential downpour had us driving the cart flat out for the shelter of the pro's shop, but by that time I'd so mastered my weird implements that my free lunch was assured.

To the best of my memory we had a quiet dinner at the hotel that evening and departed for a leisurely uneventful drive to Atlanta the following day.

There were some excesses to pay on the car when checking it in but, when it came to boarding our plane for its flight home, it was agreed that we never would have known those ten colourful days and nights in the Southern States – if it wasn't for GOLF . . . !

" I propose that 5 Day Membership for Ladies should be restricted to Christmas Day, Boxing Day, Pancake Day, Mothers' Day and Guy Fawkes Day "

20

Postscript

So what is there about this game, involving a funny ball – and even funnier sticks – that brings together such an amazing assortment of characters with a love of laughter and a zest for living?

Skinny Huggins died in May 1986. Many tributes to his memory appeared in the Nashville papers, for he was a great character and had many friends. This, my fourth book, might well have justified the title, 'If it wasn't for HUGGINS . . . !'; for it was as a direct outcome of that 1968 initial meeting in Killarney that I was urged to tell about it in *Start-off-Smashed!* And having done it once, further books followed.

Skinny's closest pal in Nashville was Cawthon Bowen. An ex-reporter with the *Nashville Banner,* Bo has a gift with words, both written and spoken, and especially for serving them Southern-style! He first came to my home with Skinny back in 1969 and, since Skinny fell ill, it has been Bo with whom I've maintained the closest contact as far as friends in Nashville are concerned. The question raised in the first paragraph cannot be answered better than the way Bo did it via a lecture tour in 1986.

He sent me his notes soon afterwards, together with some of the sources of information he used, and told me to feel free to use them any time and anyhow I wished. So, with very little change to his work, I am proud to end mine with a condensation from it. He starts with three short anecdotes he would use to warm up his audience before getting down to the 'nitty-gritty'. Here goes:

AN ANTHOLOGY OF GOLF
by Cawthon Bowen

Playing with Miller Kimbrough at St. Andrews, Scotland, a few years ago, we had a caddy wearing a long coat and bringing a dog with him. If you hit the ball into the thick and thorny gorse bushes, you don't go after it. You drop another ball and continue to play.

Kimbrough did just that. As he fumbled to get another ball out of his pocket, I noticed the dog go into the gorse. In a moment he returned carrying a ball in his mouth.

The caddy asked Kimbrough what ball he was playing.

'A Titleist', Miller replied. The dog went over and gave him the ball.

I asked the caddy, 'Suppose Mr. Kimbrough had said he was playing a Dunlop?'

'Dog wouldn't have given it to him', said the caddy.

I was introduced to a tall, blonde lady golfer at a cocktail party during the Women's Southern in 1975.

It turned out she had been Arkansas champion. 'What's your handicap?', I asked.

'Nine', she replied. I said, 'Boy, that is great, wish I could play that well' and so on.

She put her hand on my shoulder, which I did not object to, and said: 'Don't worry about your high handicap. Golf is like sex, you don't have to be good to enjoy it.'

An Eastern golfer, playing for his first time at Augusta, asked his caddy what his name was.

'Poe', said the caddy.

Trying for a witticism, the golfer said: 'Were you named after Edgar Allen Poe?'

Drawing himself up, the caddy replied: 'I *is* Edgar Allen Poe!' . . .

Both the Dutch and Scotch claim they invented golf.

It is true that a game called 'spel metten colve', a 'game played with a club', was played in Holland in the thirteenth century. 'Colve', or club, evolved to 'kolf', the Scots put a 'G' in front and called it 'gowf'. Finally it was 'G-O-L-F'.

Some kind of golf has been played at St. Andrews, in Scotland, for over eight hundred years. The links, hard by the North Sea, are known as 'The Old Course'. Perhaps they should be known as 'The Oldest Course'. This is where it all began, attained sophistication and still today weaves a magic for any player of the game.

In the beginning golf became so addictive that kings banned it. It was becoming more popular than archery and fighting men had to be kept in shape to fight, not play.

The ban was lifted when one of the kings was caught playing. Later, Mary, Queen of Scots, became the first well-known lady player. Educated in France, she called the boy who carried her bags a 'cadet'. From that we get 'caddie'.

The first great golfers were Scottish, of course. 'Old Tom' and his son 'Young Tom' Morris became legends. They were followed by many excellent players, but best known in this country, because he played here often, was Harry Vardon.

Australian-born Walter Travis was the first great American player. Remarkably, he picked up his first club in 1896 when he was 35. Four years later he was U.S. Amateur Champion. Then, at 44, he won the British Amateur, shocking that entire nation.

The game was becoming more and more popular. Rather than in hundreds, players now could be counted in the tens of thousands. Once World War I was over, Americans flew into a sports-playing, sports-loving frenzy. Flappers and the Golden Age of Sports were here.

Anyone who lived then or has read about sports since, will never forget the magical names – Bill Tilden, Ty Cobb, Jack Dempsey, Gene Tunney, Red Grange and Babe Ruth. In golf there were Walter Hagen, Gene Sarazen and a prodigy from Georgia named Robert Tyre Jones, Jr.

When flamboyant Walter Charles Hagen, his tanned face gleaming and his actor's art fine-tuned, appeared on any first tee, he lit up each and every 18-hole course on to which he strode.

Hagen cultivated the image that he was the consumate playboy. In his great days he took much better care of himself than it appeared. Serious drinking did not come until later when he was past his prime.

This splendid player won five P.G.A. championships, four in a row. He took the British Open four times and the U.S. Open twice. His charisma, plus his seemingly cavalier attitude toward life, brought him fame, fortune and great popularity.

Charles Price, who wrote the book *Golfer at Large*, lived with Hagen for a while in his later years trying to pry a book out of him. He couldn't, but admired this complex, talented man without reservation.

When Hagen died, some of his friends planned a big party in his honour. Price refused the invitation. He wrote:

'I didn't go. Like Hamlet, golf's "sweet prince", I thought, deserved a grander exit than that. He was splendid. They should have carried him out on a shield.'

Eugene Sarazen, the shortest of the major champions at five feet five inches, was the first player to win all four of the major championships during his career.

He won the Open twice, the P.G.A. thrice, the British

Open in 1932 and the Masters in 1935.

Despite all his championships and durability, Sarazen is best known for one magnificent shot. Playing his first Masters in 1935, he found himself three shots behind Craig Wood with four to play.

Facing the dangerous par-five 15th, Sarazen was 220 yards short after his drive. He selected a 4-wood and said later: 'I rode into the shot with everything I had.'

The ball flew straight as an arrow to the cup and tumbled in for a double-eagle, the rarest shot in golf. Sarazen and Wood tied after the regulation 72 holes and Gene won comfortably the next day.

Years later, almost ruefully, Sarazen commented: 'You'd think I'd never done anything but hit that shot. In the Orient I became known as "Mr Double-Eagle", which non-golfers probably took to mean I was an Indian chief.'

No figure in any sport ever achieved, and retains to this day, such king-like proportions and adulation as Bob Jones.

No player of any game ever went about his life with such talent, such style, such charm and dignity and honesty as this brilliantly intelligent and vastly loved man from Georgia.

When you consider his remarkable achievements, always remember that Jones was an amateur player with another, full-time career, variously academic, professional or business. Normally he would play only two or three tournaments a year. In-between he played in friendly foursomes. At times he went two or three months without picking up a club.

Today there are about 18 million golfers in the United States. They play some 450 million rounds and walk, or ride on carts, approximately two billion miles over 13,000 courses.

Annually they hook, slice, miss, drown, lose and

occasionally hit straight 900 million balls worth twice that in dollars. Many of these objects wind up in creeks, rivers, lakes, oceans and ponds. Enterprising divers made good livings retrieving them amid mud, slime, fish, snakes and alligators.

Golf and country clubs spend one-and-a-half billion dollars annually to maintain their indoor and outdoor facilities, which are worth 15 billion dollars. Equipment costs nine billion dollars a year and golfers spend – for the right to play – another 18 billion.

As they say in Washington, if we keep this up soon we will be talking about real money.

During the last ten years the population grew by 10 per cent while the number of regular golfers in the land grew by 30 per cent. Up and coming would-be tycoons are finding golf better suited for customer-entertaining, whereas tennis, squash, and most other activities are too adversarial.

Bo ended his notes with the closing paragraphs from Jones's book, *Golf Is My Game*. Taking the relevant excerpts from them, I couldn't think of a better way to finish *If it wasn't for GOLF . . . !*

The wonderful thing about golf is that it holds forever the interest of all who play it; and so I find myself today a member of a sort of fraternity of those who walked the fairways with me . . . Most important by far have been the avenues to friendships with individuals and groups of people. That these rewards should endure so long makes it easy to see why, for me, Golf will always be the greatest game.

Amen.

Epilogue

A photostat of the seven final chapters in typescript form was air-mailed to Cawthon Bowen, with a view to his checking with our mutual friends in Nashville there was nothing written that might embarrass or offend. He was asked to send any comments back by air and return the 'stats by surface mail, as time was vital and the book couldn't go to print until I knew whether one or two changes might be needed.

With no reply yet to hand I phoned him at home one evening about two weeks later and found him just back from losing six dollars at Belle Meade. He had not yet had my package, despite the value of stamps on it being about three times what he'd lost at golf that afternoon. Having learned the reason for my call, he promised to ring back just as soon as the missing pages arrived, but told me not to wait.

'Sam,' he said, 'you just go right ahead and print. I'm sure all your friends here in Nashville will love reading anything you write without ever wanting to change a word. When I was sports writer on the *Nashville Banner*,' he went on, 'I once interviewed a leading wrestler. When asked if he had any objection to my including a certain item that came up in our talk he replied, "Mr. Bowen, you're welcome to print anything you want to say about me – just as long as you spell my name right."'

Well, good people of the fair city of Nashville – and all others featured in these pages – I hope you feel the same as Bo's wrestler when you come across your involvement in my story, knowing that every effort was made to get the name right!

247

The Artist
by Bernard Kay, TV writer and director

I have known Jo Varney for over thirty years – first as Creative Director in the London Advertising Agency, where I was TV Director – and, of course, as the *Daily Mail* cartoonist whose VARNEY'S VIEW pocket cartoon was regularly featured in over 4,000 editions.

Other prestigious names were, and still are, on his list of clients, including the Institute of Directors, Dan Air, Building Trades journals, Wimpey, Eurogolf, Accurist Watches, and several more.

Since his retirement from the Agency he has reacted to frequent serious spells of illness with stunning energy, including a full-size portrait assignment of Falklands hero, Lt Col H Jones, VC, for the Parachute Regiment, and commemorative portraits of Dai Rees and Harry Vardon for the South Herts Golf Club; while his cat paintings for Medici make best-selling birthday cards and calendars.

Add to these his work in Sam Morley's books and a highly risible send-up of *The Diary of an Edwardian Lady*, and it's surprising where he finds the time to play golf. Let alone break four ribs falling out of a golf cart on the fifth at Hardelot!

He also talks (my God, how he talks) and demonstrates his cartoon-craft to a wide variety of audiences – from Women's Institutes and the Royal College of Midwives to high-tech business seminars.

But he is the original Golf Nut. He loves the game and finds its adherents an incessant source for laughter both on the course and on some twenty pages of this highly entertaining book.

Index

Abbott, Rodney 52–3, 58–9
Aberdeen Arms 157
Addington G.C. 31–2
Agincourt 108, 111, 122
Agnew, Spiro 204
American Football 209, 231–5
Arlington Memorial Cemetery 205
Atkinson, John 92–3, 95, 106–9, 111, 113, 115, 122, 124, 129
Atlanta, Ga. 213–14, 224, 227, 237–8

Baker, Father 160
Baker, Stanley 126, 128–9
Barber, Kath 133, 141, 149, 150, 173, 197, 199, 202, 204, 206–9, 221
Belfast, City of 154
Belle Meade G.C. 172, 177, 181, 207, 213, 230–2, 235, 237, 247
Bell's Whisky 99
Birmingham, Alabama 227–8
Bloggs, Fred 54–8
Blue Train 85, 131–2, 137, 142
Bophuthatswana 132, 148
Bottell, Nigel 134
Bourbon Street 219–20
Bowen, Cawthon 138, 207–10, 214, 230–1, 233, 236–7, 240, 247
Brickendon Grange Golf Club 164
British Embassy, US 202, 204
Brookmans Park G.C. 164
Burhill G.C. 46–9
Burning Tree G.C. 203–4

Camden, S. Carolina 188–9, 194
Campbell, Jack 155

Cape Town 84, 89, 106, 131, 137–43
Casablanca 83
Cascades, Sun City 150
Castle Beer 85
Century Inn, Atlanta 215
Chattanooga 213, 226, 236–8
CHEDDARS, The 39
Chesapeake Bay 81–2
Chickamauga 237
Choo-Choo Hilton Hotel 237
Clairwood, Durban 132, 143, 147
Colonial Cup 188, 192–3
Columbia, S. Carolina 188, 193–6
Connolly, Pat 128
Coombe Hill G.C. 125
Cornelius, Chas & Lu 169–71, 182–3
Crews Hill G.C. 7, 10, 12, 28, 39, 156, 198
Crocodile Creek 145–6
Cuffley, Herts 24, 52, 171
Cullinan Diamond 102
Cummings, Tom 170–1
Curaçao, West Indies 83

Davies, Reg 12, 31–5, 40, 46–9, 63–6, 127, 133, 145, 147–9, 150, 172, 213–16, 219–21, 224, 227, 235–6, 238
Decatur, St., N. Orleans 223
Decatur, Alabama 224, 228–30, 236
Densham, Pat 95, 106, 116
De Wet, Carel 114
Donald, Hugh 32–6, 198–9, 201–2, 211
Dorice Restaurant 33
Durban, Natal 88, 132, 142–3, 145

Eccentric Club ix, 28, 32, 45, 63, 92–3, 95–100, 102, 109, 111, 113–16, 118, 122–3, 125, 136
Edward VII 102
Elbin, Max 204
Emerson, Ralph W. 52–3
Empire State Bldg 199

Fairbairn, Anthony 134, 147, 149, 192–5
Fairmile Rest. 116
Floyd, Sue & Allen 115
Freeman, Alfred 63
Freeman, Millice 40–3

Gamages 25, 29, 104
Garner, Ron 28
Georgetown, D.C. 205
Germiston, Jo'burg (Gosforth Park) 99, 105, 131, 135
Gibraltar 80, 83–4
Gleneagles 12–16, 164
Gog Magog G.C. 40–1
Gold, Louise 134, 149–50
Gould, A. 86
GOWR, The 125, 128
Gunstone, Walter 97, 99
Gurr, Frank 134

Hay, Alex ix, 165–6
HCCG, The 40–3
Henry, Chris 172–3
Hermanus, Cape 89, 140
Hofstead, Jim 182–3, 208
Huggins, Skinny 154, 163, 165, 171, 178–80, 206, 207, 213, 235, 240

Jan Smuts Airport 93–5
J & B Whisky 69
Johannesburg 93–111, 113, 122, 131–6, 148, 151
Jo'burg Country Club 100
Jo'burg Sun Hotel 131, 134–6
Jo'burg Daily Star 96, 114
Joel, Solly 114
Johnstone, Stewart 147

John Dewar Ltd 114–15
Jones, Frank 147

Kenilworth, C/Town 131, 140
Kennedy, Jack: Robert 206
Killarney, Co Kerry 158–63, 240
Kimberley 85–8, 102
Kimbrough, Miller 171–3, 177, 241
King, Ron 24–5, 27
Knokke Le Zout 122
Kruger Park, Transvaal 105–6

Lahinch, Co. Clare 156–7
Langford, Bunny: Jack 38, 114
Laurel Park, Maryland 173, 188, 210
Lee, General Robert E. 205
Left-handers G.S. 155–6, 158, 162
LEGS, The 38
Lighting Equip News 51
LIGS, The 51, 58
Lilleywhite's 24
Limerick, Eire 159
Lincoln Memorial 206
Locke, Bobby 97
Longhurst, Henry 19, 20, 23–4

McAteer, Bill & John 203
McGaw, Bob & Libby 231
McGrath, Paul 165
McMeel, Eugene 159, 160
Maharani Hotel, Durban 132, 142, 145, 147
Mala Mala 131–2, 136–7
Matthews, Lord 59
Mayden Wharf, Durban 142
Mississippi River 221, 223
Moat House, Gatwick 69
Montieth, Alex 99–100, 135–6
Moor Park G.C. 28
Morley, John 139–41
Morley, Mark 89, 140–1
Morley, Sarah-Jane & Lauren 141
Mt Nelson Hotel 131, 139–42
Muirfield G.C. 41–2
Muller, Dr Wilgard 96

Index

Nairobi, Kenya 92–3
Nash, Ernest 95, 114
Nashville, Tenn. 153–4, 163–5, 167, 169, 173, 177–8, 180–3, 188, 197, 206–7, 209–11, 213–14, 224, 228, 230, 232, 236, 240, 247
Nell, Peter 113–14
New Club, Jo'burg 92, 94–5, 99, 103, 106, 115, 122, 135–6
New Orleans 213, 215, 217–27
New York 165, 197–202, 205, 211
Newman, Leslie 46
Newport News, Va. 83
Noble, Leslie ix, 114
Norfolk, Virginia 80, 82
Nuisance 143–4

Observatory G.C. 94–5, 97
O'Hehir, Michael 192
Olden, Charlie 7–10
OOTEGS, The 12
Orengo, Orrie 123–4, 126, 128
Oxhey G.C. 10

Pebble Beach G.C. 165–6
Peel, Robert 54
Peggy Lee 200–1
Pestriddance plc 55–6
Pink-Ball Competition 70–5
Pitt, William 54
Poplarville, Mississippi 226–7
Premier Diamond Mine 102
Preservation Hall 219–20
Przyblski, Steve 61–6

Racegoers Club 131–2, 134, 140, 147, 150, 173, 182–3, 188–91, 202–3
Racehorse, HMS 79–84
RAC G.C. 51
Ray, Ted 7, 9–16, 198
Redoubt, HMS 78–88, 142, 163
Rees, Dai 64
'Robbo' 86–8
Rock, Derek 148
Rock Island 182–3
Royal Jo'burg G.C. 106

St Andrews G.C. 242
St George's Hill G.C. 28, 115–16
SAWAS, The 86
Seretse Khama 93–4
Sewanee, Tenn. 236
Shakespeare, William 107–9
Shekey's 52
Sheridan, Richard 19
Shoney's 216, 236
Siedle-Gibson, Perla 143
Simonstown 84, 86, 143–4
Simpsons 24
South African Airways 133–4
South Herts G.C. 63, 127–8
Southport & Ainsdale G.C. 155–6, 158
Stevenson, Albert 12–16
Steyn, Louis 93–5, 103, 113
Stone, Jack 13, 15, 16
Sun City 132, 148–9
Sunningdale G.C. 3, 5, 14, 28

Table Mountain 84, 139, 141
Tebbs, Fred 32–6
Tennessee 165, 169, 174, 182, 210, 214, 236
Thorndon Park G.C. 40
Trinder, Arthur 95
Troup, Colin 51
Turfontein 99, 105
Turner, John 158, 162
TWA 194
Twain, Mark 223–4

Union Jack Club 85
Upex Cup 116, 118–19, 120

Vaderland, Die 95
Valley Brook G.C. 237–8
Van Riebeck, Jan 78
Vanderbilt University 209, 231–3
Varney, Jo 249
Vaughan Bros. 157
Victorious, HMS 80–3
Vorster, John 96–8

Waldorf, London 169, 170
Waldorf Astoria 200–1
Walker, Bob 177, 207–8
Walton Heath G.C. 69, 75
Wanderers Club, Jo'burg 99–100
Warren, Leslie 97–8
Washington, D.C. 173, 182, 188, 193,
    197, 202–3, 205–6
Webb, Larry 38, 92, 96–8, 111, 115,
    125, 129
Weigh Stations 226

Wentworth G.C. 28
West Lodge Hotel 171
Whitewebbs G.C. 7, 28, 29
Wig & Pen Club 174
Wightwick, Helen 143
Williamsburg, Va. 184–6
Wilson, Bob 221–2
Woburn Golf Club ix, 165–6
Wodehouse, P.G. 19, 20, 23
Wootton, Laurie 63